WITH ALL OUR MIGHT

WITH ALL OUR MIGHT

A Progressive Strategy for Defeating Jihadism and Defending Liberty

Edited by
WILL MARSHALL

RANDOLPH COURT and KEVIN CROKE
Associate Editors

ROWMAN & LITTLEFIELD PUBLISHERS, INC.
Lanham • Boulder • New York • Toronto • Oxford

ROWMAN & LITTLEFIELD PUBLISHERS, INC.

Published in the United States of America
by Rowman & Littlefield Publishers, Inc.
A wholly owned subsidiary of The Rowman & Littlefield Publishing Group, Inc.
4501 Forbes Boulevard, Suite 200, Lanham, Maryland 20706
www.rowmanlittlefield.com

PO Box 317
Oxford
OX2 9RU, UK

Copyright © 2006 by the Progressive Policy Institute
Published in cooperation with the Progressive Policy Institute.

British Library Cataloguing in Publication Information Available

Library of Congress Cataloging-in-Publication Data

With all our might : a progressive strategy for defeating jihadism and defending
  liberty / edited by Will Marshall.
    p. cm.
   Includes bibliographical references and index.
   ISBN-13: 978-0-7425-5198-5 (cloth : alk. paper)
   ISBN-10: 0-7425-5198-9 (cloth : alk. paper)
   ISBN-13: 978-0-7425-5199-2 (pbk. : alk. paper)
   ISBN-10: 0-7425-5199-7 (pbk. : alk. paper)
   1. Islamic countries—Foreign relations—United States.   2. United States—
Foreign relations—Islamic countries.   3. Jihad.   4. Terrorism—Government
policy—United States.   5. Terrorism—United States—Prevention.
I. Marshall, Will.
DS35.74.U6W57   2006
363.325'15610973—dc22   2006004454

Printed in the United States of America

∞ ™ The paper used in this publication meets the minimum requirements of American
National Standard for Information Sciences—Permanence of Paper for Printed Library
Materials, ANSI/NISO Z39.48-1992.

CONTENTS

Part III. Transforming Our Military

Part IV. Strengthening Collective Security

Part V. Building Our Economic Strength

Part VI. Renewing Our Fighting Faith

ACKNOWLEDGMENTS

This book was written to answer a simple question: What is the progressive alternative to the Bush administration's policies for defeating jihadist terrorism? It offers not only different ideas for making Americans safer, but a distinctly different philosophy—grounded in the tough-minded internationalism of Franklin Roosevelt, Harry Truman, and John Kennedy—about how America leads in the post–9/11 world.

First and foremost, I want to thank the contributing authors, whose analyses and ideas are updating that great tradition of progressive internationalism, and, in so doing, defining clear choices for Americans on national security and international affairs. In addition to their contributions, Jeremy Rosner and Steven J. Nider deserve special mention for helping to inspire and shape this book.

I also want to offer special thanks to my associate editors, Randolph Court and Kevin Croke, whose strong editorial and writing skills, and meticulous attention to detail, helped to make our case more clearly and concisely. Also offering indispensable editorial assistance were Tom Mirga, Ed Kilgore, and Jim Ludes. Thanks to Tyler Stone for helping to create an attractive cover for this volume. Eitan Hersh checked facts and endnotes with great care and diligence.

Rachel Chute served as production manager, coordinating all aspects of the project, and PPI chief operating officer Paul Weinstein provided overall direction. Finally, let me thank Chris Anzalone of Rowman & Littlefield for his interest and assistance in this project.

INTRODUCTION

A Progressive Answer to Jihadist Terror

Will Marshall and Jeremy Rosner

S ometimes it takes a national calamity to bring out the best in people. Americans grieved after the September 11, 2001, terrorist attacks, but we were also seized by a newfound spirit of unity and moral purpose. We knew that we had to confront and defeat not just a gang of terrorists, but the malignant creed that could inspire such atrocities. We realized that the end of the cold war had not brought an end to history, and resolved to defend ourselves and our democratic way of life against a ruthless new foe.

That robust sense of unity has since eroded and that clarity of vision has blurred. After initial successes against al Qaeda and the Taliban in Afghanistan, the Bush administration pursued a course that bitterly divided Americans, alienated many of our closest allies, ran down our military, dissipated our country's moral authority, and stoked anti-Americanism around the world.

At the same time, we have experienced stalling momentum in the struggle against jihadist terrorism. Osama bin Laden remains at large, the U.S.-led coalition has yet to quell a vicious insurgency in Iraq, and Muslim extremists have launched barbaric attacks from Indonesia to the Middle East, and from North Africa to Western Europe. In fairness, there have been gains as well: the stirrings of authentic democracy in Afghanistan, Iraq, and Palestinian areas, the expulsion of Syrian forces from Lebanon, Libya's renunciation of mass destruction weapons, and growing global collaboration against transnational terrorist networks. But on balance, the contagion of jihadist violence is growing, not contracting. The worldwide death toll from terrorism is mounting: More people were killed in each of the last two years than in 2001.[1]

Americans should not be lulled into complacency by the fact that terrorists have not struck the United States since 9/11. While we may be safer in our homeland, at least for now, the battle has shifted to other fronts, especially Iraq and European capitals. A series of shocking events—from the deadly attacks on Madrid and London, to the murder of Dutch filmmaker Theo van Gogh, to the murderous worldwide riots over Danish cartoons depicting the prophet Muhammad—has riveted the world's attention on Europe's poorly assimilated Muslim immigrants as a prime and ripe source of terrorist recruits.

Those attacks have underscored an ominous reality: the jihadist creed is spreading virally in many Muslim communities. Incredibly, the White House appears to be losing the ideological war to fanatics who exult in the

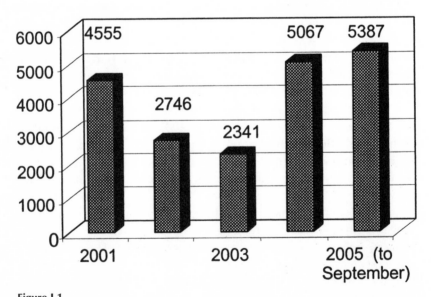

Terrorist Deaths 2001-2005

Figure I.1.

Credit: RAND Corporation. This chart was created at the authors' request, by Hillary Peck of the RAND Corporation. It is based on data from the Terrorism Knowledge Database cited in note 1; www.tkb.org/Home.jsp.

murder of innocents and dream of restoring the medieval caliphate. Throughout the Middle East, there is disturbingly broad sympathy for bin Laden and copycat extremist groups. In much of Europe, official and public antipathy to the Bush administration overshadows a mutual transatlantic interest in confronting Islamist violence. Partly because of his errors in Iraq, partly due to his own shortcomings as a communicator, and partly due to the myopia of his top aides at the Pentagon and elsewhere, President George W. Bush has failed to rally progressive forces, both in the west and in the Middle East, against an ideology that is profoundly hostile to liberal values and to the humane ethos of genuine Islam.

The president's penchant for simplistic, us-versus-them rhetoric has failed to convey to Americans the true nature of the threat we face. The struggle is first and foremost between the violent fringe of jihadists and the vast majority of moderate Muslims, who do not subscribe to their warped interpretation of Islam. But by stressing an unending war against the former rather than empathy with the later, the White House too often has played into the jihadist strategy of portraying the struggle as one between a humiliated Islamic world and its western oppressors, led by America.

Indeed, bin Laden has made it clear that his primary targets are Arab regimes whom he regards as corrupt and insufficiently pure in their commitment to his peculiar brand of Islamic chauvinism. These regimes are the "near enemy"; America is the "far enemy." The jihadists say America has propped up these regimes to achieve its own selfish ends—access to Middle East oil, the safety of Israel, a neocolonial strategy to weaken Muslim nations and prevent them from unifying—and must be driven from the region. The White House effort to counter these claims—including dispatching presidential image-meister Karen Hughes to the Middle East, where she misquoted the U.S. Constitution, distorted the history of U.S. diplomacy in the region, and invoked the joys of motherhood—has been almost laughably inept.

To be sure, President Bush has tried to recast the "war on terror" as an ennobling struggle for freedom and democracy in Muslim lands. That is the right message—in fact, it's a progressive message—but the president's policies are woefully at odds with his high-flown rhetoric. The White House prescribes democracy for Iraq and Iran while turning a blind eye to repression and corruption in Egypt and Saudi Arabia. It preaches respect for human rights while failing to take full responsibility for the torture and mistreatment of captives in U.S. custody. And it has failed to launch political and economic initiatives commensurate with its grandiose rhetoric about promoting democracy. These glaring contradictions do not go unnoticed in the greater Middle East.

The Bush administration's failures are not simply a matter of incompetence. They are the systematic reflection of a worldview—conservative unilateralism—that believes America can shape international affairs simply by flexing its military muscle. Even before 9/11, conservatives looked at the growing "power gap" that America enjoys over the rest of the world and reached two flawed conclusions. First, they overestimated what can be achieved by military power alone. The continuing carnage in Iraq, three years after U.S. forces easily toppled Saddam Hussein, is a tragic measure of their error. Second, they underestimated the value of international alliances and institutions that augment and help to legitimate the use of American power.

In short, the Bush Republicans have been tough, but they have not been smart. Their purblind policies have opened up the greatest chasm in modern memory between the scope of American power and our actual sense of security and standing in the world. Rarely has our public been more dissatisfied with an administration's conduct abroad. By early 2006, only about 40 percent of Americans approved of the president's handling of Iraq, while less than 40 percent approved of the broader job he was doing on foreign policy.[2] The Republican security formula of military dominance, ad hoc "coalitions of the willing," and preemptive war has failed to make Americans safer or the jihadists weaker. It is time for progressives to step forward with a new and better plan for victory.

PROGRESSIVE INTERNATIONALISM VERSUS CONSERVATIVE UNILATERALISM

We should begin by reaffirming the Democratic Party's commitment to progressive internationalism—the belief that America can best defend itself by building a world safe for individual liberty and democracy. We support the bold exercise of American power, not to dominate others but to shape alliances and international institutions that share a common commitment to liberal democratic values. The way to keep America safe and strong is not to impose our will or pursue a narrow, selfish nationalism that betrays our best values, but to lead the world toward political and economic freedom.

Progressive internationalism occupies the vital center between the neo-imperial right and the noninterventionist left, between a view that assumes our might always makes us right, and one assumes that because America is strong it must be wrong.

Progressive internationalism stresses the responsibilities that come with our enormous power: to use force with restraint but not to hesitate to use it when necessary; to show what the Declaration of Independence called "a decent respect for the opinions of mankind"; to exercise leadership primarily through persuasion rather than coercion; to reduce human suffering where we can, and to bolster alliances and global institutions committed to upholding an increasingly democratic world order.

This book outlines a new strategy that applies the organizing principles of progressive internationalism—national strength, equal opportunity, liberal democracy, U.S. leadership for collective security—to the new challenge of defeating Islamist extremism. We recognize, of course, that terrorism is not the only security problem facing America today. It is vital that our leaders keep a vigilant eye on China's rapid rise, Russia's creeping authoritarianism and still-extensive arsenal of nuclear chemical and biological weapons and materials, populist demagogues like Venezuela's Hugo Chavez, failed states and communal violence in Africa, and more. But now and for the immediate future, jihadist terrorism poses the most acute danger to the American people and to our democratic way of life. It has claimed nearly 3,000 lives on our own soil, thousands more in allied and friendly countries from Madrid to Bali, and inflamed a deadly movement that is sworn to the destruction of the United States, our allies, and our system of liberal, religiously tolerant democracy. To reduce this danger, and to demonstrate their capacity for national leadership, progressives must unite behind a clear, principled plan to combat the sources and consequences of jihadist terrorism.

That plan, as set forth in detail in this book, revolves around five progressive imperatives for national security:

- First, we must marshal all of America's manifold strengths, starting with our military power but going well beyond it, for the struggle ahead.
- Second, we must rebuild America's alliances, because democratic solidarity is one of our greatest strategic assets.
- Third, we must champion liberal democracy in deed, not just in rhetoric, because a freer world is a safer world.
- Fourth, we must renew U.S. leadership in the international economy and rise to the challenge of global competition.

- Fifth, we must summon from the American people a new spirit of national unity and shared sacrifice.

USE ALL OUR STRENGTHS

A progressive strategy would marshal America's economic, political, and moral strengths, as well as our armed might, to win the ideological war against jihadist extremism.

Make no mistake: we are committed to preserving America's military preeminence. We recognize that a strong military undergirds U.S. global leadership and that our diplomacy works best when it is backed by the credible threat of force.

Therefore, we must give high priority to repairing the damage done by the Bush administration to America's all-volunteer force. We must expand our armed forces, which have been stretched to the breaking point by repeated deployments in Iraq, enlarge the Special Forces, which are well-suited to unconventional warfare, and train more units for the specialized tasks required for counterinsurgency, post-conflict reconstruction, and nation-building. Most important, we believe a fundamental transformation of the U.S. military is necessary to better align it with America's new security priorities.

But it's also important to be clear about what military force can and cannot accomplish in the struggle against radical Islam. Without question, hard-core terrorists must be captured or killed and we mean to revamp America's military forces and intelligence services with this goal in mind. Yet it is also true that armed might has less deterrent power against stateless terrorists who hide in the shadows—especially those willing to sacrifice their lives to kill others—than hostile states. Our real enemy is the jihadist ideology, and you cannot kill beliefs with a gun.

Victory will come only when this creed is delegitimized in the eyes of the overwhelming majority of Muslims throughout the world. As President Harry Truman, Secretary of State George Marshall, and other architects of America's cold war strategy understood, America cannot win a clash of ideas and values using only the blunt instrument of military power. Progressives will supplement that instrument with our other national assets—the world's largest economy, prosperous democratic allies, collaborative diplomacy, a pervasive cultural presence, and the broad appeal of liberal ideas and institutions. To prevail in the struggle with jihadists, we must work with moderate

Muslims to change the conditions that breed anger and despair throughout the greater Middle East. These include repressive and corrupt governments, economic stagnation, technological backwardness, military weakness, and a humiliating sense of cultural decline. Such conditions do not excuse terrorism, but they do help to explain the attraction of the Salafist slogan: "Islam is the answer." As British Prime Minister Tony Blair has repeatedly said, the democracies need a strategy that is both tough on terrorists and tough on the conditions that breed terrorism.

The United States and its democratic allies can offer a different remedy to the pathologies that afflict the greater Middle East than the military-centric approach the Bush administration has followed. We should launch a sweeping program of economic, political, and social reform in the region. Trade and financial investment, aid tied to open governance and modern education systems, and consistent backing for human rights and pro-democracy reformers are the keys to a comprehensive, patient strategy for banking the fires of jihadist violence.

Such measures are especially important in Iraq. While Democrats (along with many other Americans) differ about the justification for invading Iraq in early 2003, they should unite behind the imperative of giving the Iraqi people the best possible chance for a peaceful, secure, and broadly representative state. The fact that President Bush and his team have mismanaged virtually every aspect of post-war reconstruction does not justify an immediate or precipitous withdrawal from Iraq. Our national interests demand that we not leave Iraq until we are assured that it will not become a threat to Americans' safety. And our national honor demands that, having invaded their country, we not abandon the Iraqi people to chaos and sectarian violence. Instead, we should rally the American people for an extended and robust security and reconstruction presence, even as we push the administration to gradually transfer security responsibilities to improving Iraqi forces, help to build truly national rather than sectarian institutions, and shore up regional as well as international backing for the Iraqi government.

REBUILD OUR STRATEGIC ALLIANCES

As progressives we believe the United States needs more friends to ensure our mutual safety in a turbulent world.

We will rebuild America's strategic alliances, cultivate better relations with rising democratic powers, such as India, and strengthen institutions for collective security. Rather than constraining U.S. freedom of action, as conservative unilateralists complain, our alliances have more often extended America's reach, amplified our voice in world affairs, and increased global trust and confidence in the exercise of our immense power.

When our country has stood for a cause larger than itself—namely, liberal democracy—it has won the admiration of people around the world. Yet the Bush administration has frittered away America's hard-earned moral authority in unbelievably cavalier fashion. Our country has paid a stiff price. Imagine, for example, how differently events might have unfolded in Iraq if the United States had enjoyed the unstinting and generous support of all of its allies, rather than the truculent resistance of France, Germany, and others. Few of the great global problems we face today—combating terrorism, halting the spread of mass destruction weapons, slowing climate change, dealing with rogue and failing states, confronting pandemics, reducing poverty—can be solved by any one nation, no matter how much power, hard or soft, it has at its command. In fact, U.S. internationalism from its inception has been premised on the need for cooperation with European democracies. Renewing the democratic solidarity of "the West" is a top strategic priority for progressives.

At the same time, we have no illusions that multilateralism can be a substitute for vigorous U.S. leadership. It is sadly the case that our allies too often lack the will, the cohesion, or the means to undertake difficult assignments. This is why the United States had to lead the way in the Balkans during the 1990s, as well as in Iraq. We are also skeptical of the European left's claims that the United Nations presents a credible alternative to U.S. power. From Kosovo to Rwanda, and from Iraq to Darfur, the United Nations has often been paralyzed by a lack of consensus among its leading powers and tarnished by corruption among those who execute its mandates. While we should always try to build such a consensus, we cannot let its absence stop us when the case for armed intervention is strategically or morally compelling.

The answer is not to give up on collective security, but to dramatically transform the U.N., or create new institutions that enable the international community to muster the will and means to act on its responsibility to protect people from ethnic cleansing, genocide, and catastrophic terrorist attacks. At the same time, we should be expanding rather than reducing our capacity to carry out antiterrorism missions through NATO. The Bush administration unwisely rebuffed NATO offers to assist in the war on terrorism. Progressive internationalists will strengthen NATO's antiterrorism capabilities and nurture a growing political consensus within NATO for tackling the shared threat posed by jihadist extremism.

RECLAIM LIBERAL DEMOCRACY

Progressives must champion liberal democracy in deed, not just in rhetoric, as an integral part of a strategy for preventing conflict, promoting prosperity, and defending human dignity. Unfortunately, President Bush's rhetorical embrace of Middle East democracy has led some Democrats to the reflexive conclusion that if a Republican supports promoting democracy in other countries, it must be a bad idea. It is troubling that a 50–43 percent majority of Democrats now oppose the goal of promoting democracy abroad, according to a recent German Marshall Fund survey, while a strong 76–19 percent majority of Republicans support this goal.[3]

We believe Democrats must reclaim, not abandon, their own tradition of muscular liberalism as exemplified by Presidents Truman, Kennedy, and Clinton. While conservative "realists" have traditionally sought to separate foreign and domestic policy, those Democrats insisted that America's conduct in the world must also reflect the nation's core values and be linked to progressive purposes at home. We recognize, moreover, that spreading economic and political liberty is a strategic imperative for the United States, not simply an expression of those values. The intentions and actions of states are as powerfully shaped by their internal character and governance arrangements as by abstract concepts like the balance of power. Countries with accountable political institutions are better global citizens than autocratic regimes. They tend to be more open, more prosperous, more likely to seek peaceful solutions to conflicts, to keep their agreements, and to abide by civilized norms of conduct. It is hardly an accident that, of the many rogue and failing states in the world, none is a genuine democracy.

Just as cold war liberals fashioned America's response to communism, today's progressives should assume responsibility for confronting the jihadist ideology. After all, the jihadist creed, in its bigotry and intolerance, its glorification of mass murder, and its contempt for liberal democracy, bears a sinister resemblance to the totalitarian ideologies of twentieth-century Europe. Even if its adherents do not have massed armies threatening to invade our allies, we cannot ignore the fact that violent jihadism, like fascism and communism, poses both a threat to our people's safety and a moral challenge to our liberal beliefs and ideals.

Progressives, who championed human rights and democratic freedoms from Central Europe to South Africa, need to take the lead in showing how a belief in the universality of these concepts can strengthen America's security.

One clear area where progressives can draw that line between themselves and the Bush administration is on the use of torture as an instrument of American military policy. The prisoner abuses at Abu Ghraib and the promotion of extreme interrogation techniques at Guantanamo not only invite others to mistreat U.S. prisoners; they also erode our moral standing with advocates of human rights and democracy abroad. Principled conservatives, notably Senator John McCain (R–AZ), know that "water-boarding" is incompatible with freedom fighting. It is disgraceful that many others, including Vice President Dick Cheney, do not.

Progressives and Democrats must not give up the promotion of democracy and human rights abroad just because President Bush has paid it lip service. Advancing democracy—in practice, not just in rhetoric—is fundamentally the Democrats' legacy, the Democrats' cause, and the Democrats' responsibility.

LINK PROSPERITY AND SECURITY

Progressives believe America must lead the world toward greater prosperity as well as greater security. One of President Bill Clinton's primary goals and clearest accomplishments was to ensure that America's foreign policy encompassed a stronger economic dimension. To that end, he worked to open markets and lower global trade barriers, as part of a strategy to support democracy and development abroad, while also increasing domestic investments in education and training, so that America could "compete, not retreat" in the face of sweeping economic changes. Progressive internationalists will work to restore that emphasis—sorely lacking since President Clinton left office—on making global economics work to the benefit of both our global goals and economic prospects of working Americans.

The Bush economic agenda, by contrast, has weakened America's competitiveness while undermining the public consensus for economic engagement abroad. This administration praises outsourcing and then wonders why trade liberalization efforts turn into a strictly partisan affair, as Democrats mistakenly although understandably line up against free trade agreements for Central America and other poverty-struck regions. The Bush administration subsidizes Hummers, blocks improvements in auto fuel efficiency, and deepens our dependence on oil, but then pleads innocent when Americans face punishingly high gas prices at home.

The Bush fiscal policy provides another example of how this administration has weakened America's strength by decoupling security from sound economics. Wartime presidents typically raise taxes; President Bush has repeatedly cut them, shifting the cost of today's security to our children, while also shifting the tax burden from wealthy to working families. Wartime presidents typically subordinate everything to the war effort; President Bush has presided over an unprecedented orgy of federal spending at the behest of special interests. On his watch, nonmilitary spending has grown by an astonishing 27.9 percent.[4] As a result of these choices, America today faces a national fiscal emergency—big budget deficits and an exploding national debt, even before the stupendous costs of the baby boom generation's impending retirement are factored in. Under the Bush Republicans, Americans borrow more heavily from foreigners than ever before to make up the difference between what we consume and what we produce. This makes our nation's financial health dangerously dependent on the willingness of investors in China and other foreign capitals to finance our debts.

Progressives believe that a balanced economic strategy is an ethical as well as a material imperative. Wartime presidents commonly foster an ethic of shared sacrifice; President Bush with two glaring exceptions has asked Americans to give up virtually nothing. That first exception, of course, is our voluntary military; they and their families have borne almost the entire physical burden of the struggle against jihadist extremism. The second exception is America's children and future generations, onto whom President Bush has shifted the bulk of the financial cost of this war.

In trying to conduct his war on terror on the cheap, the president has done a grave disservice to our armed forces. They were sent into Iraq in insufficient numbers, with inadequate equipment, and without any clear plan of what to do once they had toppled the regime of Saddam Hussein. They have borne the brunt of the administration's blunders, from the calamitous decision to set up a high-profile occupying authority, to the lack of guidance as to how to treat and interrogate prisoners, to the failure to adopt proven counterinsurgency tactics from the outset.

Progressives believe that a strategy of robust internationalism is only sustainable if we ask Americans to share its costs and risks equitably. That is why we would repeal the tax cuts for the wealthiest among us, and use part of the proceeds to invest in equipping, enlarging, and modernizing America's armed forces. And we would create new opportunities for young Americans to make contributions to our battle against terrorism, such as enlarging national service to assist with emergency preparedness, and expanding training of young people in languages that could help the State Department and CIA in counterterrorism.

Progressives also understand that our leaders can't preach democracy to others while ignoring the deep flaws and injustices of our own democracy. We must not flinch from tackling these problems, including comparatively high rates of poverty among working families and children, the shameful fact that over 40 million of our fellow citizens still lack basic health insurance, a persistent education achievement gap between minority and white students—our number one civil rights challenge—and the lack of public supports for people who lose their jobs in the fast-changing global economy.

"ASK NOT" . . . AGAIN

Finally, progressives will work to rebuild the spirit of mutual sacrifice and the bipartisan consensus that are necessary for sustaining America's confrontation with jihadism and our broader international responsibilities. President Bush bears a heavy burden of responsibility for the stark partisan polarization of American national security policy. At several critical junctures—just after 9/11 and after his 2004 reelection—the president had an opportunity to rally the country behind a comprehensive response to jihadist terrorism that would have confronted pressing domestic problems as well as our overseas enemies. Instead, he and his advisers chose to turn national security into a partisan wedge issue.

For example, they filled our highest post at the United Nations with an anti-U.N. ideologue, John Bolton, who helped wage the Bush Florida recount litigation in 2000. They wielded the Patriot Act as a partisan bludgeon and routinely impugned the patriotism of Democrats who criticized their policies. They turned key homeland security positions into dumping grounds for unqualified cronies, like the hapless Michael Brown at the Federal Emergency Management Administration. They filled sensitive public diplomacy positions with political operatives like Karen Hughes who lack the international experience or bipartisan backing to speak for America and improve the country's image abroad. They waged a savage war of reprisal against critics of their policies, in one notorious case triggering an investigation that resulted in the indictment of a top aide to Vice President Cheney.

It was once said that politics stopped at the water's edge where America's security is concerned. But today's Republicans stop at nothing, turning our troops into political props and leaking classified information to settle political scores.

Progressive internationalists know that America's national security policies are doomed to fail if they are designed to be either "red" or "blue," and will work to rebuild the badly shredded national consensus for engagement abroad that existed during most of the cold war and the years immediately following it.

In sum, the progressive strategy detailed in this book takes advantage of all of our country's strengths, not just the big stick of military power. It seeks to unite, not polarize and divide, our people. It links the defense of liberty abroad with a new determination to press progressive reforms at home. It calls on all Americans—not just our men and women in uniform—to share the burden of prevailing in what is likely to be a long, arduous, and costly struggle.

THE CHALLENGE FOR DEMOCRATS

Developing a successful strategy against jihadist terror is a security imperative for all Americans. But there is a particular political imperative here for the Democratic Party. For more than three decades, Democrats have suffered from a "national security confidence gap."[5] The public has consistently expressed higher confidence in Republicans when it comes to keeping the country strong and confronting external threats. The gap, a legacy of anti-Vietnam war protests, mattered less during the 1990s, when security moved to the sidelines and economic concerns took center stage. Since 9/11, it has become a crucial barrier preventing the party from reclaiming national leadership—even as public dissatisfaction with President Bush and the Republican Congress has reached record highs.

The American electorate will not turn over national leadership to a party it does not trust to defend the country and lead our military. Surveys by Greenberg Quinlan Rosner for Democracy Corps show that in October 2005, likely voters associated "security and keeping people safe" with the Republicans more than with the Democrats by a double-digit, 48–34 percent margin.[6] Moreover, while Democrats made gains on virtually every other issue and leadership attribute across the course of 2005—from "cares about people" to "reform and change"—they failed to make any significant gains during the year on national security issues, much less erase their deficit.

The reasons are not hard to discern. Virtually the only thing the public knows at this point about the Democrats on national security is that a large number of them want to pull out of Iraq. But that communicates very little—even to those who might favor withdrawal—about the positive steps Democrats would take to prosecute the war against jihadist extremists and make the country safer. Of course Democrats have an obligation as the opposition party to hold the administration accountable for its failures in Iraq. But discrediting President Bush's stewardship of U.S. foreign policy does not by itself establish Democrats' credibility on national security. It's important that Democrats avoid too narrow a preoccupation with Iraq and lift their sights toward the broader challenge of protecting Americans and the civilized world from the destructive fury of jihadism. Democrats should be defining themselves not just by their Iraq critique, but by their post-Iraq strategy.

It is notable that, in addition to national security, the one other area on which Democrats still trail Republicans by big margins is on whether voters "know what they stand for." The two liabilities are linked: Democrats need to articulate a clear and principled strategy for making Americans safer, both to show what they stand for, and to prove they can be trusted to protect the country. That is the mission of this book.

In the last two national elections, the party has failed to rise to this challenge. In 2002, party leaders and candidates tried to change the topic, putting aside terrorism and national security and focusing instead on domestic concerns such as jobs and health care. The results were disastrous, as a worried, post–9/11 electorate gave Republicans control of the Senate and an expanded majority in the House. In 2004, the party sought to neutralize GOP advantages on national security by nominating a war hero for president, while maintaining an ambiguous posture on the party's position on Iraq and terrorism. But the public was looking for a battle plan, not just a war record; and they wanted the clarity of fixed principles rather than a straddle across party factions.

It may well be, as William Galston and Elaine Kamarck have argued,[7] that Democrats will not be able to rebuild their credibility on security issues until they have a president in office who successfully addresses a major international crisis. Yet the party needs to start uniting around a positive security agenda, like the program of progressive internationalism outlined here, if a

Democratic president is ever going to be ready to respond successfully when that moment arises.

What holds the Democratic Party back from adopting a rigorous and credible national security program? The lack of an internal consensus on America's role in the world. Most rank-and-file Democrats, we are convinced, remain faithful to the tough-minded liberalism of Presidents Franklin Roosevelt, Harry Truman, and John Kennedy. On the other side are the antiwar, noninterventionist views held by an influential minority in the party—disproportionately upscale, liberal, Internet-active, and important in fundraising for Democratic candidates and causes. Yet liberal activists and elites often have little contact with people in uniform, feel culturally estranged from the military, and seem more focused on restraining our armed forces than on ensuring their readiness and effectiveness.[8]

As some Democrats drift away from an understanding of the military, the military has drifted away from the Democrats. Even though there is reason to believe some recent surveys overstate the case, the Republican tilt in military voting seems undeniable, as is the fact that about 60 percent of the armed forces now come from Red states, even though those states account for only 51 percent of the country's population.[9]

This is unhealthy and potentially dangerous. Already, we have seen the top ranks of the uniformed military prove themselves overly deferential to the GOP White House in the run-up to Iraq. At the same time, the Clinton administration's lack of standing with the officer corps tended to make it excessively deferential to the Pentagon, which, for example, strongly opposed American intervention in Bosnia. A well-balanced civil-military relationship, and an effective military component to the war on terror, requires a stronger relationship between the Democratic Party's own rank-and-file and the armed forces.

Democrats therefore need to move on two fronts if they are to unite around a successful set of strategies for addressing jihadist terror and the country's other national security challenges. On one front, the party's strategists need to put forward an uncompromising program for strengthening all the sources of American power and projecting them against the threats we face.

At the same time, Democrats need to distance themselves from elite attitudes that are antithetical to the party's best foreign policy traditions and to its prospects for building a new progressive majority in America. More leaders within the party need to start making the case for a stronger and larger military—even as we move toward an end-game in Iraq. More party leaders need to speak out about the need for promoting democracy abroad, even if they rightly object to the highly rhetorical and inconsistent ways that the current administration has pursued that concept. The party needs more activists, like the leaders of the promising Truman National Security Project, who engage young Democrats in discussions about strong national security policies. And the party needs to do more—as leaders like Representative Rahm Emmanuel (D-IL) have now begun to do—to reach out to veterans from the wars in Iraq and Afghanistan to tap their experience and eagerness to serve.

Our hope is that this volume will provide some of the strategic ideas to fuel those conversations—so that more progressives can unite around national security policies that give the public confidence, and so that we can give America the tools to win the battle against jihadist terror in the years ahead.

NOTES

1. "Terrorism Knowledge Base," The RAND Corporation and The National Memorial Institute for the Prevention of Terrorism, January 2006, www.tkb.org/Home.jsp.

2. Connelly, Marjorie, and Robin Toner. "Economy Lifts Bush's Support in Latest Poll," *New York Times*, December 8, 2005, final ed.: 1A.

3. Kennedy, Craig, "America Must Make Democracy a Global Cause," *Financial Times*, September 7, 2005.

4. De Rugy, Veronique, and Nick Gillespie, "Bush the Budget Buster," *Reason*, October 19, 2005, http://reason.com/links/links101905.shtml.

5. Marshall, Will, "Closing the National Security Gap," *Blueprint*, July 25, 2004.

6. Democracy Corps. "The Change Electorate on the Eve of More Change," October 2005. Washington, D.C.: Greenberg Quinlan Rosner Research, Inc., 2005. www.democracycorps.com/reports/surveys/Democracy_Corps_October_1923_2005_Survey.pdf.

7. Galston, William, and Elaine Kamarck, "The Politics of Polarization," Third Way, October 2005, www.third-way.com/products/tw_pop.pdf.

8. "The Dean Activists: Their Profile and Prospects," the Pew Research Center, April 6, 2005, http://people-press.org/reports/display.php3?ReportID=240.

9. The figures of 60 versus 52 percent are based on our own analysis of census data on state origins of military personnel. A September 2004 online survey commissioned and published by *The Military Times* found that uniformed military personnel had voted for Governor George W. Bush over Vice President Al Gore by a margin of 66–12 percent, and planned to vote for President Bush over Senator John F. Kerry by an even greater 73–13 percent margin. This survey almost certainly overstates the actual margin. Online surveys of this kind are notoriously susceptible to biases of self-selection, and the high share of respondents from upper military ranks and from Red states (66 percent, compared to about 59 percent actually from Red states) speaks to the biased nature of the sample. Even generous corrections for these biases would likely still yield a significant Republican tilt among the uniformed military.

I

WINNING THE WAR OF IDEAS

1

THE STRUGGLE FOR ISLAM'S SOUL

Reza Aslan

A few blocks east of the massive fissure where the World Trade Center once stood is St. Paul's Chapel. Here, in the days following the attacks of September 11, 2001, a spontaneous "wall of memories" was erected to record the grief, pain, and, most vividly of all, defiance of those whose lives were forever altered by that tragic day. The wall is gone now; it has become part of a permanent memorial at St. Paul's. Most of the flags, ribbons, notes, and photographs that were pinned to it have either been placed in storage or abandoned and forgotten. But there was one memento taped to that battered wall that, while surely lost by now, burned itself into my memory as the perfect expression of the anger felt by most Americans in the wake of the attacks on New York and Washington, D.C. It was a small, hand-painted sign that read in bold, red letters, "We will find whoever did this and they will pay!"

As a Muslim American, I remember thinking how quickly such raw, unfocused rage could be directed at me and my fellow Muslims if it did not find a proper outlet. Thankfully, President George W. Bush acted quickly and decisively by concentrating America's wrath at a single target, Osama bin Laden, and launching a full-scale operation, in tandem with America's European and Arab allies, to bring him and his murderous followers to justice. Like a great many Muslims throughout the world, I applauded the president's decision, recognizing that moderate, pluralist, and peaceful believers like myself, who make up the vast majority of the world's 1.2 billion Muslims, are just as endangered by bin Laden's fanaticism as is any Westerner.

Yet, four years after that tragic September day, it is clearer than ever that the angry, inchoate vow scrawled on that wall of memories during the first fuming moments after the collapse of the Twin Towers, has become the pervading sentiment behind the president's ill-defined, easily distracted, and poorly executed "War on Terror." Four years, two wars, and countless lives lost and there is still little understanding on the part of the Bush administration about who we are fighting, why we are fighting, or, most importantly, how we can win this struggle against global Islamic terrorism (what is more precisely called *jihadism*).

Part of the problem is that in all this time, the president has yet to realize what most of the Muslim world already knows: that the United States has not so much launched a war against Islamic terrorism as joined a war already in progress. Indeed, while a great many Americans continue to view September 11 as the spark that ignited a worldwide "clash of civilizations" between Islam and the West, for many in the Muslim world, the attacks on New York and Washington resulted from a larger *internal* conflict—a civil war, really—that has been raging within Islam for more than a century.

This civil war, or *fitnah*, as Muslims call it, can be traced to the colonial era, when some 90 percent of the world's Muslims were forced, under oppressive colonial rule, to confront a rapidly modernizing, aggressively secularizing, and repressively Westernizing world. The colonial experience fractured the Muslim community into rival factions, each with its own ideas about how the Islamic world should confront a distinctly Western conception of modernity. While some Muslims pushed for the creation of an indigenous Islamic Enlightenment by eagerly developing Islamic alternatives to European Enlightenment values, others advocated a total separation from Western cultural ideals in favor of the complete "Islamization" of society. With the end of colonialism in the twentieth century these factions expanded and refined their arguments over Islam and modernity into a larger, more general debate about how to form a distinctly *Islamic* state.

During this long and often bloody process to define the postcolonial Middle East, as Muslims were compelled to regard themselves less as members of a worldwide community of faith than as citizens of individual nation-states, a new sense of individualism began gradually to creep into this once quintessentially communal religion. Over the last fifty years, this process of "individualization" in Islam has accelerated, due in large part to dramatic increases in literacy and education, greater access to different sources of knowledge, the rise of globalization, and perhaps most importantly, the influx of Muslim immigrants into Europe and North America. Throughout the world, new generations of Muslims have been actively reinterpreting traditional Islamic beliefs and practices to fit the changing needs of their own communities. For the first time in history, Muslim individuals have begun to claim for themselves the traditional authority of the clerical institutions to interpret the meaning and message of their religion. In doing so, they have launched what many scholars of Islam and observers of the region are enthusiastically calling, "The Islamic Reformation."

Reformations, as we know from Christian history, can be apocalyptic events. Thus far, the Islamic Reformation has proved no different. Indeed, as long as there are people of faith who strive to reconcile their values and traditions with the realities of the modern world, there will be those who, perhaps because they feel left behind, react to those realities by retreating (sometimes violently) to the so-called fundamentals of their faith. After all, fundamentalism, in all religions, is a reactionary movement. It is an attempt to retard and reverse the natural evolution of a religion as it encounters and adapts to the changes of society. It was therefore inevitable that as more Muslims throughout the world began to actively engage in the process of reformation, more of their co-religionists began turning toward fundamentalism, puritanism, and even extremism in an effort to turn back the tide of reform and modernism.

It is against this historical backdrop that the rise of modern jihadism must be understood. Jihadism has its *theological* roots in a small, puritanical sect of Islam popularly referred to as *Wahhabism*. From its inception in the Arabian Peninsula during the latter half of the eighteenth century, Wahhabism was a militantly evangelizing movement. Yet, as is the case with most puritan sects—whether Jewish, Christian, Muslim, or Hindu—the Wahhabists directed their missionary enterprise at other Muslims, rather than at those outside of the Muslim faith. Their aim was to strip Islam of its cultural, ethnic, and religious diversity, so as to restore the religion to its original, unadulterated (if imaginary), and exclusively *Arab* origins. By allying themselves with an ambitious tribal shaykh named Muhammad ibn Saud, the Wahhabists were ultimately able to wrest political control of the Arabian Peninsula from Ottoman hands, thus paving the way for the founding of the Kingdom of Saudi Arabia.

Armed with nearly unlimited funds from Arabia's oil fields, the Wahhabists expanded their missionary enterprise to the rest of the Muslim world, where their crude brand of puritanism developed into an appealingly simplistic alternative to the complex theologies of modernism and reform that had dominated much of the region during the first half of the twentieth century. Wahhabism had a particularly deep impact on the poorer, less developed regions of the Muslim world, like southern Pakistan and Afghanistan, where scores of religious students—*taliban* in Arabic—were indoctrinated into its austere, puritanical worldview.

Of course, in those years, Wahhabism was considered an important ally of the United States in the "Great Game" being played out against the Soviet Union, so much so that throughout the Soviet occupation of Afghanistan, the CIA actively promoted it as a counterideology to "godless" communism. The strategy was an unmitigated success. Fueled by their religious zealotry, funded by the Saudis, and eventually armed by the United States, the Afghani and Pakistani *taliban* played a key role in forcing the Soviet army out of Afghanistan through a frightening combination of Wahhabi puritanism and radical militancy inspired by the political philosophies of Sayyid Qutb in Egypt and Abu Ala Mawdudi in India. The result was what is now called jihadism.

With the collapse of the Soviet Union and the end of the cold war, little attention was paid to the jihadists who left Afghanistan to wage jihad in their home countries of Chechnya, Palestine, Lebanon, and Egypt. However, in 1991, when the Saudi government asked the United States to expel Saddam Hussein's Iraqi army from Kuwait, a small group of Saudi dissidents and former Afghan fighters rallied together by Osama bin Laden reignited the ideals of jihadism not only in defense of what they perceived to be Western aggression, but also as a tool for achieving political dominance over the whole of the Muslim world. In true puritan fashion, bin Laden and the jihadists divided Muslims into two groups: "the People of Heaven" (meaning themselves), and "the People of Hell" (meaning all other Muslims). In their view, any Muslim whose interpretation of scripture and observance of Islamic law did not fit the Wahhabi model belonged to the latter group and must be converted or killed.

For more than a decade, the jihadists used the existing infrastructure of Saudi evangelism, often with the blessing of the Saudi regime, which was eager to appease religious critics at home, to spread their militant ideology across the Muslim world. At the same time, they mercilessly targeted both Muslim and non-Muslim governments through a horrifying wave of suicide and terrorist attacks. Yet while their message had great appeal to those Muslims who may have shared the jihadists' grievances regarding the oppression of the Palestinians, the autocracies of the Arab world, and the unrelenting cultural hegemony of the West, few Muslims accepted their puritan ideology, and fewer still their murderous tactics. In fact, in the years prior to September 11, 2001, most scholars and observers of the Muslim world were confidently predicting that the tide of modernism and reform in Islam would soon wash away the dying remnants of puritanism and extremism represented by bin Laden and his jihadist allies.

Then, New York and Washington, D.C., the two strongest symbols of American economic and political power, were brutally attacked. In a single day, the jihadists had achieved the kind of international recognition for which they had been striving for more than a decade. If the primary purpose of terrorism is to provide the illusion of power, the jihadists had managed a near magical feat by spectacularly attacking the seemingly impenetrable United States. For many Americans, bin Laden became the terrifying face of Islam, and September 11 the beginning of a worldwide clash of civilizations. A few days after the attack, President Bush stood on the smoldering ruins at Ground Zero and defiantly announced the beginning of a new and somewhat woolly war on terrorism—or "crusade," as the president regrettably christened it—that even then appears to have involved plans for an invasion of Iraq.

At the time, few Americans could have known that, by bin Laden's own admission, the attacks on New York and Washington, D.C., were deliberately meant to goad the United States into just such a retaliation against the Islamic world. The idea was to mobilize Muslims to choose sides in this civil war over the future of Islam by framing America's inevitable response to September 11 as a war not against terrorism but against Islam. The plan worked. Since the launch of the wars in Afghanistan and Iraq, a growing number of Muslims throughout the world, marshaled by jihadist propaganda that the "clash of civilizations" is in fact a "clash of monotheisms" between Christianity and Islam, have turned their backs on modernism and reform and have instead embraced bin Laden's militant brand of puritanism.

Part of bin Laden's success in capturing the imaginations of so many in the Muslim world—he has over 50 percent approval rating in some Muslim countries—stems from his ability to take advantage of the internal struggle taking place within Islam.[1] He offers himself and his jihadist ideology as an alluring alternative to those Muslims who do not identify with the cause of reform and whose sense of alienation has made them yearn for more radical sources of leadership. That is why if the United States is going to defeat jihadism, it must take a page out of the jihadist playbook, as it were, and also take advantage of this civil war for the future of Islam.

The Bush administration has launched a war against terrorism by relying on brute military force and polarizing, religious rhetoric. But to win this war against violence and extremism in Islam, the United States must pursue a two-part strategy: one that relies heavily on military and intelligence services to destroy terrorist networks across the globe, while simultaneously taking advantage of America's unique position to champion the cause of reform and progress in the Muslim world. The simple truth is that the United States has a national security interest in the outcome of the Islamic Reformation currently underway throughout the Muslim world. It must therefore do whatever it can to tip the balance of power away from the extremists and back to the massive yet voiceless majority of Muslims who are as much victims of jihadism as is the West. This may seem a daunting task, but it can be accomplished through five practical steps.

Change the rhetoric of the war on terrorism.

Almost immediately after September 11, 2001, President Bush initiated a war of words with Osama bin Laden, the man the president dubbed, "The Evil One."

"This is a new kind of evil," President Bush declared a week after the attacks on New York and Washington, D.C. "[And] this crusade, this war on terrorism, is going to take a while."[2]

Few would argue with the idea that the indiscriminate murder of noncombatants is a horrific and unforgivable act of evil. But the charged religious rhetoric that has consistently poured out of both the White House and the Republican leadership has had a devastating impact on the fight against Islamic extremism. By equating this struggle with "a crusade" against "evil-doers," and by referring to the global fight against international terrorism as a battle between "good and evil," the president has, from the start, allowed the jihadists to frame both the scope and meaning of the war against terrorism.

The jihadists, it must be understood, are fighting a war of the imagination, a "cosmic war" that cannot be won in any measurable terms. Their stated goals—the creation of a worldwide caliphate, the eradication of Israel, the destruction of the American army, and so on—are as hopelessly improbable to the jihadists themselves as they are to us. This is why they have been forced to recast their earthly struggle for religious and political dominance over the Muslim world as a cosmic struggle against the forces of evil. Put simply, they want Muslims to believe that the world is locked in a contest between Christianity and Islam. In some ways, the violent overreaction in large parts of the Muslim world to the Danish cartoons of the prophet Muhammad is an indication that the jihadist propaganda that says Islam is under attack by the West is gaining traction.

Yet instead of debunking this twisted ideology, the Bush administration has legitimated it, not only through its own morally reductive rhetoric, but also through a foreign policy that is viewed in large parts of the Muslim world as being unapologetically driven by an evangelical Christian agenda. Instead of treating bin Laden as a criminal who must be brought to justice, the president has transformed him into a mythical being who cannot be found, let alone defeated. In short, instead of fighting the war on terrorism on our terms, we are allowing the jihadists to fight it on their terms.

Obviously, much of the president's rhetoric is meant for a domestic audience, and perhaps no politician can be blamed for indulging the American people's innate sense of moral righteousness and divine favor. However, when Franklin Graham, whom President Bush chose to give the invocation at his second inaugural, publicly calls Islam "an evil and wicked religion;"[3] or when Congressman Tom Tancredo (R–CO) suggests bombing Mecca in retaliation for the actions of a handful of extremists;[4] or when Senator James Inhofe (R–OK) insists that the ongoing conflicts in the Middle East are not political or territorial battles but "a contest over whether or not the word of God is true,"[5] their words reverberate throughout the Islamic world. They practically invite Muslims to accept the jihadist propaganda that the United States is fighting a war not against terrorism, but against Islam. While the president has strived in recent years to distance himself from some of the more radical statements of his Republican allies by noting that the terrorists do not represent all Muslims, he has neither publicly condemned nor privately discouraged this kind of morally reductive rhetoric. On the contrary, he has only furthered suspicion in the Muslim world by suggesting, as recently as two years ago, that God had instructed him to both strike at al Qaeda and remove Saddam from power, as reported in the Israeli newspaper *Ha'aretz*.[6]

As commander-in-chief of the American military, the president must take a firm and public stand against this kind of religiously polarizing rhetoric. In a war as rife with zealotry and fanaticism as the war against terrorism, the United States must do whatever it takes to avoid even the *appearance* of a religious motivation for pursuing and destroying Islamic terrorists. After all, there is but one way to win a cosmic war: refuse to fight in it.

Work with Muslim Americans to create an effective public diplomacy program aimed at the Muslim world.

Six years of arrogant unilateralism and unconsidered belligerence has utterly shattered America's reputation across the globe, especially in large parts of the Arab and Muslim world. Perhaps at no other time in American history has there been a more urgent need to develop a robust program of public diplomacy aimed not at making American foreign policy more palatable (probably a fruitless exercise as long as President Bush remains in charge) but rather at communicating American *values* and *traditions* to Muslims of all nations. Who better to express to the Muslim world what it means to be American than we Muslim Americans?

Muslims are now the largest religious minority in the United States. And yet the American Muslim community, while infinitely diverse in its faith, practice, ethnicity, and political persuasion, has for the most part managed to avoid many of the problems of identity and integration that are currently plaguing Muslim communities throughout Europe. This is partly due to the fact that the majority of European Muslims come from impoverished immigrant families who have formed insulated ethnic communities cut off from the rest of European society, while the majority of Muslims in the United States are either middle class converts (primarily African Americans) or educated immigrants from a wide array of ethnic backgrounds. America's long and storied history of assimilation and multiculturalism tends to prohibit the formation of insulated communities, meaning American Muslims are united less by their individual ethnic identities than by a shared political and cultural ideal (one that we could simply call "Americanism"). It is precisely this shared sense of national identity, coupled with the socioeconomic advantages of living in the United States, that has made American Muslims far more resistant to the pull of jihadism than their European counterparts. As such, American Muslims are ideally suited to become the public face of the United States to the Muslim world.

From my discussions with American Muslim organizations and individuals, I can say with confidence that Muslims in the United States are eager to play an active role in counteracting the influence of bigotry and extremism in their faith. Thus far, however, there has been little attempt by this administration to seriously harness the creative energies of the American Muslim community. The best way to do so is by forming an advisory committee of American Muslim clerics, leaders, activists, and academics charged with the task of drawing up a list of initiatives aimed at reaching out to Muslims across the world. Once finalized, these initiatives can be given to a carefully vetted ambassadorial council of American Muslim leaders responsible for implementing them through a robust program of public diplomacy aimed first at Muslims in allied countries like Jordan and Egypt, where America's image has been particularly damaged by its conduct in the War on Terror, and then (with the help of these allies) at countries like Saudi Arabia and Pakistan, where the internal battle within Islam is being most fiercely fought. The task of this ambassadorial council would not be to convert hard-core jihadists, who would likely view them as apostates, but to show America's best face to the silent Muslim majority.

As the embodiment of the freedoms of faith and conscience for which America is revered in all parts of the world, American Muslims are already at the front lines of the Islamic Reformation. If given the chance, and made to feel that their opinions matter, they can also form the front lines in the war against Islamic extremism.

Actively encourage religious groups in the Arab and Muslim world to participate in the democratic process.

For more than half a century, America's dictatorial allies in the Arab and Muslim world have convinced the West that their antidemocratic policies are necessary because "fundamentalists" in their countries allow them but two possible options: despotism or theocracy. Thus they base their very survival on what a recent U.N. Arab Human Development Report termed "a legitimacy of blackmail."[7] Putting aside for a moment the role these draconian policies have played in creating Islamic extremism in the first place, the notion that, if given a voice in their governments, Muslims would inevitably choose a stifling, archaic theocracy over a free and independent democracy is utterly absurd.

The truth is that the majority of Muslims already accept the fundamental principles of democracy.[8] Democratic ideals such as constitutionalism, popular sovereignty, government accountability, pluralism, and human rights are widely acknowledged throughout the Muslim world, even if many rulers in the region are not willing to implement them. However, what most Muslims do not acknowledge is the notion that their religious values should play no role in their government. The interplay between faith and government has for centuries been the hallmark of political culture in the Muslim world. That is why political opposition in the region is so often religious in nature: not because opponents seek to establish a religious state, but because the language of religion holds the most currency with the Muslim community. Thus, for example, in Iran both the liberal left and the ultra-conservative right use the same "Islamic" rhetoric to fight for either democratic reform or theocratic intransigence.

If democracy is to have a chance in the Middle East, religious factions must be encouraged to participate in the political process. This is especially true with regard to relatively moderate groups like the Muslim Brotherhood in Egypt or the Islamic Action Front in Jordan. But even more extremist groups like Hezbollah in Lebanon and Hamas in Palestine must eventually be brought into the democratic fold. In fact, Hamas's electoral victory offers a key test of whether political participation can moderate extremist ideologies. Hamas must now transform itself from an unaccountable terrorist organization dedicated to nothing less than the destruction of Israel and the creation of a theocratic state in Palestine, to a governing party that must show it can improve the lives of ordinary Palestinians and reach some sort of modus vivendi with Israel. If it wants to retain the support of its constituency—the majority of whom are fed up with the cycle of violence in their country—Hamas must not only distance itself from its military wing (the Qassam Brigades), but also publicly accept a two-state solution that would involve the creation of a secular democratic Palestine. Otherwise, the United States and Europe should feel no obligation to subsidize a Hamas-dominated Palestinian authority. Still, there is every reason to hope that, as with the IRA in Ireland, the more political Hamas is allowed to become, the more accountable it will have to be to the Palestinian people.

Certainly there exist extremist religious groups who have no interest in taking part in any kind of democratic process. They must be opposed by all means necessary. But when even legitimate religious opposition is discouraged or outlawed, the unfortunate result is that it becomes radicalized. As the same Arab Human Development Report cited above concluded, it is precisely the lack of avenues for peaceful opposition that has become the underlying cause of religious extremism in the region. If the United States wants to present itself as being on the side of modernism and reform in this battle for Islam, it can no longer allow itself to be blackmailed into compliance with those rulers whose political interests are served by stifling all opposition—religious or otherwise—in their country.

Begin a serious "dialogue between civilizations" to combat the "clash of civilizations" mentality gripping both the Western and the Islamic worlds.

The war on terrorism is, at its core, a war of ideology. But one cannot win an ideological battle solely with guns and bombs. On the contrary, the only way to defeat an ideology of hatred and fanaticism as defined and spread by Muslim terrorists and extremists is with an ideology of hope and tolerance as defined and spread by Muslim moderates and reformers. Unfortunately, while the jihadists have at their disposal the absolute attention of the worldwide media and a nearly endless supply of funds from wealthy Saudi backers (many of whom remain unaccountable to the Saudi government), moderate Muslims, who have little money or media attention, have thus far been unable to make themselves heard. By engaging moderate Muslim groups, foundations, parties, and individuals to promote shared values like human rights, pluralism, rule of law, and democracy, the United States can play an active part in facilitating the development of an effective ideological counterweight to jihadism.

During the last two decades, the Saudi government, in an attempt to maintain ideological control over their theocratic empire, has funneled more than $75 billion to aid the spread of Wahhabi puritanism across the globe.[9] There is no longer any city in the world with a significant Muslim population that does not have either a mosque, a school, a charitable organization, or a religious institution flush with Saudi funds and, consequently, Wahhabi ideology. To counter this trend, the United States must strive to give the forces of modernism and reform an equal voice in the debate over the future of Islam by providing a forum for moderate Muslims to organize, publish, and transmit their ideas to the rest of the Muslim world. By far the best way to accomplish this task is through a series of initiatives designed to further the exchange of ideas between Islam and the West. These initiatives could include (1) the creation of "translation projects" that would allow Muslim American and Muslim European scholars to translate and disseminate their work in Arabic, Persian, and Urdu, while simultaneously offering Americans and Europeans an opportunity to read and engage with ancient and contemporary works of the Middle East; (2) the support of international think-tanks where moderate Islamic scholars from every corner of the world—people like Tariq al-Bishri and Fathi Osman in Egypt, Abdulkarim Soroush and Shirin Ebadi in Iran, Abdelwahab El-Affendi in Sudan, Mohammad Habash in Syria, and others—can come together to develop and publish new and innovative interpretations of Islamic law to counteract the more traditionalist and fundamentalist interpretations infiltrating much of the Muslim world; (3) the formation of a cultural exchange program under the auspices of USAID, through which artists, writers, scholars, and thinkers from the United States and across the Muslim world could spend a year traveling, working, and teaching in each other's home countries; (4) and finally, the funding of educational scholarships for Muslim high school and college students that would allow them to visit and study in the United States in an intensive cultural awareness program designed to introduce them to American values and traditions.

Of course, the international reputation of the United States is such that it must be wary of appearing to force American values upon the Muslim world or of compromising Muslim groups with its support. However, by working in tandem with the United Nations and other international organizations, the United States could quite easily foster a dialogue between Islamic and Western cultures that would counter the clash of civilizations mentality preached by extremists on both sides of the war on terrorism. If it is true that the war against terrorism is a war of ideology, then the United States must do whatever it can to give moderate Muslims the tools to develop and foster their own ideologies of peace, tolerance, democracy, and pluralism.

We must win the war against the insurgency in Iraq and help create a lasting, viable, and stable Iraqi democracy.

The jihadists have framed the war on terrorism as a cosmic war, which cannot be won in any measurable terms. Sadly, the war in Iraq has, for the first time, transformed their cosmic war into a *real* war, and one that they have every chance of winning in spectacular fashion.

In essence, the war in Iraq has deteriorated into a war of attrition, meaning all the jihadists must do to claim victory is outlast the occupation long enough to destroy any attempt by the Iraqi people to create a modern, pluralistic, and truly indigenous Islamic democracy. It is therefore time to put an end to the endless debates about why and how the war came about and instead set about the overwhelming task of helping Iraqis build a new, freer, more democratic country by (1) destroying the foreign jihadists who make up the most ruthless elements in the insurgency, and (2) giving the indigenous Sunni insurgents an opportunity to take part in the political process while gradually withdrawing our troops from Iraq.

It is true that the Bush administration's arrogance and ignorance has made success in Iraq a more difficult and distant prospect. However, by working with the international community, and in particular with Iraq's neighbors, the United States can still overcome the incompetence and dishonesty of the administration to create a lasting, stable, and democratic Iraq. The fact is that, for better or worse, a democratic Iraq can become the best tool to fight the forces of Islamic extremism because it represents everything the jihadists disdain. That is why the jihadists have focused all of their efforts toward making sure the political experiment in Iraq collapses into chaos before it can have an opportunity to flourish. The United States cannot allow that to happen. The cost of success in Iraq may be high, but the cost of defeat would be unimaginably higher.

Four years after the tragic events of September 11, the unfocused rage of those early days is slowly being replaced with a sense of reflection and contemplation. More encouragingly, many American Muslims who feared they would be the victims of a widespread backlash against Islam in the United States have now begun to consider themselves as part of the solution, rather than part of the problem, in the global war against Islamic terrorism. Now more than ever, the American people are ready for frank talk about what kind of war we are fighting and, more importantly, what it will take to win this ideological battle against jihadism. For this is a war that can be won; indeed, it *must* be won. But to do so will require an administration dedicated to combining military might with a willingness to fully engage in this internal battle for the future of Islam.

NOTES

1. According to a recent poll, support for bin Laden varies significantly by country. While 60 percent of Jordanians and 50 percent of Pakistanis claim to have a lot or some confidence in bin Laden as a leader, fewer among Indonesians (35 percent), Moroccans (26 percent), Turks (7 percent), and Lebanese (2 percent) express this level of support. "Islamic Extremism: Common Concern for Muslim and Western Publics," Poll, Pew Global Attitudes Project, July 14, 2005, http://pewglobal.org/reports/display.php ?PageID = 814.

2. Bush, George W., "Remarks of the President upon Arrival," September 16, 2001, www.whitehouse.gov/news/releases/2001/09/20010916-2.html.

3. "Graham Stands by Characterization of Islam as 'Wicked,'" State and Local Wire, *Associated Press*, November 19, 2001.

4. Kamen, Al, "Brave Nuke World," *Washington Post*, July 20, 2005.

5. "Of Theology and Mideast Policy," *St. Petersburg Times*, March 17, 2002.

6. Regular, Arnon, "'Road Map Is a Life Saver for Us,' PM Abbas Tells Hamas," *Ha'aretz*, July 3, 2003, www.haaretzdaily.com/hasen/pages/ShArt.jhtml?itemNo = 310788&contrassID = 2&subContrassID = 1&sbSubContrassID = 0&listSrc = Y<br%20/>.

7. Quoted in "A Long Way to Go," *The Economist*, April 7, 2005, www.economist .com/agenda/displayStory.cfm?story_id = 3855160.

8. Pew, Poll, http://pewglobal.org/reports/display.php?PageID = 809.

9. Alyami, Ali, and Micha van Waesberghe, "Defenders or Enemies of Islam?" The Center for Democracy and Human Rights in Saudi Arabia, June 8, 2005, www.cdhr .info/pressroom.asp?id = 52.

2

A GRAND STRATEGY FOR
THE MIDDLE EAST

Kenneth M. Pollack

The United States has never had a grand strategy for the Middle East.[1] In truth, we did not "discover" the Middle East until World War II, when we feared German designs on its oil and rushed to defend it with our British and Soviet allies from panzer columns threatening from North Africa and southern Russia. During the cold war, our Middle East policies were adjuncts of American grand strategy toward the USSR. Our principal mission was to prevent Soviet expansion and our policies everywhere were based almost entirely on containing the Russians.

We have not developed an overarching foreign policy design since the fall of the Soviet Union to replace the strategy of containment. Yet, especially since September 11, 2001, we now realize that the gravest threats we face are from the Muslim Middle East. This troubled part of the world is riven by conflict, mired in backwardness, and seething with anger at America and other countries it holds responsible for its problems. What's more, global economic dependence on cheap oil is so great that we cannot tolerate the instability for which the Middle East has become famous. A major calamity there could bring down the entire international economic order. Thus, we have every reason to make the Middle East our preeminent concern.

There are many problems with the Bush administration's Middle East policies. The greatest, however, has been its failure to conceive and pursue a grand strategy toward the region. As a result, many of our policies are mutually contradictory: They hinder one another and make it harder for us to achieve our principal goals in the region. Just as we tailored our policies toward every other country during the cold war to support the strategy of containment, we must now fashion a similar strategy toward the Middle East if we are to meet the challenges it poses.

THE HEART OF A NEW GRAND STRATEGY

At West Point, Annapolis, Sandhurst, St. Cyr, and wherever else strategy is taught, the first lesson is that any strategy must begin with an idea of the end state the strategy seeks to create. The end state that America's grand strategy toward the Middle East must envision is a new liberal order to replace a status quo marked by political repression, economic stagnation, and cultural conflict. These conditions—much more than reactions to U.S. policy—have generated the two principal threats to America's vital interests today. The first and most obvious is terrorism—9/11 demonstrated that the Middle East's problems are not confined to the region and can cause catastrophic damage to Americans at home. Troubles there can have a very real impact on our lives here.

The second principal threat stems from the world's dependence on Middle East oil. Our global economy was built on a foundation of cheap, plentiful oil. It underpins our way of life and a major supply disruption could cause chaos on the order of the Great Depression. Unfortunately, the Middle East represents a major slice of oil production, holds the vast majority of proven reserves, and has the most easily recovered oil, making its exports absolutely vital. More unfortunately still, many of the region's most important states suffer from disaffected populations, militant Islamist oppositions, social unrest, and deep economic distress. Many of these countries show signs of internal instability that could lead to coups, revolutions, civil wars, and failed states. Oil's importance to the global economy makes the region's instability a global problem.

THE CASE FOR TRANSFORMATION

During the cold war, we worried about conflict among the region's states escalating into conflict between their superpower backers. We assumed that the best way to achieve stability in the region was to focus on its international relations. Consequently, we ignored problems festering *within* Middle Eastern states and let Arab autocrats rule as they saw fit. Those problems have produced Islamic terrorists seeking to harm the United States and its allies and desperately unhappy populations increasingly willing to challenge illegitimate and insecure regimes.

The Arab states' economies are stagnant. Many have failed to diversify beyond oil and now suffer from crippling unemployment and under-employment. Many of their citizens have retreated into religious revival, often of particularly noxious new hues. Arab educational systems produce graduates qualified to do little of value to society. The problem is not just the predominance of Islamic learning in their curricula, but a teaching method that reveres rote memorization and smothers creative thinking, interdisciplinary learning, and other entrepreneurial skills. Politically, the Arab autocracies have largely ossified into massive bureaucracies that provide virtually no services to their people, no outlets for them to express their grievances, and no hope for political action to address their many difficulties.

This situation is not unique to the Middle East or even new. Indeed, it is broadly similar to the problems that have beset every traditional society confronted by modernity. In every case, transformative reform of virtually every sector of life has been the only "solution." It means economic reform along free-market principles. It means educational reform to produce graduates who can compete in the global economy. It means social reform that adapts traditional values to modern necessities. It means establishing the rule of law. It means making government more responsive to people's needs and more reflective of their beliefs and aspirations.

East Asia, Latin America, and now South Asia and Eastern Europe are all in some phase of this reform. While hardly a panacea, it has vastly improved conditions in all of those regions. There is no reason why it cannot do the same in the Middle East. There is every reason to believe that it will and, quite frankly, no one has ever proposed a better alternative. Helping the Muslim Middle East undergo such a transformation will be a long and daunting task. It must be led principally from within the region's states, will require overcoming countless obstacles, and has no guarantee of success.

But until someone can pose a better solution, this is the only one that we know *can* work.

HARMONIZING THE CACOPHONY

To its credit, the Bush administration has recognized the importance of bringing reform to the Middle East. However, it has *not* made transformation its highest goal for the Middle East. It has paid only a modest amount of attention to political reform and even less to economic, social, educational, legal, and other reforms. Its efforts in the political realm have been inconsistent at best and have often amounted to little more than rhetoric. And it has singularly failed to revise its other regional policies to advance reform. Recent developments in Palestine are the best example of this. The election of Hamas was not a triumph of democracy, but a demonstration of the barrenness of the administration's policy of rhetorical support for elections without any effort to create the underpinnings of a democratic society.

Instead, the administration seems to have made advancing reform in the region its lowest priority. Iran and Syria's rogue regimes seem to be the only exceptions. The administration insists on democratic change there in a manner it eschews for Egypt, Saudi Arabia, and other allies, which only fuels Middle Easterners' cynicism about America. The right grand strategy would make transformation of our friends and foes alike our agenda's foremost issue.

The administration is committed to the transformation of Iraq, but is handling the situation in such a wrongheaded way that it is actually retarding this critical goal. The right grand strategy would recognize that transformation is so vital that other considerations arguing for these failed policies (like an unwillingness to admit past mistakes—too few troops, too little planning, a focus on terrorists rather than the real sources of instability in Iraq) are luxuries that cannot be afforded.

Finally and most notably regarding Israel and the Palestinians, the administration's policies are actually antithetical to the cause of reform. The right grand strategy would reverse such policies. As with Iraq, the specific rationales that motivate current approaches fade into insignificance when judged against the importance of achieving the nation's most important goal and defeating its gravest threats.

IRAQ

For better or worse, whether you supported the war or not, it is all about Iraq now. All of America's policies and interests in the region are tied to its fate.

The issue can be stated fairly simply. If some day, Iraq becomes a stable, pluralist society, others in the region will eventually follow. Democratic dominoes would not begin to fall overnight, of course. Rather, Arabs (and Iranians and others) would finally have a model of a "liberal" Arab state that reflects Arab history, traditions, culture, and values. Its existence would provide a powerful counterargument to the claims of the region's autocrats and Islamists. And as has been the case elsewhere in the world, its success might slowly help convince others to adopt a similar system in their own country. It would be akin to how Japan showed other East Asian nations over a period of decades that democratic principles can coexist with East Asian traditions, values, and aspirations and so made the transformation of East Asia possible.

On the other hand, liberal reform in the Middle East might well be doomed if Iraqi reconstruction fails. Autocrats and their Islamist opponents alike could claim that if America cannot make democracy work in Iraq with 150,000 troops and $300 billion, there is no chance it can work anywhere else in the Muslim Middle East. And many other Middle Easterners (and Americans and Europeans) would agree.

If we fail in Iraq, the most likely scenario would also be the worst-case scenario. Iraq almost certainly would slide into chaos and civil war and destabilize many, if not all, of its already fragile neighbors—the great oil-producing states of Saudi Arabia, Kuwait, and Iran; our NATO-ally Turkey; our Jordanian friends; even our Syrian foes. We would be lucky if their governments merely survived, let alone reformed themselves as our grand strategy should seek.

Failed states are the perfect breeding ground for the worst kinds of terrorist groups. Lebanon and Afghanistan are prime examples. Iraq was decidedly not the central front of the war on terrorism before we invaded it, but by our actions we have made it such. Today, any would-be Salafi jihadist is traveling to Iraq to learn the trade of terrorism and test his mettle in combat with the Americans. If we leave Iraq in chaos and it spreads across the region, these groups will establish even more training camps and other bases from which to conduct attacks against Americans and our allies, just as al Qaeda used Afghanistan to mount the East Africa bombings, the attack on the USS *Cole*, and the horrors of 9/11.

We cannot simply walk away from Iraq without repercussions. In that sense, Iraq is decidedly not Vietnam. Failure in Iraq would almost certainly destabilize the Middle East and thereby expose Americans to even graver terrorist and economic threats. As Andrew Krepinevich has remarked, the war in Iraq began as a war of choice but has become a war of necessity.[2]

The Bush administration seems to understand the danger of failure in Iraq. But during the nearly three years after it toppled Saddam it neglected and in some cases contributed to problems that are making Iraqi reconstruction harder to achieve.

For example, it spent too much time chasing insurgents in remote areas and too little protecting Iraq's population and infrastructure. It failed to give

Iraq's nascent security services enough training, resources, and time to become an effective substitute for American forces. It was unwilling to cut deals with Sunni tribal shaykhs who broadly hinted they would help keep the peace if the price were right. It failed to address corruption in the Iraqi government that skims away billions of dollars in oil revenue that could be spent on reconstruction. It failed to decentralize power and the distribution of resources beyond Baghdad. And it was unwilling to either pressure Iraq's existing political parties to develop wider constituencies or force those with little popularity out of the currently skewed political process.[3]

The Bush administration needs to correct these mistakes if it is serious about stabilizing, let alone succeeding in Iraq.[4] In the short term, it should de-emphasize offensive operations against insurgents in the Sunni triangle and redouble security operations in southern and central Iraq, where the vast majority of Iraq's Shi'ah and urban Sunni populations live. This would mean concentrating more coalition forces in these areas and making their priorities presence, dismounted patrolling, protection of critical infrastructure, and creating a secure environment for Iraq's economic and political life to revive and for the Iraqi armed forces to train and cohere. Ideally, it would also include a much greater emphasis on creating mixed formations of Iraqi and American troops, and the embedding of whole U.S. formations (ideally of platoon or company strength) in new Iraqi units. It should actually slow the pace of training Iraqi security forces to give them ample time to hone their skills and become capable successors to coalition forces. And as unpalatable as it might be, the administration needs to cut the deals that Sunni shaykhs seem anxious to make. The best intelligence suggests that tribal Sunnis make up a considerable proportion of the insurgency. Buying them off might not end the insurgency, but it might reduce it to the most extreme fringe.

In the longer term, once we have created a secure space for much of the population we must focus on building Iraqi political, military, and economic institutions strong enough to hold the country together without a massive U.S. military presence. This would include a thorough vetting of Iraq's police coupled with lengthy re-education for those who remain. Iraq's police need to be taught that their job is to protect and serve, not oppress and steal as was the case under Saddam Hussein and continues to be today. Similarly, too many judges are Saddam holdovers and the most upright live under constant threat from both insurgents and criminals. The bad ones need to be ejected, the good ones protected, and a slew of prosecutors, detectives, public defenders, and others hired, trained, and set to work.

In a similar vein, the administration needs to press Iraq's government to fight graft to the greatest extent practicable. It needs to demonstrate that corruption will not be tolerated in the new Iraq and educate the citizenry that graft, nepotism, and other forms of traditional Middle Eastern patronage are unacceptable in a democracy.

In addition, the administration needs to empower Iraqi local and municipal governments until the central government develops the capacity and self-discipline to administer reconstruction properly. It must make a major effort to promote new political parties in Iraq and encourage the existing ones to widen their constituencies and act more in the interests of their constituencies. It must work with the Iraqi government to oust corrupt officials and provide Iraq's ministries with the resources and knowhow they need to govern the nation properly.

Until such time as they are able to do so, the administration must work with international and nongovernmental organizations to push contracts and other aid down to levels of government closer to the Iraqi people. This means getting more Americans who can speak Arabic out of the Green Zone and into towns and villages where they can learn about and address local needs firsthand. This also probably means relaxing rules that otherwise would prevent Iraqis who speak little or no English and are unfamiliar with Western accounting and legal practices from securing contracts.

As a final note, although the Bush administration deserves criticism for mishandling the reconstruction of Iraq, those calling for a hasty American withdrawal are committing a far graver sin. Iraq's military and political institutions are simply unready to handle the burden of reconstruction on their own. Even if the steps enumerated above are implemented completely and immediately, we will not see results for several years. An American withdrawal from Iraq before its military and government can cope with the country's myriad problems will almost certainly lead to civil war. And nothing could be worse for America's interests in the region and the world.

THE ISRAELI-PALESTINIAN CONFLICT

The Bush administration's abdication of responsibility for a peace process between Israelis and Palestinians is seriously hampering the transformation of Iraq and its neighbors in the Middle East.

Trouble between Israelis and Palestinians is a major obstacle to persuading wary Arab populations and their reluctant governments to embrace political, economic, or social reform. Liberal reforms like the establishment of truly independent opposition parties and truly free elections are typically portrayed as being Western. And whenever there are problems between Israelis and Palestinians, anyone advocating anything that smacks of Westernization quickly loses favor.

In fact, to some extent, these reforms are often portrayed in Middle Eastern conspiracy theories as being inspired by the Israelis to weaken the Arabs. The governments themselves often hint that an opposition figure is supported by Israel, or that the voicing of dissent is a trick to weaken the government. Along similar lines, many Arab regimes steadfastly maintain that they cannot begin reform while remaining on guard against the Israeli enemy. They claim they must maintain martial law, command economies, wasteful levels of military spending, crippling legal codes, and other inefficiencies to mobilize national resources to combat the "Zionist entity."

Moreover, anger at Israel among Arabs inevitably turns into anger at the United States for supporting Israel. When such tensions run high it makes all Arab rulers wary of introducing reforms or taking other actions that could further inflame their populace, regardless of whether they think it the best course of action. King Abdullah of Jordan has courageously introduced a series of liberal reforms to his kingdom, even allowing Islamist parties to participate in parliamentary elections. But his government has complained bitterly that the breakdown in meaningful peace negotiations has forced him to move slower than he would have liked.

The Israeli-Palestinian dispute is also a convenient excuse for Arab regimes to ignore the travails of reconstruction in Iraq as well as the threat (which they themselves frequently voice) from the region's rogue states. It also becomes a convenient issue for outside powers seeking to gain purchase in the region. Remember that the Soviets made vast inroads into the Middle East by supporting the rejectionist Arab states against Israel. So too could China, India, Russia, or other countries should they desire.

The Israeli-Palestinian conflict makes everything else that the United States wants to do in the region harder. By the same token, when negotiations between Israelis and Palestinians move along, everything the United States wants in the Middle East suddenly becomes easier. That is why the Bush administration's neglect of the Israeli-Palestinian conflict is so deleterious to the pursuit of American interests in the Middle East.

Moreover, the Bush administration's utter neglect of the Israeli-Palestinian conflict has produced a potentially catastrophic Hamas victory in Palestinian parliamentary elections. As former U.S. ambassador to Israel Martin Indyk has observed, this places the "card" of the region's touchstone problem into the hands of the radical Islamists, for them to play as they see fit. It is not necessary for Washington to conclude a final peace between Israel and the Palestinians (although it is something for which we should all hope). The peace processes of the 1970s and the 1990s showed that the *appearance* of progress is enough to help advance other American policy objectives in the region. This sets the bar pretty low for the United States and the Bush administration should be ashamed for failing to clear it.

Make no mistake: Keeping the Arab-Israeli peace process moving forward is central to America's grand strategy for transforming the Middle East. That will be doubly difficult with Hamas in power. The United States must now exert itself to curb Hamas' violence and undercut its appeal to the Palestinian people. Above all, we must hold the new Palestinian government accountable for its behavior. The Palestinian Authority signed a series of important agreements with Israel that created the foundation for eventual statehood and immediate benefits in the form of trade, aid, and political engagement. Washington must make crystal clear to the Palestinians that the continuation of those benefits is contingent upon the new government's continued adherence to all of the terms of those agreements (including those requiring the disarming of militias). We must put the onus on the Hamas government: either they give up their terrorist war against Israel, or the international community will give up on their new government.

At the same time, the United States should lead an international effort to increase all forms of assistance to NGOs and civil society groups within Palestinian society to provide the Palestinian people with basic services and necessities, coupled with micro-enterprise loans and infrastructure development. The goal should be to jumpstart the Palestinian economy, and so weaken Hamas's hold on average Palestinian families for whom it provides jobs, money, food, and medical care.

All of this is not to suggest that there aren't changes that need to occur on the Israeli side as well. For instance, Jerusalem needs to exercise greater restraint when retaliating against terrorist attacks so as not to inflame the Palestinian sense of victimhood, on which extremists feed. However, today the greatest problem on the Israeli side is that there are pitifully few Israelis who believe they have a real partner for peace among the Palestinians: Those willing to make peace seem too weak to deliver, while those strong enough to deliver seem to have little desire for peace. This is why it is critical for the United States to lead an international effort to empower moderates who seek peace, and simultaneously punish the extremists who oppose it. When Abu Mazen was elected president after Yasser Arafat's death, the United States faced a rare opportunity to bolster moderates in the ruling Fatah party. Unfortunately, the Bush administration chose to do nothing, and that chance is gone. Now we must cultivate and fortify moderates throughout Palestinian society in the hope that they will get another chance to govern. Only then will the desire for a negotiated peace reemerge among the majority of Israelis, and changes in Israel's own political landscape will inevitably follow.

DEALING WITH ROGUE REGIMES

Iran, Libya, and Syria have long been among the worst supporters of a range of international terrorist groups, and all participated in terrorist attacks against Americans at one time or another during the past twenty-five years. Likewise, all have supported efforts to subvert and destabilize various governments in the region. In short, they have helped cause or exacerbate terrorism from and instability within the Middle East.

After a decade of sanctions, the United States and Great Britain used economic and political incentives to persuade Libya to stop supporting terrorism and give up its nuclear program in a verifiable manner. It was a triumph for Western diplomacy and should be a model for our dealings with Iran and perhaps Syria as well. However, while the Libyans have largely kept up their end of the bargain, the Bush administration has been rather niggardly when it came to making good on its promises to Tripoli. Such stinginess makes it more likely that the Iranians and Syrians will reject something like the Libyan deal and continue to defy us. It also makes it less likely that our European and Asian allies will back such deals if they question our commitment to provide benefits in return for good behavior.

In both cases, the administration simply seems to be unwilling to make the necessary concessions. This is especially baffling with respect to Iran since the administration already accepts the basic premise of a deal with the Europeans in which they would wield the stick of economic sanctions to punish bad Iranian behavior if we agreed to use the carrot of economic integration to reward good behavior. The problem is that the Iranians are being recalcitrant (exactly as could have been expected) and the administration has been unwilling to offer up carrots big enough to convince the Europeans to use sticks big enough to convince the Iranians to budge. The administration's rationale seems to be little more than visceral dislike of the Iranian regime. Such stubbornness is losing us the best chance we have to convince the Iranians to end their pursuit of nuclear weapons and their support of terrorism, two critical elements of what should be America's grand strategy.

Instead, the combination of the administration's stubbornness and Iranian truculence is propelling the nuclear confrontation toward a U.N. Security Council totally unready to deal with the issue. Iran's deceitful and defiant behavior has been egregious enough to convince other states to refer its nuclear program to the Council. But the absence of a consensus among Europeans and Americans as to how Iran's bad behavior should be punished (and its potential good behavior rewarded) threatens to hamstring the Council. It is crucial that the United States engage with like-minded states to develop a multilateral approach that would impose graduated economic sanctions on Iran if its intransigence continues. At the same time, the United States should offer Tehran security guarantees, properly safeguarded nuclear energy, and economic incentives (including the lifting of U.S. sanctions) if Iran is willing to sever its ties to terrorist groups, renounce its efforts to develop the nuclear fuel cycle, and accede to a comprehensive inspections and monitoring regime to verify their compliance. Such an approach, combining bigger sticks and bigger carrots, is the only way to build a united front against proliferation that includes the Europeans, Japanese, Indians, and even the Russians and Chinese.

The United States is in a similarly advantageous position with regard to Syria. The Mehlis report,[5] finding Syrian officials and pro-Syrian Lebanese officials complicit in the assassination of former Lebanese Prime Minister Rafiq Hariri, has mobilized international opinion against the Syrian regime, leaving it vulnerable to diplomatic pressure. The danger is that the Bush administration will once again fall under the spell of its own extremist supporters and demand outright regime change in Damascus.

The United States cannot topple the Syrian regime without a major military intervention, and such a step is unthinkable in light of our commitments in Iraq and Afghanistan. The international community, moreover, probably would part ways with Washington if it hijacked the Mehlis report to promote regime change. In the end, we probably would fail to change the regime and lose the considerable leverage we currently have with Damascus. What's more, none of the likely alternatives to the current regime appear more palatable than the status quo. True democracy in Syria would likely result in the immediate election of a government dominated by the Islamic fundamentalists of the Muslim Brotherhood—an outcome that would be difficult for anyone to see as progress.

Instead, the United States should continue to work with its allies through the U.N. to force Syria to sever its ties to Lebanon, end its support for terrorism (including those crossing Syria on their way to Iraq), abandon its pursuit of weapons of mass destruction, curb its human rights abuses, and begin the same processes of gradual reform and liberalization needed throughout the Arab world. It would be a major boon to our position in the region if we used the opportunity created by the Mehlis report to accomplish these goals.

DEALING WITH FRIENDLY REGIMES

Since 9/11, we have finally faced up to the fact that even our friends in the Muslim Middle East are part of the problem. It is worth remembering that fifteen of the nineteen hijackers were Saudis and much of al Qaeda's core leadership was Egyptian. In Saudi Arabia, Egypt, Jordan, Morocco, and other U.S. allies, economic distress, political stagnation, educational failings, and a sense of cultural threat have combined to produce terrorists and populations sympathetic to their goals (and sometimes even their methods). It is not enough just to press the countries in the region we don't like to end their support for terrorism and halt subversive activities that destabilize the region. It is critical that friendly governments embark on a gradual process of reform as well.

The Bush administration has embraced this cause rhetorically and has even made some small steps in the right direction. Washington pressed Hosni Mubarak hard enough to convince him to hold elections that were more competitive than any previously seen in Egypt, and the administration even followed the French lead in demanding Syrian withdrawal from Lebanon, thereby sparking the "Cedar Revolution." Likewise, the administration created a Middle East Partnership Initiative designed to funnel modest amounts of money to some regional states to help them move in the direction of change, and is planning other initiatives as well.

These are useful steps. But they are so tentative and so under-resourced that they mostly demonstrate the administration's failure to make this effort the centerpiece of American strategy toward the region. The Bush administration has a bad habit of saying all the right things but then failing to live up to its own rhetoric.

As with our adversaries in the region, the United States must use big carrots and big sticks to promote reform among our allies. We must provide very sizable inducements to governments that adopt progressive reforms and we must penalize those that refuse.

The handling of U.S. aid to Egypt is an obvious example. Although the Bush administration pressured the Mubarak government, it was only willing to use small sticks and no carrots. The result was an election that was certainly better than any in the past but hardly a great leap forward for democracy. What's more, many of the rules governing this election could actually make the long-term prospects for democratization worse, not better.[6] It would be much better to work out a long-term plan for political and economic changes in Egypt and then tie American aid to such a "road map." The precise nature of these steps could be left largely to Cairo to ensure that the average Egyptian does not believe that the United States is forcing changes on them. But Washington would still need to certify that the steps were progressive. Of greatest importance, we should be willing to *increase* our aid to Egypt beyond the current level of $2.1 billion per year as long as Egypt moves along this path and *decrease* it if Egypt fails to do so.

Likewise, we must move aggressively and creatively to help reformists throughout the Arab world. Prodding the governments to move in the right direction is barely half the battle. Ultimately, the West cannot impose reform on the Middle East, our efforts to do so in Iraq being the exception that proves the rule. If some form of liberalism is to take hold in the Muslim Middle East, it will have to emerge from Arab society itself. It will have to be seen as authentic, and that automatically disqualifies "made in America" reforms. It will also have to be consonant with Arab traditions and values, and that too can only come from Arabs themselves.

Consequently, we must look beyond traditional ways of providing aid so as to distance it from the United States or any other country. For example, Senator Richard Lugar (R–IN) has proposed creating an international foundation funded by the G-8 nations that would provide merit-based grants to any individual, institution, or even government in the greater Middle East seeking to build civil society and advance the cause of reform.[7] This is precisely the kind of idea that the United States should explore to speed the process of reform.

MONEY AND MULTILATERALISM

The transformation of the Arab states will require far more resources than we have so far been willing to commit (again, Iraq being a notable exception) and will require us to cooperate with like-minded allies in a way that we have so far resisted.

Many European and East Asian states recognize that transforming the Middle East is the only long-term way to solve the threats we face from terrorism and instability in the region. Many of their governments have tried to persuade the United States to embark on multilateral efforts to promote reform, provide resources to Middle Eastern reformers, and even create positive and negative inducements for Middle Eastern governments to adopt key reforms. Unfortunately, there has been little receptivity to these offers in Washington. This must be reversed. An effort as great as this will require more resources than we can furnish alone. It will require us to coordinate our policies with those of our allies and (heaven forbid!) perhaps even make some compromises with "old Europe." Given the importance of these goals, it is a price we must be willing to pay.

ADDRESSING FUTURE CHALLENGES

Finally, a true grand strategy for the Middle East must be dynamic. We must anticipate major changes in the region and design a grand strategy that can adapt to them. It is already possible to discern likely changes in the Middle East's geopolitical landscape. The most obvious and potentially most important is China's growing interest in the region as its demand for oil surges.

China is now the world's second largest consumer of oil and its dependence on foreign oil is expected to grow. This is already pushing China to become more involved in Middle Eastern affairs. In particular, China has signed multi-billion dollar oil deals with Iran and is seeking the same with Saudi Arabia and other Gulf oil producers. To smooth their entrée into the region and generate additional export revenues, the Chinese have shown a willingness to sell a wide range of weaponry—including ballistic missiles and possibly nuclear weapons technology—to Middle Eastern states.

So far, the United States has seen the growth of Chinese interests in the Middle East as wholly pernicious. The Bush administration has long viewed China as an inevitable rival and America's newest threat. It has viewed Chinese efforts to secure oil concessions in the Middle East as part of a zero-sum game, meaning that there would be less oil available for Western consumers (a view the Chinese generally share). It has also grown alarmed at Chinese arms sales to some of the region's worst rogue regimes, including Iran.

In this light, China could become the replacement for the Soviet Union in the Middle East. Throughout the cold war, the USSR competed with the United States for power and position in the region. This was a source of tremendous tension in the superpower balance: The two sides backed different states that were themselves adversaries and, in some cases, far more aggressive and risk-tolerant than either of their superpower backers. As a result, whenever regional states went to war, it threatened to escalate into a superpower conflict. Even on a day-to-day basis, the region's rogues always believed that they could get away with a lot, knowing that their superpower patron (typically the Soviet Union) would protect them from harm. This injected even more instability into an already volatile region.

However, seeing the Middle East from the perspective of a unified grand strategy focused on the region opens up a different view on China's growing interest in the region (and its burgeoning military, political, and economic clout). The principal reason that the United States and the Soviet Union clashed so frequently in the Middle East during the cold war was that Moscow had virtually no interests in the region other than to cause problems, and thereby distract and weaken the United States and its allies. In marked contrast, China has very specific interests in the region and these interests happen to be identical to those of the United States: Beijing needs cheap, plentiful oil to flow from the region, and it needs stability in the region to ensure its first interest. These are also America's priorities in the region, and this commonality of interests creates the possibility for the two countries to cooperate, rather than compete, in the Middle East. Imagine if Washington and Beijing were to jointly demand that the region's rogue regimes shape up, and that all of the states embrace the kind of liberal reforms that are their only chance to diminish the threat of violent political change.

This is one of those revelations that seems obvious once it has been said. It opens up new possibilities and suggests that the United States would do best to include China in a range of new initiatives—on security, politics, and economics in the Gulf—to make Beijing feel that Washington sees it as a partner and is not trying to exclude it from the region. For instance, the United States, and its allies in the Gulf (including Iraq), have begun to explore new security architectures for the region based on the successful OSCE (Organization of Security and Cooperation in Europe) model in Europe; Washington would do well to invite China to participate in that process from start to finish. Doing so could send a powerful signal to Beijing that the United States recognizes China's legitimate interests in the Middle East and seeks to accommodate rather than block them. It is also the best way to prevent the Chinese from concluding that such a new security framework is merely the cover for a regional alliance against them.

Moreover, such Sino-American agreements could make clear to Middle Eastern states looking to try to play one great power off against the other that such divide-and-conquer tactics will be impossible. Unfortunately, the Bush administration seems determined to see China as a threat, and in so doing, will doubtless reinforce Chinese predilections to approach the relationship in the same manner. It is yet another manifestation of the pressing need for a unified American grand strategy toward the Middle East to harmonize our policies and rationalize our priorities.

NOTES

1. The one possible exception to this rule was during the Clinton administration, when some members of the Clinton foreign policy team, notably Assistant Secretary of State for Near Eastern Affairs Martin Indyk, conceived the strategic approach of making a major effort to hammer out a comprehensive peace to settle the Arab-Israeli dispute in the expectation that this was both achievable given the circumstances of the early 1990s, and that doing so would then make solving the region's other problems considerably easier. For reasons to be explained, I consider that a "proto-grand strategy," and indeed draw upon some of its key features, but do not consider it a true grand strategy aiming to address all of America's problems in the region.

2. Quoted in "Complete Victory: Bush Offers a Strategy Beyond 'Stay the Course' in Iraq," *Wall Street Journal*, December 1, 2005, A16.

3. This phenomenon is the most important factor feeding the growth of Iraq's militias. Iraqis increasingly feel that the central government and the Americans simply cannot or will not help them, so they will have to turn to some local power broker—a shaykh, a clergyman, a former general, or some other would-be warlord—to secure the basic necessities of life. This is the classic path that other societies have taken in the descent to civil war.

4. For a more detailed discussion of the military, political, and economic changes needed to stabilize Iraq, see Pollack, Kenneth M., "A Switch in Time: A New Strategy for America in Iraq," The Saban Center for Middle East Policy at the Brookings Institution, February 2006.

5. Report of the International Independent Investigation Commission Established Pursuant to Security Council Resolution 1595 (2005) accessible at www.un.org/new/dh/docs/mehlisreport/.

6. On the problems in the Egyptian electoral system, see Cofman Wittes, Tamara, "The 2005 Egyptian Elections: How Free? How Important?" The Saban Center for Middle East Policy at the Brookings Institution, Middle East Memo #8, August 24, 2005, http://brookings.edu/views/papers/wittes/20050824.htm.

7. See Senator Lugar's March 29, 2004, speech at the Brookings Institution, http://www.brookings.edu/dybdocroot/comm/events/20040329lugar.pdf.

3

SEEDING LIBERAL DEMOCRACY

Larry Diamond and Michael McFaul

President George W. Bush came to the White House with very modest goals for American foreign policy. Before September 11, in the tradition of Presidents Richard Nixon and George H.W. Bush, President George W. Bush disparaged President Bill Clinton's use of American power to advance democratic ideals. Instead, Bush and his foreign policy team called for a return to realism, a code phrase for disengaging from nation building in peripheral countries and focusing instead on managing relations with the great powers.[1] This so-called realist framework, however, provided little guidance for understanding the security challenges facing the United States after September 11. After all, a non-state, ideologically motivated movement, not a powerful state, attacked us that day. Moreover, this enemy, al Qaeda, could carry out this attack in large measure because of the safe haven provided by a weak state, Afghanistan, ruled by an antidemocratic regime, the Taliban.

To his credit, Bush understood that his original ideas about foreign policy no longer worked. As one element of his new approach to fighting terrorism, Bush started to highlight the importance of promoting freedom around the world. In particular, he stressed the need to foster democratic development in the wider Middle East, the most autocratic region of the world.

In this new embrace of democratic reform in the Middle East, Bush has been correct in intent, even if late to the cause. Although the link between promoting democracy and fighting terrorism and extremism has been

49

greatly oversimplified, there is a relationship between the two broad goals. Over time, expanding political freedom and accountability through democratizing reforms would help to change the political and socioeconomic conditions that have spawned terrorist groups and ideologies in the region. In the broad arc of lands from Morocco to Indonesia, radical Islamist terrorist creeds and organizations have been bred in the humiliating conditions of oppression, injustice, and stalled or failed development. Globally, the perpetrators of terrorist acts have emerged overwhelmingly out of conditions of dictatorship.[2] Of course, not all terrorists are themselves poor, oppressed, or living in autocratic countries with Muslim majorities, and the problem of radical Islamic alienation in Europe is increasingly evident and troubling. But ideologically and symbolically, radical Islamist violence feeds on the perception that regimes in this part of the world are both unjust and illegitimate because they are corrupt, abusive, and unaccountable to the people or to any higher law or code. Radical Islam appeals to many young people and even to well-educated people in this region, in part because its moral condemnations reflect what they see and experience personally, including the support that the United States and "the West" more broadly have given to corrupt dictatorships and the blind eye we have turned to terrible abuses of state power. Democracy is the only reliable constraint on abusive state power, the only tonic for illegitimacy, and the only political system that offers the disenfranchised a way to participate nonviolently in the political process. Moreover, when democratic institutions are well designed and consolidated, the incentives they generate to appeal to and represent moderate, "swing" voters push extreme elements to the political sidelines over time.

Governments that are accountable to their own people and respect the rule of law are also more likely to behave responsibly abroad, especially when interacting with other democracies. In the greater Middle East, the consolidation of liberal democratic regimes within states would reduce the threats between these states, which in turn would decrease the demand for weapons of mass destruction among regimes in the region, and also reduce the need for a large American military presence in the region, which has heightened the mobilization of some terrorist groups. For both moral and strategic reasons, then, promoting freedom is the right thing to do.

To date, however, George Bush's far-reaching rhetorical embrace of democracy promotion has vastly exceeded his real achievements in advancing democratic institutions and norms in the greater Middle East. According to Freedom House, 2005 saw "a measurable improvement in freedom in several key Arab countries," such as Lebanon and Iraq, but most of these gains were modest.[3] Our military interventions to remove the Taliban regime in Afghanistan and Saddam Hussein's regime in Iraq have opened the possibility of democratic development in both countries, but each confronts daunting obstacles to stabilization and democratic development, which have been enlarged in Iraq by the administration's blunders and astonishing lack of postwar planning and preparation.[4] Moreover, the chaos in Iraq is increasingly cited by neighboring Arab regimes as a reason not to move forward with democratic reforms. Lebanese sovereignty has been restored, but democracy in this combustible country still remains a goal. Presidential elections in the Palestinian Authority in January 2005 gave hope for a new more effective and accountable government. However, in the January 2006 parliamentary elections, Hamas's victory dealt Fatah's corrupt and incompetent ruling elite a harsh and necessary wake-up call. Those elections were a dramatic exercise in accountability, and thus contained seeds of democratic development. But by empowering radical, fundamentalist forces whose commitment to democracy is dubious at best, the outcome raised the specter of worsening civil unrest and further damaged the prospects for peace. In 2005, Egypt held for the first time a multicandidate presidential election, but nothing approaching a free and fair election, and fraud was rampant in the subsequent parliamentary elections as well. Saudi Arabia has taken some slight steps to expand popular participation at the local level, but it remains a corrupt dictatorship of the sprawling royal family. Tunisia has been praised and rewarded by the Bush administration for its economic reforms, but it has yet to allow any real political pluralism or freedom. Morocco has gone furthest in terms of a genuine civic opening, with political competition and a visible loosening of repression, but it remains in the end an absolute monarchy where power is not accountable to the people. Throughout the Arab Middle East, reform is stymied and independent expression and organization are repressed by the heavy and pervasive hand of the secret police.[5] Iran, perhaps the country with the greatest potential for democratization in the region four years ago, has lurched backward away from political opening to hard-line clerical control. Pakistan has held rigged elections to sustain General Pervez Musharraf's tight grip on power—and then called them "democratic" in the hope of winning international acceptance. No progress toward freedom has been made in Syria or Libya.

Globally, the progress of democracy has also been mixed. Without question, the struggle for freedom has made some important gains in recent years: the "colored revolutions" in Georgia, Ukraine, and then (at least partially) Kyrgyzstan; continued democratic reform under a moderately Islamist elected government in Turkey; and democratic progress in the world's most populous Muslim-majority country, Indonesia. However, democracy remains fragile in each of these countries (save Turkey), and these recent breakthroughs have largely been offset by other, countervailing trends, such as the virtual demise of democracy in Venezuela, growing instability in the Andes, and intensified repression in much of the rest of the former Soviet empire. Overall, the number of democracies in the world today (122) is only slightly higher than the 120 that existed in 2000. By the count of Freedom House, there were three more relatively liberal democracies ("free states") at the end of 2005 than there were at the end of 2000, and three fewer "not free" states, but these included such entrenched brutal regimes as those in North Korea, Syria, Burma, and Zimbabwe. Moreover, on Bush's watch, the largest country in the world, Russia, also has moved from "partially free" to "not free."

This mixed record of achievement has led many critics to call for abandoning democracy promotion as a priority in American foreign policy. A new generation of self-described "realists" from both the left and right argue that the efforts to confront tyranny and promote democracy have been a fool's errand; that to make America secure, we need instead to pull back to more narrow, conservative conceptions of the national interest, militarily, politically, and economically; and that to win the war on terror, we must ally with whoever will work with us, without reference to our values or principles.

We disagree. Bush's limited success in advancing democracy in the greater Middle East does not mean that the objective is wrong. Rather, his strategy for achieving it needs fundamental revision. In fact, a more effective strategy for promoting democracy in the wider Middle East will make Americans safer and more prosperous, as well as more faithful to the liberal values that have made our country a beacon of hope to others. You do not win a war of ideas and values by abandoning precisely those ideas and values that are most admired in the world. To meet the new security challenges of our era, we as a nation must reaffirm our commitment to promoting democracy at home and abroad as both the smart and right course of action.

DEMOCRACY: A UNIVERSAL VALUE AND U.S. INTEREST

At the time of America's birth as a nation, most of the world lived under tyranny. Our founding democratic ideas were seen as idealistic and naive. Few gave this new country any chance of success. Of course, we now know that the naysayers were wrong. American democracy was born imperfect;

our nation had to endure tragic wars and heroic struggles to deliver democracy to all of our people. But democracy in America did grow and improve, and eventually inspired millions of aspiring democrats around the world. That leaders should be freely elected, constrained by the law, and bound to respect human rights are ideas that cross cultural and geographic boundaries, from Botswana to Bulgaria, from Italy to India, from Argentina to Australia. Until recently, the American example has been the most effective tool for promoting these democratic values abroad.

The success of democracy in America and the inspiration it provided others produced some unintended but very positive consequences for Americans. The expansion of democracy around the world went hand in hand with the spread of prosperity. It is no accident that the richest nations in the world today are also the oldest democracies. Democratic diffusion also fostered peace between democratic states. Likewise, the dissolution of autocratic regimes in Germany, Italy, and Japan after World War II and the Soviet Union in 1991 has made the United States and its allies more secure. No country in the world has benefited more from the expansion of democracy than the United States. Every enemy of the United States in the past has been a dictatorship, while the United States has never been threatened or attacked by a democratic state. On the contrary, democratic nations have always been our most trusted and longest lasting allies. Not all dictatorships in the world today are foes of the United States, but nearly all foes of the United States are dictatorships or movements that espouse antidemocratic creeds. Virtually all the countries that provide safe haven to non-state enemies of the United States have been autocratic regimes.

In addition, a growing body of scholarly research is showing that democracies in general do a better job of promoting development, securing human rights, protecting the environment, preventing famine, fighting corruption, and preventing or containing extremist violence.[6] Moreover, the more truly democratic regimes are, the more likely they are to be at peace with one another.[7]

We cannot know if the process of democratization in the wider Middle East will have in the near term the same positive benefits for American national security that democratization did first in Europe and Asia after World War II and then in Eastern Europe and the former Soviet Union more recently. With the Hamas victory, we now have a case in which a radical, violent, and anti-American movement has come to power through elections that international observers considered free and fair. However, it is important to keep in mind that Hamas actually did not win a majority of the vote, and many Palestinians who voted for its candidates were protesting corruption and bad governance, not voting for radical Islam, terrorism, or the destruction of Israel. More broadly in the region, while most Arabs oppose the U.S. intervention in Iraq, this criticism has not translated into a surge of support for radical groups like al Qaeda or for radical ideas such as the creation of an Islamic state.[8] Osama bin Laden and his supporters, like the Bolsheviks in Russia or Ayatollah Ruhollah Khomeini in Iran, can most certainly take advantage of fragile autocratic regimes to seize power, but if they do come to power it is not likely to be through the ballot box. Moreover, there are some signs that when Islamists have to compete, govern, and share power under democratic institutions and restraints, this can, over time, exert a moderating influence on these groups. If the process of transition to democracy is carefully crafted, in ways that limit majoritarian power and allow time for secular and more moderate Islamist political forces to organize and compete, there is reason to believe that these same stabilizing and peaceful benefits of democracy in other parts of the world would become manifest in the Middle East.

People around the world recognize both the intrinsic desirability and the practical benefits of democracy. Now, more than ever, democracy and human rights are transnational values, which extensive public opinion polls tell us are embraced and aspired to by large majorities of the people in every region of the world.[9] Democracy and human rights are also increasingly embedded in regional and international covenants, declarations, treaties, and institutions, while democracy promotion is a policy objective of many countries and multilateral organizations.[10] This nearly universal demand for freedom may be the most compelling reason why the United States should be promoting democratic development around the world.

Certainly, the advance of democracy in the greater Middle East will not eliminate all terrorist threats to the United States. Democracy is not a panacea. Even consolidated democracies are the birthplace and residence of extremists, who resort to terrorism as a tool of their politics or an expression of their rage. Just as democratic institutions did not stop the Unabomber, Timothy McVeigh, or the 2005 terrorist attacks in London, the emergence of democratic regimes throughout the wider Middle East will not eliminate all security threats to the United States from the region. As this book makes clear, we need a bigger and better military, more effective intelligence gathering, a more strategic and collaborative approach to counterterrorism, and a vigorous readiness to deploy force if we are going to preempt deadly terrorist attacks and defeat the forces of hatred and terrorism. Afghanistan may not be the last time we need to attack and root out terrorist training camps and operations.

But we also need to attack and root out the political and social conditions of oppression and injustice in which Islamist extremism and other terrorist ideologies gain adherents. In this sense, America finds itself still, as the newly inaugurated President John F. Kennedy observed forty-five years ago, in "a long twilight struggle . . . against the common enemies of man: tyranny, poverty, disease, and war itself."

THE SHORTCOMINGS OF THE BUSH STRATEGY

President Bush was right to make the advance of freedom a goal of his foreign policy after September 11. But he did not come to Washington to promote democracy worldwide. Consequently, in embracing this new objective midstream in his presidency, Bush was an inexperienced and unprepared democracy promoter, and it shows. His rhetoric has vastly exceeded his policies, not to mention their execution.

Most detrimentally, Bush has relied much too heavily on military force to bring down autocracy and build democracy. Our military intervention in Iraq underscores the lesson that war—and especially a war of choice bereft of broad international support—is not a sustainable (much less broadly applicable) means for promoting democracy. In fact, the Bush administration's bungled intervention in Iraq has embroiled the United States in a vicious, debilitating insurgency while eroding our moral standing and soft power, and thus our ability to promote democratic norms and institutions elsewhere in the world. Rather than launching a new wave of democratic transitions in the Arab world, it has stiffened the backs of autocrats in the region while frightening liberal forces in civil society who want democracy in principle but fear that rapid change could unleash Islamic extremism, violence, and chaos. Though it has gradually drawn back from its self-defeating unilateralism, the Bush administration has yet to fully recognize that promoting democracy in the Middle East requires a long-term, sophisticated, and truly multilateral strategy.

General John Abizaid has stated that the battle to defeat terrorism is 10 percent military, and 90 percent nonmilitary. However, Bush's budgets do not reflect this distribution of needed efforts. Expenditures for the military have hovered above $450 billion over the last four years, yet spending on democracy assistance programs is at most about $1.5 billion, while public diplomacy to advance democracy has withered. When budgets for Iraq and Afghanistan are removed from the count, democracy assistance around the rest of the world has decreased during the Bush administration. Development assistance has increased under President Bush (an achievement for which he deserves some credit), but it remains far short of the United Nation's Millennium Development Goals.

Like the cold war, the war against our current enemies involves much more than armed struggle and requires much more than the force of arms. The war against terrorist organizations and their supporters is also very much a war of ideas and a struggle between competing political visions and systems. Yet, our effort to engage in the nonmilitary components of this war is still well below the level needed to win. Four years after September 11, tens of thousands of students from the greater Middle East should be studying politics, philosophy, history, and economics in our universities, but they are not. An equal number of Americans should be learning Arabic, Persian, and Pashto, and studying and researching these countries, but they are not. American funding for the development of independent media in the Arab world and its neighborhood should have increased tenfold in the last four years, but it has not even come close. Likewise, economic assistance, tied to political reform, should have increased dramatically for those regimes taking real steps toward democracy and good governance, but the Millennium Challenge Account—a worthy start—has lagged badly in implementation and funding. Countless op-eds and task forces have decried our abysmal efforts at public diplomacy, yet President Bush and his administration have responded to this failing as if it were simply a public relations problem. New multilateral institutions dedicated to the defense of human rights in the greater Middle East should have been created long ago, but they have not been. In response to September 11, Bush has tried to reorganize our government to provide for better homeland defense and better intelligence, but a similar effort at reorganization of government bureaus and resources to provide for a better offensive strategy of democracy promotion has not been attempted.

Bush also has chosen to promote a narrow vision of democracy. He focuses rightly on fostering the emergence of political systems that protect individual liberties. Yet he speaks little of equality and justice, values that past American leaders have always considered fundamental to shaping our system of government. The promotion of economic development must also accompany efforts to advance democracy, since simultaneous progress on both fronts can create a virtuous circle of sustainability. In the developing world, new democracies without economic growth are much more likely to fail than democracies which do produce economic growth. A final shortcoming of the Bush approach to democracy promotion is a pronounced unilateralism. Much of the genius of the postwar generation of American foreign policy leaders lay in their construction of multilateral institutions that reflected American values and extended American power. The Marshall Plan, the World Bank, and NATO all served to buttress and unify a community of democratic states. Later in the century, new transnational networks such as the Helsinki movement in the twilight of communism and the World Movement for Democracy[11] after the fall of communism helped to connect democrats from around the world while furthering the globalization of democratic values. In tackling the new challenge of defeating antidemocratic movements and the despotic governments that help to breed them, American leaders should be working in close alliance with fellow democrats from around the world. But what is striking about our present moment is how deeply distrusted, resented, and isolated the United States has become. On September 11, 2001, most governments and people around the world stood in solidarity with the United States and the American people. President Bush has squandered this extraordinary asset.

The Bush administration has done serious damage to America's moral standing as a beacon of liberty and thus to our soft power in the world. We cannot inspire others to respect human rights and embrace democratic principles if our own government officials do not do the same. The abuses at Abu Ghraib offset years of democracy promotion work by American nongovernmental organizations in the region. The human rights eyesore that is Guantanamo Bay serves as a giant albatross to any American—from President Bush to the junior embassy officer in Bahrain—trying to press for greater freedom abroad. As Senator John McCain (R-AZ) stated eloquently in seeking to introduce amendments to the 2006 Pentagon bill to prevent torture of detainees, "Our enemy doesn't deserve our sympathy. But this isn't about who they are. This is about who we are."

THE RIGHT WAY TO
PROMOTE DEMOCRACY

To restore America's moral authority and regain the trust of friends and allies around the world, U.S. leaders must live up to democratic ideals at home and promote them more consistently abroad. We need to design new policies to meet the special challenges of promoting better governance in the greater Middle East and at the same time reaffirm and recommit to those principles and practices that made the United States a catalyst for democratic change in the past.

Key Principles

The first principle of a more effective strategy for promoting democracy is that we must lead by example. Our greatest tool in advancing democracy is the example of our own system. This asset, however, has been severely damaged in recent years, especially by the horrific acts of prisoner abuse by Americans in Iraq and Guantanamo, and by the failure of our leaders to accept accountability for these acts. To reverse our plummeting image abroad, we have to recommit to behaving more justly. First and foremost, our leaders must pledge to adhere to the U.N. Convention Against Torture, to which the United States is a signatory. Behavior inconsistent with this treaty or other American laws must be investigated swiftly and accountability for infractions must be assigned to the highest levels of government. The effort of Senator McCain to forbid the United States by law from ever using torture and degrading punishment on detainees should have been readily embraced by an administration that is trying to promote democratic norms in the broader Middle East, and to convey to the peoples of the region a message of solidarity with their struggles for dignity and human rights. To help rehabilitate our image abroad as a country dedicated to democracy, we have to show that we are serious about promoting genuine democratic change and willing to sustain a credible commitment even in the face of short-term risks and costs. A dose of humility would also help. We need to stop trumpeting the United States as the paragon of democracy and recognize that democracy comes in many forms, takes a long time to build, and, even in our own country, suffers flaws that must be constantly addressed.

Second, democracy cannot be imposed; it must be homegrown. Only under the rarest of circumstances has the United States been successful at dictating democratic rules from the outside. We have been much more successful in fostering democratic governance abroad when we supported local, grassroots democrats who were fighting to change their own countries. Supporting democratic political parties, women's groups, trade unions, and human rights activists—those fighting for democracy from the bottom up—will have a much more lasting impact than trying to impose democracy from the top down. The *kifaya* ("enough!") movement for free elections in Egypt, the recent "Cedar Revolution" to end Syrian domination in Lebanon, the long, continuing effort to deepen democracy in Turkey, and the incremental steps to liberalize authoritarian rule and create a freer civil society in Morocco all show the importance of local initiative and ownership for democratic change in the region, even as these reform efforts draw moral and practical support from the outside.

Third, our approach must be multilateral. Contrary to the myths sometimes propagated in Washington, European democracies, especially the new European democracies, are also committed to promoting freedom and human development around the world.[12] A serious strategy for promoting democracy must include a rejuvenated transatlantic partnership dedicated to enlarging the borders of the democratic community even farther. India, Japan, and other Asian democracies, beneficiaries of previous waves of democratic development, also have vital contributions to make to the next one. Not only do our allies have resources, special talents and, especially in Europe's case, deep connections with the Muslim world, they are also alternative sources of democratic legitimacy. Our efforts to support democracy are powerfully reinforced when America joins forces with the larger democratic community.

Fourth, we must be consistent. We must remain true to our values all the time and everywhere, even if we cannot always advance them with equal speed or effect. We cannot claim to be concerned about democratic development in Iraq but then ignore the absence of democratic progress in neighboring countries. Of course, the United States must sometimes work with unsavory regimes around the world to pursue urgent national security interests. Whenever possible, we should cooperate with dictatorships and democracies alike in tracking down and eliminating terrorists and preventing the proliferation of weapons of mass destruction. But in doing so, we do not have to check our values at the door. Just as Presidents Harry Truman, John Kennedy, and Ronald Reagan did with the Soviets during the cold war, we can and we must pursue both agendas simultaneously. Words matter, and we can use them to denounce repression and support and inspire democratic forces. We can stand up for the rights of dissidents and embattled minorities. We can make clear, publicly and privately, our expectations for democratic progress and for the defense of human rights.

A fifth principle must be bipartisanship. The United States anchored a successful global alliance against communism because American foreign policymakers and the American people shared a common assessment of the nature of the enemy and a broad strategy for defeating it. A bipartisan commitment to democracy promotion does not exist today. It must be cultivated by leaders who put American interests ahead of Democratic or Republican Party interests.

Taking New Action

A serious strategy for promoting democracy would include the following actions:

Provide Incentives for Autocratic Regimes to Change. The United States enjoys cordial if not close relations with most of the autocratic regimes in the greater Middle East. We must seek to use these relationships to spur democratic change. We must generate concrete incentives, through trade concessions, increased aid and foreign investment, and (for poorer countries) debt relief, for regimes to implement liberalizing and democratizing reforms. Political reforms should be seen to pay off for regimes and countries, by bringing substantial tangible and symbolic benefits from the United States and the international system. Economic aid to regimes that liberalize politics and improve government accountability and transparency should be increased while aid to autocratic regimes refusing to reform should be reduced. In the same way that assistance provided by the Millennium Challenge Account (MCA) is poised to reward improved governance in countries like Mali, Madagascar, Georgia, and Ghana, the United States and Europe should establish a new multi-billion dollar challenge fund to greatly increase aid to non-oil states of the Middle East that bite the bullet of real political reform. During the cold war, when the threat of communist takeover served as an excuse to sustain American-friendly dictatorships, careful American diplomacy nonetheless played a decisive role in edging out of power autocratic rulers in South Korea, Chile, the Philippines, and South Africa. Diplomats committed to democratic change can play a similar role in the wider Middle East today.

Mobilize Multilateral Pressure on Truly Bad Governments. For some leaders, no amount of positive incentives will compel them to end repression or begin a process of political liberalization. For these worst offenders, American foreign policymakers, including the U.S. Congress, must seek to weaken them, first and foremost through targeted sanctions. The bank accounts of the most brutal and irresponsible despots and their families should be tracked down and frozen; visas must be denied; criminal charges can be brought. Obviously, such measures must always meet some standard of feasibility, but more will be feasible if we work in close coordination with our democratic allies. This kind of moral and practical ostracism did begin to isolate ruling military elites in Nigeria under the tyrant Sani Abacha, and may have expedited a democratic transition there at the end of the 1990s. This strategy also succeeded in helping to push out of power a corrupt regime in Ukraine in 2004.

Provide More Direct Assistance to Democratic Reformers. Since autocratic regimes still govern most of the greater Middle East, our democratic assistance efforts in the region must focus heavily on nongovernmental actors. We should aid democratic reformers in the state where we can find them. But through technical and financial assistance, we should support and empower democratic civil society organizations, mass media, think tanks, parties, trade unions, business groups, and social networks. Finding democratic allies in these societies will require that American NGOs adopt a more expansive definition of "democrat" or "liberal" than they have had to use in the postcommunist world, Africa, Latin America, or Asia, so that moderate Islamists committed to democracy and nonviolence can be engaged. Throughout the greater Middle East, autocrats have determined which nongovernmental groups can receive foreign democratic and developmental assistance. This practice, which long prevailed in Egypt until the United States finally got tougher with the Mubarak regime, must fully stop.[13]

Press for Negotiated, "Pacted" Transitions. It is false to assume that autocratic regimes in the wider Middle East are providing real stability today. Demographic pressures, economic conditions, and competing societal forces have already launched a process of change throughout the region. The only question is whether these forces for change will produce evolution or revolution, democracy or a new form of dictatorship. Especially in conversation with autocratic rulers with friendly ties to the United States, American policymakers should press authoritarian rulers to initiate pacts, negotiations, and roundtable discussions with democratic forces in society. The goal should be a deliberate, gradual process of democratization and increased power sharing that would provide mutual guarantees of restraint and marginalize blatantly antidemocratic forces in the opposition. Such political pacts could buy time for moderate forces (both secular groups and Islamic democrats) to develop their platforms, constituencies, and organizational strength, while creating new political space for such opposition forces, and for democratic civil society in general. The leaders of autocratic regimes must start these processes of pacted transition now while they can still help to manage the process of change rather than waiting for radical Islamist forces to gain strength. Leaders in the United States and Europe should encourage their counterparts in the region to emulate the evolutionary transition from autocracy to democracy in Spain and avoid the revolutionary transition from autocracy to a new form of autocracy in Iran.

Multiple Society-to-Society Contacts. The greatest American asset in promoting democracy is the American people. All kinds of contacts—

between students, businesses, artists, city councils, civil society leaders, religious organizations, trade unions, and universities—must be expanded dramatically. To do so requires a fundamental reform of the American visa and customs process, including a vast increase in the number of consular staff interviewing people in embassies abroad. Just as we have a list of known terrorists and criminals who will not be granted entry to the United States, so we should establish a positive "fast-track" list of known democrats and advocates of peaceful reform whose visa applications should be greatly expedited. In addition, we should build on the examples of the Asia Foundation and Eurasia Foundation (NGOs which receive substantial annual U.S. government funding to promote democracy, strengthen civil society, and conduct exchanges), and establish a Middle East Foundation to greatly expand democracy assistance efforts and social, educational, and cultural exchanges on a society-to-society basis. Ideally this new foundation would have multiple donors in addition to the U.S. government. Above all else, the U.S. government must take advantage of mobile phone and Web-based technologies to expand contacts between communities in the Arab world and the West, with a particular focus on integrating Arab young people into networks both in their region and around the world. Ignorance and false information about the United States can only be fought through greater, deeper engagement of these societies. English-language training programs offered on communication platforms sponsored by American resources is another way to help integrate Middle Eastern people into global society. Finally, we should exhibit much greater respect for our *guests* when they arrive at our airports.

Replicate the Helsinki Experience in the Greater Middle East. More than any other region in the world the greater Middle East is devoid of multilateral security institutions. The United States, Canada, the European Union, and other consolidated democracies should partner with their Middle Eastern counterparts to establish regional norms, confidence-building measures, and other forms of dialogue and political reassurance. The goal should be to establish a regional architecture to affirm human rights and promote regional security on the model of the Helsinki process in Eastern Europe during the last phase of the cold war, which gave rise to the Organization of Security and Cooperation in Europe (OSCE) and extensive human rights monitoring within and across borders.[14] The impetus for creating such regional structures must come from within the region, but the initiative should be supported from the outside. Such efforts can draw inspiration from past experiences in Europe and elsewhere. At the heart of the Helsinki process was the recognition that true security depended not only on relations between states but also on the relationship between rulers and ruled. Many Middle Eastern governments have signed statements committing themselves to democratic reform. What is lacking is a regime that can empower the societies to hold their own rulers accountable to such pledges at home and in their relations with their neighbors. This regime might be launched at a conference in the capital of the one Arab country that has known democracy in the past, Lebanon, and so we propose a new "Beirut process."

Disseminate Knowledge about Democracy and Comparative Experiences with Democracy. One of the most powerful forces for democratic change—crucial ultimately in the triumph of liberty in Eastern Europe—is the flow of independent information and democratic ideas and values. The United States has many mechanisms to disseminate independent news, information, and knowledge about democracy, including through embassies, nongovernmental organizations, satellite radio and television stations, and university scholarships and international exchanges. The entire effort, however, is still woefully inadequate. Moreover, international public broadcasting has been politicized in recent years in a way that has damaged our democratic credibility and standing. While creating a new international broadcasting vehicle to reach the Arab world (Al Hurra), the Bush administration foolishly shut down the Arabic service of the Voice of America (VOA), leaving us less able to reach this crucial part of the world with independent news and information. The Arabic service of VOA must be revived and expanded as a vehicle to explain U.S foreign policy. In addition, however, other U.S.-sponsored international broadcasting must be truly independent and not simply an information department of the U.S. government to be credible and effective. Al Hurra, which today only enjoys a tiny viewing audience, must be overhauled and made more substantive and independent, and a new independent broadcasting effort in Farsi must be initiated to reach the people of Iran with democratic ideas, competing viewpoints, and credible information.[15] Both of these television networks, as well as new radio programs, websites, and Internet publications targeted for the wider Middle East, should be reconstituted under a new corporation with funding from the United States but an independent board and an autonomous editorial policy—that is, something similar to Radio Free Europe/Radio Liberty. Like Radio Free Europe/Radio Liberty, this new media corporation should also develop an extensive research capacity on the greater Middle East, both to inform programming and to educate policymakers in the United States. The current level of resources is simply inadequate for the task at hand.[16]

In addition to basic news coverage, the United States must do more to provide basic information about the practice of democracy to the peoples of the greater Middle East. Most basic texts on democracy and democratization have yet to be translated into the languages of the region. Courses on democracy or social science departments more generally are in short supply in the institutions of higher learning in the region. Meetings between Arab and Western scholars working on issues of democracy are few and far between. Exchanges of students interested in democratization are still underfunded. The United States, working closely with other democracies around the world, must do more to fill this informational vacuum.

Know Thy Enemy, Know Thy Friend. As a country, we still know very little about the greater Middle East. As in the cold war, the war against Islamic extremism will not be won in months or even years. And as in the cold war, the nonmilitary components of the war will play a crucial role. To fight the decades-long battle against communism, the United States invested billions in education and intelligence. The U.S. government sponsored centers of Soviet studies, provided foreign-language scholarships in Russian and Eastern European languages, and offered dual-competency grants to get graduate students to acquire expertise both in security issues and in Russian culture. We need a similar effort today to help us better understand our friends and foes in the wider Middle East. Although some scholars today do study Islam and the languages and countries of the people who profess it, we suffer from severe shortages of intelligence analysts, linguists, academic scholars, and senior policymakers trained in the languages, cultures, politics, and economics of the wider Middle East and the entire Islamic world. The National Security Language Initiative announced by the Bush administration in early 2006 promises over time to significantly increase the number of Americans speaking critical languages such as Arabic and Farsi (as well as Russian and Chinese). Yet while welcome, the program is too closely tied to the government's defense and intelligence apparatus. It does not do enough to support the rapid training of a new generation of academic and policy experts on the broader Middle East, who need a combination of overseas experience, deep cultural knowledge of the region, and linguistic expertise. Universities, with government support, should encourage the study of Islam from within the various social sciences and humanities, the better to promote truly interdisciplinary conversation, while greatly expanding the teaching of Middle Eastern languages such as Arabic, Persian, and Turkish. We urgently need a revamped Foreign Languages and Area Studies Act to greatly expand U.S. government support for university centers, classes, and overseas studies and training programs focused on this broad part of the world, and on other areas vital to our national security. During the cold war, future diplomats such as Strobe Talbott and Condoleezza Rice learned Russian (and in Rice's case, Czech), read Pushkin, but also studied throwweights, Soviet military doctrine, and communist thinking about international relations. Today, we need a new generation of scholars and policymakers who speak Arabic, know the Koran, understand the geopolitics of the Middle East, and are also well versed in theories of democratization.

Department of International Development and Reconstruction. To demonstrate a real commitment to the agenda outlined in this chapter, the United States should create a cabinet-level department to lead and coordinate U.S. governmental efforts to foster economic development, democracy, disaster relief, and postconflict reconstruction. The rationale for this step is simple. The State Department's principal mission is diplomacy between states, not providing political and economic assistance or managing reconstruction. The Pentagon's mission should remain defense; many of its assets for regime reconstruction should be moved into this new department, which would begin by incorporating the U.S. Agency for International Development (USAID) while drawing resources and talent from other government departments and agencies. Currently, USAID lacks the authority and stature to lead the interagency process on these challenges of development and reconstruction, nor does it have the authority and status it should in interaction with the cabinet-level development assistance departments of other donor countries. The new department should be endowed with prestige, talented people who pursue rewarding career tracks, and, above all, resources. It should be clearly designated as the lead actor in U.S. government efforts to promote democracy and human development—broad-based sustainable economic development that improves the living standards and productive capabilities of people. Our capacity to help build new states must be as great as our capacity to destroy them.

In calling for a reorganization of the United States government to create greater capacity to help promote democracy, our intention is not to nationalize the democracy promotion business. On the contrary, nongovernmental organizations and independent foundations, such as the National Endowment for Democracy, the International Republican Institute, the National Democratic Institute, the AFL–CIO's Solidarity Center, the Center for International Private Enterprise, the Asia Foundation, the Eurasia

Foundation, Freedom House, Internews, IREX, and the International
Foundation of Electoral Systems, should remain the main providers of funding and expertise on democracy promotion. Government-based programs
for democracy assistance, such as the recently created Middle East Partnership Initiative (MEPI) within the State Department, should be transferred
to the private, nonprofit sector as soon as possible. And only in the rarest of
situations should democracy assistance be a for-profit activity. Those individuals and organizations fully committed to democracy as a cause—and not
as part-time focus or as a way to make money—will be our best champions
for democratic change abroad over the long haul.

FIGHT FOR FREEDOM

The fight for freedom in this new era will be—as it was during the cold
war—a "long twilight struggle." But now, much more than the harsh days
of the global struggle against communist totalitarianism, the forces of democracy are ascendant politically, morally, and organizationally. Freedom is
the fundamental antidote to all forms of tyranny, terror, and oppression. If
we craft a more adept, consistent, bipartisan, cooperative, compelling, and
yet patient strategy for promoting freedom, we can ultimately defeat this
new wave of antidemocratic movements and creeds. We prevailed before;
we can prevail again.

NOTES

1. The most cogent statement of this approach is Rice, Condoleezza, "Promoting
the National Interest," *Foreign Affairs* 79, No. 1 (January/February 2000): 45–62.

2. In its 2005 annual report, Freedom House observed: "Between 1999 and 2003,
70 percent of all deaths from terrorism were caused by terrorists and terrorist groups
originating in Not Free societies, while only 8 percent of all fatalities were generated by
terrorists and terror movements with origins in Free societies." Karatnycky, Adrian,
"Civic Power and Electoral Politics," Freedom House, *Freedom in the World 2005: The
Annual Survey of Political Rights and Civil Liberties* (Lanham, MD: Rowman & Littlefield
Publishers, 2005), p. 10, www.freedomhouse.org/template.cfm?page = 130&year =
2005.

3. "Middle East Progress Amid Global Gains in Freedom," press release, Freedom
House, December 19, 2005, http://www.freedomhouse.org/media/pressrel/122005
.htm.

4. For details, see Diamond, Larry, *Squandered Victory: The American Occupation and
the Bungled Effort to Bring Democracy to Iraq* (New York: Times Books, 2005).

5. MacFarquhar, Neil, "Heavy Hand of the Secret Police Impeding Reform in the Arab World," *New York Times*, November 14, 2005.

6. Feng, Yi, *Democracy, Governance, and Economic Performance: Theory and Evidence* (Cambridge: MIT Press, 2003); Halperin, Morton H., Joseph Siegle, and Michael Weinstein, *The Democracy Advantage: How Democracies Promote Prosperity and Peace* (New York: Routledge, 2004).

7. Brown, Michael, Sean Lynn-Jones, and Steven Miller, eds., *Debating the Democratic Peace* (Cambridge: MIT Press, 1996).

8. Telhami, Shibley, and Zogby International, "Arab Attitudes Toward Political and Social Issues, Foreign Policy and the Media," unpublished manuscript, November 2005. These polls, conducted in six Arab countries in October 2005, showed that 76 percent of respondents believe that Iraqis are worse off after the war, a more negative result than what Iraqis themselves believe. Only 6 percent of these respondents, however, sympathize with the al Qaeda goal of creating an Islamic state. A published account of the poll's findings can be found in "Arab Nations Deeply Suspicious of U.S. Motives— poll" Reuters-Alertnet, December 2, 2005, www.alertnet.org/thenews/newsdesk/ N02305592.htm.

9. Inglehart, Ronald, "The Worldviews of Islamic Publics in Global Perspective," in Moaddel, Mansour, ed., *Worldviews of Islamic Publics* (New York: Palgrave, 2005) p. 16; Zogby, James, *What Arabs Think: Values, Beliefs and Concerns* (Washington: Zogby International, 2002); Tessler, Mark, "Do Islamic Orientations Influence Attitudes toward Democracy in the Arab World?: Evidence from Egypt, Jordan, Morocco, and Algeria," *International Journal of Comparative Sociology* 43, Nos. 3–5 (June 2002): 229–49; and the cluster of articles under the rubric, "How People View Democracy" in *Journal of Democracy* 12, No. 1 (January 2001): 93–145.

10. McFaul, Michael, "Democracy Promotion as a World Value," *Washington Quarterly* 28, No. 1, (Winter 2004–2005): 147–63.

11. A network of different regional and sectoral democratic networks, including parliamentarians, parties, think tanks, democracy promotion foundations, civic educators, and a diverse array of other civil society organizations, the World Movement for Democracy is sponsored by the National Endowment for Democracy and is about to hold its fourth World Assembly in Istanbul in April 2006.

12. See Asmus, Ronald, et al., *Democracy and Human Development in the Broader Middle East: A Transatlantic Strategy for Partnership, Istanbul Papers No. 1* (Washington: German Marshall Fund and Turkish Economic and Social Studies Foundation, June 2004).

13. In November 2005, Egypt blocked a final declaration at a regional summit in Bahrain launching a new multilateral Foundation for the Future to promote democratic political reforms in the region with American, European, and Arab funding. Egypt insisted that the new foundation should only provide aid to "legally registered" groups— which, perversely, would again enable authoritarian regimes like Egypt's to decide which of its NGOs should be allowed international assistance.

14. Thomas, Daniel, *The Helsinki Effect: International Norms, Human Rights and the Demise of Communism* (Princeton: Princeton University Press, 2001); and Sharansky, Natan, *The Case for Democracy: The Power of Freedom to Overcome Tyranny and Terror* (New York: Public Affairs, 2004).

15. The October 2005 poll conducted by Shibley Telhami and Zogby International that is cited above in note 8 showed that only 1 percent of respondents viewed Al Hurra most often when watching international news, compared to 45 percent for Al Jazeera.

16. For instance, Radio Free Europe currently sponsors a weekly report on Iran, which is one of the best English-language sources on current events in Iran, but which could also be expanded tenfold.

4

REVIVING MUSLIM ECONOMIES

Edward Gresser

Four years into the war on terror, America and its allies can claim genuine achievements. Al Qaeda has lost its Afghan base and some of its ability to train recruits. Many of its leaders are jailed and others dead. Allied groups in Southeast Asia, Central Asia, and North Africa have been weakened. And if any of these groups have tried to strike the United States since the September 11 attacks, they have failed.

But victory seems far away. Attacks continue, from Indonesia to Jordan, Morocco, Istanbul, London, and Madrid. New terrorist leaders emerge to replace the old. Broad trends of public opinion in the Muslim world seem little changed.

Why? Perhaps the explanation is that the war effort has a blind spot. Al Qaeda and its allies are threats. But they are also symptoms of deeper problems. The environment from which they emerged in the 1990s is much like those that produced the twentieth-century totalitarian movements of Europe and Asia: one of undemocratic governments, unresolved conflicts, and least recognized in the West, a deepening economic crisis.

For a quarter-century, and from Morocco to Central Asia, populations have boomed as unemployment rose and living standards fell. This is an environment in which extremism will flourish. Al Qaeda's religious orientation is very different from the false nationalism of fascist Germany or the pseudo-egalitarianism of the Chinese Cultural Revolution. But its basic themes are similar—an idealized past, a foreign threat, a purified society, a utopian future—and seem to appeal to the same urban, disenfranchised, and angry young men who joined the earlier totalitarian movements.

To defeat al Qaeda and its allies, military and intelligence targeting of the groups themselves is not enough. The West and its Muslim-world allies also need an economic initiative that can change lives in city neighborhoods and rural districts. This is precisely the achievement of the liberal internationalists of the 1940s, who used the Marshall Plan, the International Monetary Fund and World Bank, the invention of a foreign aid program, and regional trade initiatives to help Europe (and later Asia and Latin America) return to growth, create jobs, and drain away the anger that once fueled the extremists of the right and left.

The war on terror today needs an initiative on a similar scale—but not one that is precisely the same. The Marshall Plan was meant to help an industrially advanced but financially broke Europe recover through a massive infusion of cash. The Middle East today has the opposite problem. As Dr. Rima Khalaf, principal author of the United Nations' *Arab Human Development Report* series, noted in 2002, the region is "richer than it is developed."[1] It has lots of cash, but too little industry and too few urban jobs. Therefore it needs ways to put the cash to better use more than it needs financial aid, and to develop policies that encourage investment and job creation.

The West's main policy tools should therefore be trade and investment policies rather than aid. The Bush administration's call for a U.S.-Middle East Free Trade Area (MEFTA) is not, however, the best approach. For one thing, this proposal excludes Pakistan, Turkey, Afghanistan, Central Asia, Bangladesh, and Indonesia, or two-thirds of the Muslim world. Even for the Arab world its benefits are far away, as the MEFTA would not go into effect for nearly a decade—and its prospects are very uncertain in any case. The United States cannot impose such a project; all the countries in the Middle East need to agree to it. Given the region's turbulence and diversity, the MEFTA is a far bigger challenge than the Free Trade Area of the Americas, which the Bush administration has famously been unable to finish.

The MEFTA project need not be scrapped. But the centerpiece of a new trade strategy for the Muslim world needs to be different in three basic ways. First, it needs to provide tangible investment and job creation quickly, rather than a decade from now. Second, it needs to help the entire "greater

Middle East," rather than one slice of it. And third, it needs to be something the West can deliver without relying on local governments and elites.

This chapter proposes a "Greater Middle East Prosperity Plan": a large-scale trade preference program, modeled on America's African Growth and Opportunity Act (AGOA) but on a larger scale and enlisting the European Union as well. It could be implemented within a year, based on Congressional legislation, and would begin delivering results almost immediately. Under this program, both the European Union (EU) and the United States would dismantle their main barriers to Muslim-world goods. The hope would be to double manufacturing and agricultural imports from the region by the year 2010 (roughly the same time it took the AGOA program to double clothing and value-added agricultural imports from Africa) and bring a wave of labor-intensive investment and jobs to the region.[2] In pursuit of this goal, the program would do two things.

First, it would abolish America's discriminatory trade barriers against Muslim-world manufactured goods. Our tariffs on clothes, household linens, and other textiles—the main exports and urban job creators for Pakistan, Afghanistan, Egypt, and Turkey—are ten times higher than the tariffs we apply to the high-tech products and heavy-industry goods of the wealthy world. Meanwhile, seventy countries in Africa and Latin America have been exempted from the tariff system, trapping Muslim-world exporters between giant competitors China and India and dozens of smaller duty-free competitors. Dropping the tariffs—not over years but immediately—could create hundreds of thousands or even several million new jobs from Morocco to Central Asia.

Second, the program would scrap the EU's exclusionary agricultural policies. EU farm subsidies and trade protection keep the olive oil, grains, and fruit of the Maghreb and the Levant not only out of Europe but off the world market. Were Europe to abolish production-linked subsidies for these goods, and end tariffs and quotas on them, billions of dollars would flow to rural districts in North Africa, the Middle East, and Central Asia, easing pressure to move to cities and creating wealthier rural communities.

BACKGROUND: THE MUSLIM WORLD'S ECONOMIC CRISIS

The case for this approach begins with one of the great and tragic economic phenomena of the late twentieth century. This is the deep and prolonged crisis of the greater Middle East, the historic heartland of the Muslim world, spanning twenty-seven countries from Morocco to Afghanistan and Central Asia. Statistics describe it in an impersonal way, whether one measures demographic change, growth and trade, or living standards.

Population

The World Bank's tables show that between 1980 and 2005, the population of the Middle East rose from 175 million to 305 million, while that of Pakistan, Afghanistan, and Central Asia from 225 to 350 million.[3]

Trade

The World Trade Organization and the International Monetary Fund tell us that the region's share of world exports has dropped from thirteen percent in 1980 to 4 percent in 2000.[4]

Investment

The U.N. Conference on Trade and Development tells us that in 2004, the Arab states, Iran, Pakistan, Afghanistan, Bangladesh, and Central Asia combined to receive $14.5 billion in foreign direct investment. This is not much more than the $9 billion that went to little Ireland alone, less than the $16 billion that went to Singapore, and barely two percent of total world FDI.[5] In 1980, the figure was close to 5 percent.[6]

Jobs

The International Labor Organization finds youth unemployment rates in the Middle East at 25 percent, higher than the rate in any other developing region,[7] and the U.N. Development Program's Arab Human Development Reports say the same about the general unemployment rate in the Middle East.

Income

The Arab Human Development Reports show that per capita income in the Arab world has fallen from $2,300 to $1,650 between 1980 and 2000.[8]

Two personal and anecdotal observations, recorded in the weeks after the September 11 attacks, give such statistics a bit of life.

One is from the Moroccan writer Fatima Mernissi. Drafting a new introduction to her 1992 book *Islam and Democracy,* she recalls a conversation with a young economics graduate from Rabat University. Karim (whose last name goes unrecorded) has been unable to find a permanent job. Despite his degree, he was making ends meet through part-time work as a cashier in newspaper shops and Internet cafes. As the Afghanistan war approached, he has an idea:

> I wish I could advise Mr. Colin Powell . . . . A good military leader is one who can imagine turning a conflict into equal opportunities for both adversaries. In a situation where people can make a living trading peacefully, violence becomes an absurdly costly choice.[9]

The other is from a more influential person four thousand miles east. Abdul Razak Dawood, then Pakistan's Minister of Commerce, echoed Karim's thoughts almost precisely in an interview with the *Financial Times.* "If you want Pakistan to be a liberal and modern state," Dawood said, "you are not going to get that unless you've got people employed."[10] Mr. Dawood was not influential enough; the Bush administration turned down his request for a textile tariff concession.

THE GREATER MIDDLE EAST: ISLANDS IN THE DESERT

Both Karim and Dawood suggest that growth prospects and more healthy rates of job creation could help drain the pool of recruits for terror groups. The U.N. Development Program's (UNDP) first report speaks of the Arab world in particular, but in terms that apply to the greater Middle East as a whole. It suggests that to do this, the region must return to the global economy:

> Domestic markets are too small to provide the basis for sustainable growth based on manufacturing and services. For this reason, the most viable response to globalization is openness and constructive engagement in which Arab countries both contribute to and benefit from globalization.[11]

History elsewhere in the world suggests they are right.

A generation ago, Southeast Asia and Central America were as prone to violence and warfare as the Middle East and South Asia are today. Both are now peaceful, growing, and generally stable places, having used exports of manufactured goods and farm products to create jobs, develop more diversified economies, and discredit violence and extremism. There is no reason to believe the greater Middle East is utterly different.

In fact there is good reason to believe its present condition is abnormal. For most of history, after all, this region was the world's "globalizing" culture. It was famous not as a region full of violence and prejudice, but as the birthplace of religions, the inventor of the library and the alphabet, and the commercial bridge between Europe and Asia. Today it is more economically isolated than ever before. This reflects not mysterious cultural or religious factors, but some basic matters of policy.

Trade Barriers, Sanctions, and Boycotts

First, trade barriers are higher in the greater Middle East than elsewhere, and boycotts and sanctions are more common there than anywhere else in the world. Syria, for example, imposes a 200 percent tariff on cars, though it makes no cars, and requires a separate signed permit for every import. On top of these national policies are sanctions from within and without, which for most of the last twenty years have isolated Israel and Pakistan from their neighbors, and Iran, Libya, Iraq, and Afghanistan from the entire world.

Together these policies deter investment and reduce the economies of scale that create growth. They also all but wreck regional trade, reducing the stake of each country in the others' prosperity and security. In 2004, only 6 percent of Middle Eastern trade was internal—a far lower rate than we see in Africa, Latin America, or Asia. Egypt barely trades with Lebanon and Syria, Iran barely trades with Saudi Arabia and Turkey, Morocco trades mainly with France and Spain.[12] The greater Middle East, with a tenth of the world's people, accounts for barely one percent of global farm and manufacturing exports.[13] As King Abdullah of Jordan has said, it is more like a series of "isolated islands of production" than a single integrated region.

Policy Isolation

Second, the Arab world and Iran participate less in trade policymaking than any other region of the world. Ten of the Arab League's twenty-two members, including Algeria, Iraq, Lebanon, Libya, Syria, and Yemen, remain outside the World Trade Organization (WTO). Saudi Arabia joined only last December. Iran is outside too, as are Afghanistan and three of the five Central Asian states, unable to defend themselves against discrimination, win reduction of barriers to their exports, or reshape their own economies through improved services policies, intellectual property rights, and transparency.

SIGNS OF CHANGE

The environment is depressing. But the fact that—at least in part—ordinary policy failures can explain it, is reason for optimism. Mistaken economic policies can be replaced with better ones. In many countries this is already happening.

Most dramatically, the sanctions on Afghanistan, Iraq, and Libya are gone. Meanwhile, governments in other major countries are reshaping their own policies. Turkey has long since chosen a European destiny, and opened talks on membership in the European Union last fall. Pakistan has deeply cut tariffs, limited state involvement in the economy, cautiously begun to reopen trade with India, and backed an ambitious approach to the Doha Round. Egypt, starting later, has also cut tariffs, begun to simplify its notorious bureaucracies and regulatory systems, and opened a small economic integration project with Israel to take advantage of duty-free privileges in the United States. Smaller economies, led by Jordan, have done much more.

WTO membership has become a higher priority in the Middle East. Jordan and Oman joined in the 1990s. Saudi Arabia joined late last year, with a thorough "accession" agreement extending to renunciation of secondary and tertiary boycotts of Israel. Afghanistan, Algeria, Iraq, Kazakhstan, Lebanon, Yemen, and even Syria and Iran have applied as well.

THE UNITED STATES AND EUROPE:
BLIND SPOTS IN POLICY

These are the policy equivalents of "green shoots" after winter. An energetic response from America and Europe can help them grow. Europe deserves credit for its decision to begin formal negotiations on Turkey's EU membership. The United States has helped to negotiate Saudi Arabia's

WTO accession, and concluded bilateral free trade agreements with Morocco, Oman, and Bahrain. But neither the Bush administration nor the bland commissioners of Europe have been willing to touch their own most discriminatory and damaging policies. Both Western giants, in fact, are making life harder for reformers, as the United States preserves openly discriminatory manufacturing tariffs, while European farm subsidies and trade barriers push rural Muslim produce out of the world market.

THE UNITED STATES, TEXTILE TARIFFS, AND THE WORKING WOMEN OF KARACHI

Afghanistan, Bangladesh, Egypt, Pakistan, and Turkey are together home to over 400 million of the region's 600 million people. All rely on textile exports to the United States to support urban jobs and acquire foreign exchange. These products make up 90 percent of Pakistani and Bangladeshi exports to the United States, and support half of all industrial jobs in both countries. Figures for Afghanistan, Egypt, and Turkey are only slightly less dramatic.[14] In all five countries, these jobs are especially important for poorer urban women, for whom garment-factory jobs are an almost unique opportunity.

America's tariff system hits them very hard. The average American tariff rate, excluding textiles, is 1.4 percent. This means that Japan's cars, Singapore's medical equipment, Malaysia's televisions, France's wine, and Britain's medicines all flow easily into the United States. The tariff rate on clothes and textile products like fabrics and linens is 12.5 percent, or about ten times higher than the rate on other goods.[15] So Turks, Egyptians, Pakistanis, and Bangladeshis see a much more closed U.S. market than their wealthier Asian and European neighbors encounter.

Table 4.1 illustrates the effect, comparing treatment of the top hundred imports from the major Muslim states with imports from some other large trading partners in Europe, Asia, Africa, and Latin America.

A second inequity makes matters worse. Muslim states are not only treated poorly, but much worse than their competitors. Since 1985, the United States has eliminated tariffs on two dozen Central American and Caribbean countries through the Caribbean Basin Initiative. Since 2000, four large South American states and thirty-seven African countries have joined the duty-free list. These "preference" programs were created with good intentions and often good effects, but they have inescapably created losers as they picked winners. By default, the losers are some of the large Muslim

Table 4.1.   U.S. Tariffs on Top 100 Goods from 24 Countries, 2003[1]

	Duty-free Products	Tariffs 0.1%–4.9%	Tariffs 5%–15%	Tariffs >15%
Bangladesh[2]	6	5	48	41
Pakistan	10	7	66	17
Oman	30	8	31	31
Syria	35	17	22	26
Egypt	37	17	31	15
Turkey	49	9	27	15
Indonesia	54	11	14	19
India	48	15	25	12
China	56	20	20	4
Brazil	64	18	15	3
WORLD	63	24	8	5
EU	65	24	11	0
South Africa	83	7	9	1
U.K.	69	23	7	1
Japan	57	37	6	0
Saudi Arabia	69	22	9	0
Germany	60	38	2	0

Source: U.S. International Trade Commission.
1. HTS classification, 8-digit level, full-year 2003.
2. All tariff data treat goods imported through the Generalized System of Preferences, Free Trade Agreements, the African Growth and Opportunity Act, or the Caribbean Basin Initiative as duty-free.

states most important in the war on terror—among them Afghanistan, Egypt, Pakistan, and Turkey. Meanwhile, the elimination of the textile quota system in January 2005 has freed China and India to take full advantage of their size and economies of scale, further intensifying the stress.

Even as America's terror-war partners in the Muslim world begin to rethink their policies at home, therefore, the American trade landscape is tilting against them. Their factories and workers compete head-to-head against two giant rivals, and also against seventy small countries given special advantages through exemptions from tariffs.

To illustrate the result, Table 4.2 looks at acrylic sweaters, sneakers, suitcases, and drinking glasses. These are all cheap, labor-intensive products rarely made in the United States. If a retail chain wishes to avoid the tariff payments, it can order the glasses, sweaters, or suitcases from factories in South Africa, Peru, or El Salvador. If it wants to buy a huge number of sweaters, Guangdong or Bombay might be the best choices. Why would it buy from Karachi? Or Beirut? Or Cairo, Bursa, Dhaka, and Kabul?

A Clinton-era experiment in trade policy with Jordan shows that

Table 4.2.   Sample U.S. Tariffs

	Acrylic Sweaters	Sneakers	Suitcases	Drinking Glasses
China	32%	20%–48%	22%	28.6%
India	32%	20%–48%	22%	28.6%
Pakistan	32%	20%–48%	22%	28.6%
Egypt	32%	20%–48%	22%	28.6%
Turkey	32%	20%–48%	22%	28.6%
El Salvador	0%	0%	0%	0%
Honduras	0%	0%	0%	0%
South Africa	0%	0%	0%	0%
Kenya	0%	0%	0%	0%
Peru	0%	0%	0%	0%
Colombia	0%	0%	0%	0%

Source: U.S. International Trade Commission.

scrapping this inequity brings quick results. With a small tariff benefit awarded in 1997, Jordan lifted its exports from $16 million to $400 million within three years. Despite its unlucky location in an arid desert between the intifada and Iraq, Jordan attracted dozens of new factories and created nearly 50,000 export jobs.

A similar program on a large scale would do the same throughout the region. Former U.S. Trade Representative Robert Zoellick seemed to hint at the idea as early as 2001, when he wrote that trade policy could help fight terrorist groups by promoting growth and economic integration in countries susceptible to radicalism.[16] But the administration rejected each attempt to implement the idea. Minister Dawood's request for a temporary exemption from tariffs in 2001 went nowhere. The administration publicly ignored, and quietly killed, a much larger tariff relief bill for eighteen countries in the Middle East and South Asia introduced by Senators John McCain (R-AZ) and Max Baucus (D-MT) and Representatives Calvin Dooley (D-CA) and Adam Smith (D-WA) in 2003.

EUROPE: OLIVE OIL, AND THE MOROCCAN ORCHARD WORKER

European farm programs do for rural districts what American tariff policy does for factory workers.

Olive oil is a typical example. The olive tree grows in Morocco, Tunisia, Lebanon, and Turkey as well as in Greece, Italy, and Spain. Arab-world olive oil presses can produce in high volume at respectable quality, and America is a growing market. Our supermarkets sold almost 240,000 tons last year, up from 100,000 tons fifteen years ago, and California orchards supply only ten or twenty thousand tons a year. But it is all but impossible to find Moroccan or Tunisian olive oil on an American market shelf.

This is not because the United States maintains any important trade barriers to olive oil. Our tariffs are low and we have no quota program. Tunisians and Moroccans cannot sell here because the European Union drives its own oil prices down through gigantic subsidy checks to its olive growers. EU olive oil subsidies total 2.5 billion euros a year. This is two dollars for every single dollar of olive oil trade outside the European Union, or more than half of the world's $5.7 billion in olive oil production value.[17]

Modest reforms to the Common Agricultural Policy, intended to weaken the link between cash assistance and production volume, have excluded olive oil. So Spain and Italy, with a dollar of subsidies in each quart bottle of olive oil, account for 220,000 tons of oil exports to the United States at cut-rate prices, or 95 percent of the market. Moroccan and Tunisian orchards, pitted not only against Europe's good image and recognized brands but three billion dollars of free money, managed 6,000 tons.

Nor are European trade initiatives in the Middle East of much help. European subsidies—covering forty-seven separate farm commodities, including almost everything grown in the Middle East except couscous grain—keep Middle Eastern farmers from global agriculture markets, while a battery of tariffs and quotas keep Europe itself closed. Examples range from a 25.6 percent tariff on preserved apricots to flat fees of 13 euros per hundred kilograms on olives.

The EU's "association agreements" and Euro-Med program are of little help, as they seem carefully designed to keep Middle Eastern produce to a minimum. The association agreement with Lebanon is a typical example. It excludes a dizzying list of products: olives, olive oil, table grapes, wine, potatoes, pears, apples, garlic, tomatoes, as well as buttermilk, cream yogurt, sweet corn, margarine, fructose, some malt, flour, and cocoa products, pasta, tapioca, and ice cream.[18]

THE PROSPERITY PLAN

The Bush administration's proposed U.S.-Middle East Free Trade Agreement is ambitious, but also both too grandiose and too limited. It is too limited, because it is scheduled for conclusion in 2015—implying no actual benefits until 2017 or 2018—and excludes Pakistan, Afghanistan, Bangladesh, and Central Asia. It is too grandiose, because the plan is unlikely ever to materialize; the administration has been unable to complete even the much easier Free Trade Area of the Americas (FTAA). In the interim, the administration has marked time through small free trade agreements with a series of Persian Gulf monarchies. Unobjectionable in themselves, they are irrelevant to the places in which the war on terror will be won or lost: flashpoints like Afghanistan and Iraq, and giants like Pakistan and Egypt.

This is not good enough. The West faces a deadly threat, and with governments in the Middle East and South Asia reshaping their own policies, we have a chance to use trade policy to make a decisive contribution to reform. The next administration should return to the duty-free initiative suggested by Minister Dawood and offered as legislation by Senators Baucus and McCain, and Representatives Dooley and Smith, then broaden it by enlisting the European Union. The result would be a three-part program known as the Greater Middle East Prosperity Plan, along the following lines:

Greater Priority for WTO membership: for the Arab states and Central Asia, although this of course depends on the urgency their governments devote to the task.

Bilateral Agreements: Countries at the leading edge of reform— evidenced in WTO membership, economic integration with neighbors, noncompliance with the boycott of Israel, and similar self-help policies— should be eligible for expanded FTAs with the United States or Qualifying Industrial Zone concepts like the early program created for Jordan. Europe, meanwhile, should revise its series of Association Agreements in the Middle East to include fresh produce, meats, and value-added products like olive oil, preserved fruits, and vegetables.

General Duty-free Program: Finally, the United States and EU should join in a duty-free program open to the Muslim world generally, along the following lines:

- Coverage. The program should cover countries in the Middle East, South Asia, and Central Asia not already benefiting from free trade agreements, America's African Growth and Opportunity Act, or the European Union's Everything but Arms program.
- Benefits. Goods from qualifying countries would receive duty-free and quota-free access to the United States and European markets for manufactured goods and farm products. This would include removal

of tariffs on manufactured goods like shoes and clothes plus duty-free status for regional agricultural products such as dates, olive oil, and Middle Eastern grains.

- Conditionalities. Countries participating in the program should meet a set of conditions. One, participation in antiterror efforts, should be mandatory for countries receiving benefits. Others should cover economic and political issues, but serve as loose guidance for appropriate policies rather than strict eligibility requirements. Their hope would be to ensure that governments trying in good faith to do the right thing, even if imperfectly, can show concrete benefits.
- Security. Cooperation against al Qaeda and withdrawal of support for other terror-linked groups like Hezbollah.
- Political. Respect for basic human rights and core labor standards, along the lines of conditions contained in America's Caribbean Basin Initiative and African Growth and Opportunity Act.
- Economic. Domestic reform, anticorruption measures, membership or progress toward membership in the WTO, work toward regional integration, and noncompliance with the Israel boycott.

The program, though covering many countries and almost 500 million people, would initially affect a relatively small fraction of United States and European trade. Excluding oil and precious metals (where neither the United States nor Europe have meaningful trade barriers) America's imports from the Middle East, central Asia, and Muslim South Asia total roughly about $14 billion, and Europe's about $23 billion. In both cases the figure is below 2 percent of manufacturing and agricultural imports. America's $14 billion in non-oil imports from these countries is barely half the $25 billion in annual imports from Ireland.

For the United States and Europe alike, the program's disruption of domestic employment and production would be minimal or nonexistent. If it were to double the region's exports of farm products and light manufacturing to the west, however, the practical effect would be an extra $40 billion a year, directed—in contrast to oil money—to urban job creation and rural incomes rather than princes and government departments.

CONCLUSION

The four years since the September 11 attacks have been years of important achievement. Americans can take pride in the military effort that drove al

Qaeda from Afghanistan; in the clandestine services which captured Khalid Sheikh Mohammed, Riduan Isamuddin, and other terrorist leaders; and in the homeland security policies that have so far prevented a major new attack on our homeland. But Americans must also recognize that these successes have not brought victory in the war on terror.

The next administration has an opportunity to go further. Al Qaeda is a military and security threat, but also the product of an environment. Defeating the organization in detail is essential, but the aim of the West and its Muslim-world allies must be to extinguish violent fundamentalism altogether. To do this we need to change the environment. A broader vision can help us do so, joining the military intelligence battle against al Qaeda with a hopeful view of the Muslim world's future, and a practical, cooperative set of economic policies that help to make it real.

NOTES

1. Khalaf, Rima, "Arab Human Development Report," United Nations Development Program, 2002, www.rbas.undp.or/ahdr2.cfm?menu = 10.

2. This would not be disruptive. Doubling agricultural and manufacturing imports from the Middle East, Turkey, Pakistan, Afghanistan, and Bangladesh would mean an increase from about $10 billion to about $20 billion. A typical year's import growth from Canada is at least $30 billion.

3. "World Development Indicators 2005," Table 2.1, World Bank, 2005, pp. 48–50.

4. See IMF annual Direction of Trade Statistics, for example the 1984 and 2004 editions.

5. "World Investment Report 2005," United Nations Conference of Trade and Development, September 29, 2005, www.unctad.org/Templates/WebFlyer.asp?intItem ID = 3489&lang = 1.

6. "World Investment Report 2003," United Nations Conference of Trade and Development, September 4, 2003, www.unctad.org/Templates/WebFlyer.asp?intItemID = 2979&lang = 1.

7. "Youth Employment Trends," International Labor Organization, August 2005, www.ilo.org/public/english/employment/strat/download/getyen.pdf.

8. "Arab Human Development Report 2002," United Nations Development Program, 2005, 88, www.undp.org/rbas/ahdr/bychapter.html.

9. Mernissi, Fatima, *Islam and Democracy*, Mary Jo Lakeland, trans., Second Edition (Cambridge: Perseus Publishing 2002), pp. xi–xv.

10. "Pakistan Looks for Better Deal on Textile Exports," *Financial Times*, September 29, 2001.

11. "UNDP Releases the First Arab Human Development Report," Executive Summary, United Nations Development Program, www.undp.org/rbas/ahdr/ahdr1/press kit1/PRExecSummary.pdf.

12. "Direction of Trade Statistics," International Monetary Fund; See also Barshefsky,

Charlene, "Bridges to Peace: The U.S.-Jordan Free Trade Agreement and U.S. Trade Policy in the Middle East," Amman, Jordan, July 2000.

13. "World Trade Statistics 2005," World Trade Organization, 2005, www.wto .org/english/res_e/statis_e/its2005_e/its05_toc_e.htm.

14. Trade data from the U.S. International Trade Commission, available at dataweb.-usitc.gov, show textiles and clothing accounting for 37 percent of Turkish exports to the United States, 42 percent of Egyptian exports, and 40 percent of Afghanistan's infant export trade.

15. U.S. International Trade Commission.

16. Zoellick, Robert, "Fighting Terror with Trade," *Washington Post*, September 20, 2001.

17. For EU olive oil supports, see EU domestic support notifications to the WTO, available at http://docsonline.wto.org/gen_home.asp?language = 1&_ = 1; for production and consumption figures, see the U.S. Department of Agriculture, www.fas.usda .gov/psd/complete_tables/OIL-table2-162.htm.

18. "The EU's Relations with Lebanon," Office of External Relations, European Commission, December 2005, http://europa.eu.int/comm/external_relations/lebanon/intro/.

II

CONFRONTING GLOBAL
TERRORISM

5

A SMARTER WAR ON TERROR

Daniel Benjamin

In the fifth year of the war on terror, the United States faces an unnerving paradox: For all the tactical successes that have been achieved—the terrorists arrested, plots foiled, networks disrupted—our strategic position continues to slip badly. The ideology of jihad is spreading: A new generation of terrorists is emerging with few ties to al Qaeda but a worldview soaked in Osama bin Laden's hatred of the West, and new areas of the globe are increasingly falling under the shadow of this growing threat.

So much is clear from the 2004 bombings in Madrid, the 2005 bombings in London, and the murder of Dutch artist Theo van Gogh by a young Dutch Muslim militant in the same year. These incidents demonstrate the rise of the new breed of self-starter terrorists, who are self-recruited and often self-trained, and who can draw on the vast wealth of instructional materials available on the Internet. Self-starters have appeared not only in Europe but also in Morocco, where they carried out a string of bombings in Casablanca in 2003, and in Pakistan, a country with a well-established jihadist infrastructure that some new recruits have deemed insufficiently aggressive.

Geographically, the picture is one of jihadist metastasis. With more than thirty failed plots across the continent in roughly five years, Europe has become a central battlefield.[1] In Australia, a major dragnet recently wrapped up eighteen conspirators who appear to have been plotting an attack on the country's one nuclear power plant.[2] And in South Asia the incidence of Islamist violence continues to grow.

Perhaps the most damaging development is that Iraq has become the central battlefield of jihad. The number of foreign fighters in the country is disputed, but studies show that the insurgency against the U.S. occupation is drawing young men with no background in radical activities to Iraq. Even more ominously, an Iraqi jihadist movement has emerged where none existed before. Two of the major insurgent groups, the Islamic Army of Iraq and Ansar al-Sunna, embrace a radical ideology, and Abu Mussab al Zarqawi's al Qaeda in the Land of the Two Rivers claims to have all-Iraqi units. Confirmation of the rise of this new movement came in November 2005 when three hotels in Amman were bombed by Iraqi suicide operatives. The attacks were the first successful ones in Jordan and the most stunning case of spillover from the turmoil in Iraq.

But they were hardly the only ones. Kuwait, a country with no history of jihadist violence, experienced running gun battles between authorities and militants and discovered plotters within its own armed forces. Syria, which waged a campaign of extermination against Islamists in the early 1980s, has seen Sunni radicalism reemerge. Qatar had its first vehicle bombing in early 2005. Saudi Arabia suffered a series of bombings and attacks, and while the authorities have gained the upper hand against al Qaeda in the Arabian Peninsula, the group still exists. The discovery of Iraqi-style bombs in the kingdom may well be a harbinger of worse to come once veterans of the fighting to the north return home. Saudi Arabia has contributed the largest number of foreign fighters to the Iraqi insurgency.

There is a significant possibility of wider destabilization because Iraq's terrorists appear to have won a sanctuary in the overwhelmingly Sunni-dominated al Anbar province. U.S. troops have fought one campaign after another in this region, from the villages on the Syrian border to cities such as Ramadi and Fallujah. Yet terrorist attacks have often increased because the militants shrewdly move out of town when troops arrive and return after our forces depart. They will be rooted out only when there is a capable Iraqi intelligence service. Since that service is likely to be dominated by Shiites and Kurds, there are not going to be many operatives able to work in the hostile environment of al Anbar. The likelihood is that this sanctuary will be there for years.

It is not obvious now how many Iraqi jihadists will support the global jihad of bin Laden and Zarqawi and how many will focus their efforts on Iraq's fledgling state. Even if relatively small numbers opt for the global fight, though, it could make a significant difference to the terrorists' capabilities, as has been seen by the actions of the small numbers of individuals involved in the Madrid and London bombings. These attacks clearly belie the Bush administration's claim that the United States would fight terrorists in Iraq and Afghanistan so it would not have to face them, as Vice President Dick Cheney put it, "in Washington or London or anywhere else in the world."[3]

The chief reason for this failure is a fundamental misunderstanding of the ideological nature of jihadist terror. Although President George W. Bush and others have often spoken of the terrorists' "ideology of hatred," they appear to have little conception of its fundamental storyline. At the heart of it is a belief, handed down from the revolutionary Egyptian Islamist writer Sayyid Qutb, that the West is the preordained enemy of Islam. In its most bare-bones formulation, the ideology holds that America and its allies seek to occupy Muslims' lands, steal their oil wealth, and destroy their faith. Radical Islamists interpret much of history through this prism: The drawing of borders in the Middle East after World War I was aimed at dividing Muslims and destroying their historic unity. The creation of Israel was another step in this direction since it, too, created a Western foothold in the region and was designed to weaken and subjugate Muslim nations. The U.S. deployment to Saudi Arabia and the invasion of Iraq in Operation Desert Storm marked another stage in this tale of woe. Radical Islamists believe, moreover, that the United States supports the autocrats of the Muslim world as a way of keeping the believers down and undermining the faith.

The administration's blunders in Iraq have given the radicals fresh fodder for their "clash of civilizations" claims. Polling in Muslim nations over the last three years has shown that America's image has plummeted to historic lows. Although the overwhelming majority of Muslims will not turn to violence, in this environment, it appears more are turning in that direction as actors or supporters than would otherwise be the case. It is clear that Iraq provided a major part of the motivation for the Madrid and London bombers and for Mohammed Bouyeri, the murderer of Theo van Gogh. In countries such as Pakistan, it is also clear that anti-Americanism has been bolstered by the invasion of Iraq, and it is increasingly being used as a tool of mobilization for radicals.

Moreover, the effectively unilateral invasion and the botched occupation opened a new "field of jihad" for militants who were more than eager to take on U.S. forces in the Arab heartland. For the radicals, killing Americans is the essential task; by doing so, they demonstrate that they are the only ones determined to stand up for Muslim dignities. Through their violence, they have also created a drama of the faith that disaffected Muslims around the world can watch on television and the Internet. Thus, the jihadist movement's show of its determination to confront American and coalition forces as well as those of the fledgling Iraqi regime has boosted its attractiveness. However benign our intentions were in going into Iraq, in the context of the culture of grievance that exists in much of the Muslim world, the extremists' narrative has had a profound resonance.

It is true that the original al Qaeda network's ability to carry out long-distance operations has been degraded—though probably not eliminated—by the arrest or death of a number of high-level members, and numerous operatives around the world have been taken off the streets. (Many of the Bush administration's claims regarding the extent of the damage to the network cannot be confirmed and some are dubious, but progress has clearly been achieved.) But the terrorists will inevitably seek to rebuild their networks and capabilities to attack the United States at home. This is the gold standard for them, and if the overall strength of the movement is growing, reestablishing the capacity to carry off "spectaculars" will also be on the agenda. The United States already made the mistake of not taking events abroad seriously enough once, and the result was 9/11. We dare not commit this error twice.

VULNERABLE AT HOME

The threat is growing, but there is little to demonstrate that our defenses have improved commensurately. The United States may be safer today than it was on 9/11 because we are more vigilant, and for that, alas, we owe the terrorists who committed the atrocities of that day. In terms of programmatic efforts to shore up our vulnerabilities, the three years since the creation of the Department of Homeland Security (DHS) have been largely consumed by the task of merging the twenty-two different entities that were joined together in the new department—and then by a couple of rounds of reorganization. Weak leadership from the White House has meant that homeland security issues often drift along with no one driving the process.

Indeed, assessments of DHS performance have been almost uniformly bleak. A recent audit by the department's inspector general depicted a management in disarray and complained that "integrating its many separate components in a single, effective and economical department remains one of DHS's biggest challenges." The audit reported that Immigration and

Customs Enforcement has failed to maintain proper financial records, DHS's technology infrastructure remains fractured and ineffective, and DHS faces "formidable challenges in securing the nation's borders."[4] In evaluating progress on homeland security in December 2005, the 9/11 Commission's Public Discourse Project gave an array of low grades—mostly F's, D's, and C's. Private sector preparedness for a terrorist attack received a C. The effort to come up with a plan to track terrorist travel received an Incomplete.[5]

It has become somewhat harder for terrorists from Muslim countries to get into the United States. But this may be a benefit of limited duration since our visa waiver program has, in essence, optimized access to the United States for people from the part of the world where radicalism appears to be growing fastest—Europe. Those who want to commit violence within our borders can take comfort that the vast sums invested into securing air travel through the hiring of an army of Transportation Safety Administration inspectors have been of limited value since, as a study by former DHS Inspector General Clark Kent Ervin showed, it remains relatively easy to bring weapons onboard planes. Cargo and checked bags on passenger planes are still not adequately inspected.

In short, the nation has lost three years of priceless time for getting its defenses in order—time we could ill afford to waste.

A PROGRESSIVE
COUNTERTERRORISM STRATEGY

Over the last year, public confidence in President Bush's ability to keep Americans safe has taken a nose dive. This presents Democrats with an opportunity, and an obligation, to offer Americans a smarter strategy for global counterterrorism. Such a strategy should entail five key steps: delegitimating the jihadist ideology, tamping down the local conflicts that fuel terrorism, shaping the global antiterror battlefield, improving tactical counterterrorism, and getting serious about homeland defense. While the first two steps are explored in detail in other chapters, they must be the point of departure for any serious discussion of counterterrorism strategy.

1. Winning the Ideological War

It has become an administration shibboleth that all the instruments of American power must be used in the struggle against terror. Nonetheless, the Bush team has overmilitarized the fight in a way that is profoundly counterproductive, and it has ignored valuable tools that are at hand. To begin turning the conflict in our favor, the United States must work to delegitimate the terrorists in the eyes of the global Muslim community. This will be, above all, a diplomatic and economic task. Conducting this ideological battle effectively will create an opportunity for pro-Western Muslims to reassert themselves and begin separating moderates from extremists—a key part of dealing with any insurgency. Yet more than four years after the attacks in New York and Washington, the United States has failed to craft a counterstory to the terrorists, one that emphasizes that the United States is a benign power that seeks to help countries, regardless of their religion, modernize and democratize in ways that will serve their peoples' best interests.

A key element of this strategy must be the promotion of a reform agenda in the Muslim—and especially Arab—world. Democratization and economic liberalization will not end terror. But over time, they will help marginalize extremists and create political space in which radical dissent will be vented and, most of the time, dissipated. Moreover, if our democratization policy focuses only on elections and not building institutions, a democratic culture and respect for the rule of law, we risk empowering extremists whose aims are inimical to ours—this, surely, is the lesson of the Hamas victory in the Palestinian elections of January 2006. In any case, the United States cannot make such a push alone, especially because we are viewed with deep suspicion in most of the Muslim world. But if we are joined by the European Union, Japan, Australia, and other democracies, there would be a real chance for progress. Reconnecting and strengthening America's alliances will also be essential if we are to ensure that nuclear and other mass destruction weapons do not fall into the hands of terrorists. Moreover, Washington must take much more seriously foreign disapproval of some of the practices the United States has employed in the war on terror—the creation of "black sites" (secret detention centers), torture, the use of European airports for renditions, and the establishment of legal gray zones such as at Guantanamo. The Bush administration has resisted curtailing the practices that have so outraged foreign publics by arguing for the security benefits against the moral claims of critics, but it seems clear that our security will ultimately be damaged more by the inevitable erosion of our relationships with other intelligence services than by eliminating the most offensive practices.

2. Extinguish the Fires of Local Conflict

Another high priority involves tamping down through diplomatic means the regional conflicts that are feeding the global jihad, including those in the Caucasus (a region slipping into chaos), Kashmir, and Southeast Asia, particularly the Philippines, Thailand, and Indonesia. In this archipelago of disparate, local jihads, the terrorists of tomorrow are becoming ideologically radicalized and technically proficient in the tradecraft of violence. An effort to ameliorate these conflicts will not be easy. Most of the countries concerned have a strong sense of sovereignty and will resent what they will characterize as "meddling" in their internal affairs.

One of the greatest challenges the United States will face involves deepening its efforts to bring the Palestinian-Israeli conflict to a close—a task made much more daunting by Hamas's victory. As a source of Muslim grievance, nothing surpasses this struggle. Since the establishment of Israel in 1948, and especially after the 1967 war, the situation has been used by Arab regimes and their apologists to justify authoritarianism within and confrontation without. The Internet and satellite television have now ensured that the plight of Palestinians is at the forefront of Arab and Muslim grievances. This has been crippling to our image and forms the mental backdrop against which Muslims experience our intervention in Iraq and gauge our pro-democracy rhetoric. For Washington, the near-term challenge is to demonstrate its commitment to building a better future for the Palestinian people without backing into concessions to Hamas before the group abjures terrorist violence and recognizes Israel.

3. Shape the Battlefield

A key shortcoming in U.S. counterterrorism policy has been a failure to "shape the battlefield"—to make more inhospitable for terrorists the environment in which they operate. There is a vast need for counterterrorism capacity building, especially in the developing world, to improve border controls, eliminate safe havens, and expand the law enforcement and intelligence abilities of the authorities. We demand a great deal from countries that are on the front lines of the war on terror, but we give them relatively little assistance. To cite one example, the United States insists on a high level of financial controls and surveillance to restrict terrorists' ability to raise and move money, but Washington has provided only a pittance for countries that seek to build the capacity to implement these controls.

The Bush administration has increased military assistance to other allies in the war on terror. But it has neglected the civilian programs—funded largely by the State Department's Antiterrorism Assistance Program—that are vital to building counterterrorism capacity abroad.[6] It is easy to illustrate how much this kind of investment is needed: In Kenya, the police crackdown after the 1998 bombing of the U.S. embassies in Nairobi and Dar es Salaam was inefficient enough that four years later al Qaeda operatives based in the same coastal area were able to bomb a Mombasa hotel filled with Israeli guests and fire missiles at an Israeli charter plane. Much more could be done, for example, to improve border controls, eliminate safe havens, and upgrade travel documents. The logic of Antiterrorism Assistance is compelling: We need to prepare others who share our interests to be the pointed end of the spear in a global conflict in which the United States cannot do everything and be everywhere. Antiterrorism Assistance is a vital tool for combating terror, and we could probably spend several times what we are now spending without pressing up against the ability of worthy recipients to absorb the aid.

Many international organizations work on matters related to counterterrorism, but no single body focuses primarily on the issue. The United States should therefore back the establishment of an international organization to raise global norms of behavior by states to make it more difficult for terrorists to operate. Such an organization—call it the International Counterterrorism Agency (ICA)—could significantly change the environment in which terrorists operate by pressing for universal ratification and enforcement of all international counterterrorism conventions. The conventions—now numbering thirteen—have historically been an excellent means of prodding underperformers to do a better job of terrorism prevention. For example, after the spate of hijackings in the 1960s and 1970s, signing up dozens of countries to some of the early conventions, which dealt with aviation security issues, provided an excellent lever for pressing governments to improve their counter-hijacking programs. Over the years, hijacking all but disappeared as a phenomenon, until 9/11, when suicide hijacking made its debut. The conventions spell out signatory states' obligations in a range of areas including aviation security, investigation of terrorist bombings, and preventing terrorists from acquiring materials related to weapons of mass destruction. They have proven to be a particularly valuable tool because they spell out responsibilities without getting bogged down in the definitional debate about terrorism, which has plagued the international community for decades.

Additionally, the ICA could play a vital role in assessing national counterterrorism capabilities regularly on a global basis. Using an international team of experts as well as the voluntary reports of countries, such as those which are now being filed to the United Nations' Counterterrorism Committee (created by U.N. Security Council Resolution 1373), the ICA would be well positioned to recommend specific improvements in intelligence and law enforcement practices in countries in need of greater capacity. So, for example, countries with problems in the area of border security could receive technical and other assistance on how to raise the effectiveness of their police and immigration authorities. The United States has undertaken such efforts in the past, but doing so on a global scale is beyond the abilities of any one country.

Most of the countries in need of improvements are developing countries with few resources to devote to such tasks. The ICA could help them considerably by performing a task that has been identified as essential by both the U.N. and the G-8: Matching donor countries with recipients to ensure that necessary resources are being transferred as needed and best practices are being put in place. The U.N. Security Council expected that its Counter-terrorism Committee would play this role, and when it became clear that was not happening, the G-8 created a body to do the same. Neither has lived up to expectations. A dedicated international organization would be better positioned to accomplish this job.

The ICA could also institute a process of peer review in which member nations would evaluate whether a particular country was living up to its counterterrorism obligations. This would be much like the Financial Action Task Force's (FATF) practice of "naming and shaming" underperforming states. The opprobrium attached to this sanction would prompt many countries to improve their capabilities, and significant financial impact would likely also occur. Because there is no international institution dedicated to counterterrorism, no one does this now; when the United States or its European partners complain about underperformance, the charges are typically seen through the lens of North-South antipathies.

The creation of an ICA, with its emphasis on technocratic evaluation, would have the further virtue of removing the "made in America" label from the war on terror. This would reduce antagonism resulting from what many view as an overbearing superpower imposing its agenda or seeking to expand its hegemony. It would create an international constituency that recognizes the global nature of the problem. A well-conceived institution with strong support from a cross-section of the global community would reemphasize that the world faces a struggle between the forces of civilization and barbarity. Shifting the war on terror from being America's fight to that of the international community would enable Muslim countries that want to defend their own societies to join without excessive fear of being tarnished as U.S. lackeys.

The ICA could be established in a number of ways. It could be brought to life as a treaty-based organization, like the International Atomic

Energy Agency. In this case, its charter could be negotiated under U.N. auspices, which would give it great legitimacy but lessen the likelihood that the organization would "name and shame" because of the U.N.'s consensus-oriented rules. Or it could be established more informally by a coalition of the like-minded, as the FATF was. In this case, it might be established by a group of nations convened by the G-8 or G-20. It might also be desirable to have a relationship with the U.N. that would allow the referral of hard cases—countries that refuse to fulfill their counterterrorism obligations—to the Security Council.

4. Strengthen Tactical Counterterrorism

Tactical counterterrorism is the combination of intelligence, law enforcement, and military force that must deal with terrorists at the ground level. It involves identifying, locating, and neutralizing terrorist groups, denying them access to the most dangerous weapons and sanctuaries, and cutting off their resources. Our abilities in the area of tactical counterterrorism can determine whether we capture or kill terrorists or they kill our citizens.

At this level, the United States has done reasonably well in the struggle against terror—with the single and very large exception of Iraq-related jihadist activity. But reasonably well will not be good enough for long, especially given the high rate of innovation among these information-age terrorists. Consequently, the United States must adapt its intelligence collection and analysis to a constantly evolving threat.

Some steps are clear: As detailed elsewhere in this book, the military must be reorganized to optimize its counterterrorism capabilities, and the United States must continue to enhance its training of foreign forces in counterterrorism tactics and cultivate the essential long-term relationships with these forces that will make for strong joint operations. There will also need to be continual reinvestment in signals intelligence because, as the communications revolution continues, the intelligence community's capabilities must keep pace. The clandestine service must be increased to meet the current threat, though no easy, cookie-cutter solutions are available to determine how much larger the Directorate of Operations should be. And as important as any other undertaking, there must be a redoubled effort to establish a culture of information sharing between and among all levels of government, which does not currently exist. Despite the reforms instituted since the 9/11 Commission reported its findings, turf battles remain endemic, and the actual roles and missions of the proliferating entities involved in counterterrorism are uncertain because negotiations over a presidential directive have gone on for an interminable amount of time. Indeed, the lack of White House leadership in driving reorganization in the intelligence community, as in homeland security, has been a key reason for the continuing, much-documented shortcomings in the government's offensive and defensive programs.

In the area of law enforcement, it is time to do what the Bush administration won't: establish a separate domestic intelligence service. More specifically, the national security division of the FBI should be reconstituted as a separate agency to overcome continuing shortfalls in information sharing, communications between Washington and the field, among federal agencies, and with state and local governments. At the state and local levels, law enforcement personnel require more training and guidance to ensure that they are attuned to local and national collection needs. In January 2006, the administration finally appeared to recognize that the allocation of resources for state and local governments needs to be changed to a risk-based model—North Pole, Alaska, population 1,700, does not need more than half a million dollars for rescue and communications equipment.

5. Get Serious about Homeland Defense

The first step in effective homeland security must be setting priorities. Weak leadership at both the White House and in the Department of Homeland Security has meant that the new behemoth in the Washington bureaucracy has been consumed by the problems of merging numerous different institutions and cultures and by chasing the crisis of the moment. In the place of a real strategy, both White House officials and agency leaders have chosen to embrace such nostrums as voluntary compliance and aspirational goals, while building a reliance on underfunded initiatives and unfunded mandates. One sweeping reorganization has followed the other, and only after the tenure of Governor Tom Ridge did senior managers admit that the department had done little to set out a strategy for defending the United States from various kinds of attacks.

In short, we still have no real strategy, no real threat analysis or baseline study of capabilities, few requirements, and no integrated or adequate budget to meet our long-term objectives. We must proceed on the principle of defending against the most devastating potential attacks. And progressives must confront the Congressional logrolling that spreads our finite homeland defense dollars too thinly across the American landscape, while leaving our most likely targets vulnerable. Setting real priorities will both reduce the loss of life in the event of an attack *and* increase our deterrence—one of the few areas in which we can do so against terrorists who are prepared to sacrifice their lives. The list of urgent priorities is long, but some stand out:

Working together, government and industry must implement a mandatory risk-reduction strategy to reduce the vulnerability of catastrophic incidences at chemical facilities or other hazardous material sites, particularly those near population centers. There are 123 chemical plants in America that put populations of one million or more people at risk, and we have not begun seriously to mitigate this threat—nor, as former Homeland Security officials acknowledge, have we begun to deal with the dangers of transporting hazardous materials that terrorists might target.

We must accelerate the development of countermeasures to prevent attacks by the shoulder-fired anti-aircraft missiles known as "man portable air defense systems" (MANPADS). The debate over developing and installing countermeasures aboard commercial airliners has been confused by narrow-minded cost-benefit analyses that fail to recognize that a successful attack—or even a near-miss—could lead to the crippling of commercial aviation and a catastrophic impact on the economy. The nation needs to produce a contingency plan for restarting commercial aviation in case of an attack, and to expand international efforts to cap production and reclaim MANPADS that have slipped from government control. With several thousand such weapons looted from Iraqi government stockpiles, this threat is growing.

In the area of consequence management—dealing with the immediate crisis caused by an attack—we must be prepared to respond effectively to minimize the immediate impact and to recover as quickly as possible. One key element of this involves ensuring that we have fully trained and equipped police, fire, and emergency medical personnel who are prepared to handle all risks, and an emergency response system with interoperable communications. Because of the federal government's role in funding first responders, it must insist on uniform standards and practices in a way it has shied away from thus far.

We need to develop a public health infrastructure equal to the real threat of mass-casualty attacks, with a medical surveillance capability to quickly recognize a biological weapons attack; an adequate national stockpile of vaccines, antibiotics, and antivirals; the means to distribute them across the country; and the research and development base to deal with emerging bio-threats. Here, too, the key is White House leadership to drive the process. Some progress has been made, but not nearly enough.

While funds are not limitless, homeland security almost certainly requires a phased increase in funds of at least 50 percent above the approximately $40 billion we are currently spending. Additional funds are needed to develop the incidence response capabilities we need—though there should be some savings when Washington stops providing funds to low-risk areas—as well as better port security and container inspection, improvements in chemical plant protection and hazardous materials transport, continued improvement in public health surveillance, and drug development and stockpiling.

This work must become a permanent part of the national agenda, not just a one-off to deal with the threats of the moment. These investments and arrangements will pay dividends long after the jihadist threat has passed, because the future of American security will depend on our ability to defend against "asymmetrical'" threats that target U.S. citizens and the U.S. economy at home.

The urgency of these tasks cannot be overstated. The struggle against al Qaeda and its many progeny could well last for several decades. But the hurdles to real progress are not insuperable. Progressives must provide clear-eyed leadership that recognizes the ideological appeal of radical Islamism, and they must offer a bold strategy for waging a smarter war on global terrorism.

NOTES

1. Nesser, Petter, "Jihad in Europe: A Survey of the Motivations for Sunni Islamist Terrorism in Post-millennium Europe," Norwegian Defense Research Establishment, April 13, 2004, p. 9, www.mil.no/multimedia/archive/00039/Jihad_in_Europe_39 602a.pdf.

2. "Australia Terror Suspects 'Were Stopped Near Nuclear Plant,'" *Guardian*, November 14, 2005, www.guardian.co.uk/australia/story/0,12070,1642231,00.html.

3. "Vice President Richard B. Cheney Delivers Remarks at Air Force Association National Conference," FDCH Political Transcripts, Washington, D.C., September 17, 2003.

4. "Major Management Challenges Facing the Department of Homeland Security," Department of Homeland Security, Office of Inspector General, October 25, 2005, www.dhs.gov/interweb/assetlibrary/OIG_06-14_Dec05.pdf.

5. "Final Report on 9/11 Commission Recommendations," 9/11 Public Discourse Project, www.9-11pdp.org/press/2005-12-05_report.pdf.

6. For fiscal year 2006, the Bush administration requested $133.5 million for the State Department's Antiterrorism Assistance Program.

6

PREVENTING NUCLEAR
TERRORISM[1]

Graham Allison

Amerian politics may be deeply polarized, but there appears to be virtual unanimity about what constitutes the greatest threat to our national security. When asked that question during the first presidential debate of 2004, Senator John F. Kerry's immediate answer was, "nuclear proliferation," because "there are terrorists trying to get their hands on that stuff." President George W. Bush concurred: "I agree with my opponent that the biggest threat facing this country today is weapons of mass destruction in the hands of a terrorist network."[2]

Indeed, in the final weeks of the campaign, Vice President Dick Cheney made nuclear terrorism a centerpiece of his stump speech. "Nuclear weapons able to threaten the lives of hundreds of thousands of Americans . . . are the ultimate threat," he said. "For us to have a strategy that's capable of defeating that threat, *you've got to get your mind around that concept.*" (Emphasis added.)[3]

That assessment was buttressed by the 9/11 Commission's July 2004 official report, which documented in chilling detail al Qaeda's search for nuclear weapons. The report concluded, "al Qaeda has tried to acquire or make weapons of mass destruction for at least ten years. There is no doubt the United States would be a prime target."[4] In August 2001, for instance, during the final countdown to what al Qaeda calls the "Holy Tuesday" attack, bin Laden received two key former officials from Pakistan's nuclear weapons program at his secret headquarters near Kabul. Over the course of three days of intense conversation, he and his second-in-command, Ayman al-Zawahiri, quizzed Sultan Bashiruddin Mahmood and Abdul Majeed about chemical, biological, and especially nuclear weapons. Mahmood's career spanned thirty years at the Pakistani Atomic Energy Commission, and he had been a key figure at the Kahuta plant that had produced the enriched uranium for Pakistan's first nuclear bomb in 1998. Thereafter, he headed the Khosib reactor in the Punjab that produces weapons-grade plutonium.[5] Bin Laden, al-Zawahiri, and the two other as yet unidentified, top-level al Qaeda operatives who participated in these conversations had clearly moved beyond the impending assault on the World Trade Center to visions of grander attacks to follow.[6]

Yet, distracted by Iraq, political scandals, and hurricanes, the White House has failed to match its alarming rhetoric with the deeds required to dramatically reduce the risk of nuclear terrorism. As recently as December 5, 2005, the members of the 9/11 Commission, operating with private funding to follow up on their official mandate, gave the administration and Congress a "D" for their efforts to prevent terrorists from acquiring weapons of mass destruction (WMD). As Commission Chairman Thomas Kean noted, "the size of the problem still totally dwarfs the policy response."

What makes this failure so inexcusable is the largely unrecognized good news about nuclear terrorism: it is preventable. There is an agenda of specific, feasible, and affordable actions that, if taken, would reduce the likelihood of a terrorist's Hiroshima to nearly zero. A comprehensive strategy for pursuing that agenda should be organized under a Doctrine of Three No's: No Loose Nukes, No New Nascent Nukes, and No New Nuclear Weapons States. The strategic imperative is to keep terrorists from acquiring nuclear weapons or the materials from which weapons could be made. As a fact of physics: no highly enriched uranium or plutonium, no nuclear explosion, no nuclear terrorism. It is that simple.

SMALL STEPS FORWARD

To its credit, in the Bush administration's attempt to fashion a strategy for combating catastrophic terrorism, it got two things right. First, it made an important conceptual advance in recognizing that the gravest danger lies in the "nexus between terrorists and weapons of mass destruction"—terrorists armed with nuclear weapons. It rightly rejected a status quo that let terrorists and WMD threats hide behind a shield of state sovereignty. It employed the full spectrum of American military power to topple the Taliban and deny terrorists sanctuary in Afghanistan. And it has been prepared to revise traditional cold war policies of deterrence and containment in those cases where they are no longer sufficient. Deterrence, which discouraged other states from launching a nuclear attack on the United States through the threat of overwhelming retaliation, is hard to apply to suicide bombers or terrorists with no return address.

Second, the administration undertook certain specific initiatives to reduce this danger that received little notice amid the global uproar over the administration's aggressive foreign policy. President Bush successfully proposed United Nations Security Council Resolution 1540, which requires states to criminalize proliferation and "develop and maintain appropriate effective measures to account for and secure" nuclear materials. Bush also promoted the Proliferation Security Initiative (PSI), which stretches existing legal frameworks to allow the interception of suspected weapons-of-mass-destruction cargo, and now includes more than sixty nations. According to Secretary of State Condoleezza Rice, PSI partners completed eleven successful interdictions over a nine-month period.[7]

After its own initial skepticism, the administration enlisted the remaining G-8 members to match a U.S. commitment of $10 billion to secure and eliminate former Soviet nuclear weapons over the next ten years. The United States took the lead in cooperation with Russia in extracting enough material for five nuclear weapons from Yugoslavia, Romania, Bulgaria, Uzbekistan, and the Czech Republic. A new American-led program, the Global Threat Reduction Initiative, began the vital work of securing bomb-making materials at risky research reactors around the world. And during Bush's first term, Libyan leader Muammar Quaddafi renounced his nascent nuclear weapons program, and the secret black-market network of Pakistani scientist A.Q. Khan was exposed.

Despite these praiseworthy successes, if we jump to the bottom line and ask whether we are safer today from a nuclear terrorist attack than we were on September 11, 2001, the answer is no (see table 6.1). The threat of a nuclear bomb exploding in the next year is at least as high as it was on the day al Qaeda crashed airplanes into the World Trade Center and the Pentagon.

Al Qaeda remains a formidable enemy with clear nuclear ambitions. The former head of CIA's bin Laden task force, Michael Scheuer, has

Table 6.1.

Subject	First-Term Trend	Grade
No Loose Nukes	↔	D+
No New Nascent Nukes	↓	D−
No New Nuclear Weapons States	↓	F

detailed how in May 2003, Osama bin Laden acquired a fatwa from a Saudi cleric, providing a religious justification to use nuclear weapons against America. Titled "A Treatise on the Legal Status of Using Weapons of Mass Destruction against Infidels," it asserts that "if a bomb that killed 10 million of them and burned as much of their land as they have burned Muslims' land were dropped on them, it would be permissible." Scheuer, who followed terrorism and militant Islam for much of his twenty-two-year career, was particularly troubled by "the careful, professional manner in which al Qaeda was seeking to acquire nuclear weapons."[8]

Islamist websites reveal growing interest in nuclear bombs as weapons of jihad. "An Encyclopedia for the Preparation of Nuclear Weapons" has begun appearing in the virtual training library of some jihadist websites. No matter how much or how little the author knows about nuclear physics, the title, "The Nuclear Bomb of Jihad and the Way to Enrich Uranium," makes clear that intent is not the missing ingredient to a nuclear terrorist attack.

Russia's 11-time-zone expanse contains more nuclear weapons and materials than any country in the world, including more than 16,000 assembled warheads and enough weapons-usable material for 70,000 more, much of it vulnerable to theft.[9] Fourteen years after the cold war, according to Department of Energy data, less than half of Russia's nuclear weapons and materials have been secured to acceptable standards. These present attractive targets for terrorists shopping for a bomb. In her confirmation hearing, Secretary of State Rice agreed, stating, "I really can think of nothing more important than being able to proceed with the safe dismantlement of the Soviet arsenal, with nuclear safeguards to make certain that nuclear-weapons facilities and the like are well secured."[10]

But after America was attacked by bin Laden on 9/11, what happened to U.S. spending and related efforts to secure nuclear weapons, with what result? Funding for the critical Nunn–Lugar Cooperative Threat Reduction program for securing loose fissile material increased only modestly. Still harder to believe: fewer potential nuclear weapons of highly enriched uranium and plutonium in Russia were secured in the two years after September 11 than in the two years before. The pace of U.S.-sponsored advanced security measures at nuclear weapons storage sites in Russia has dropped from three-and-a-half additional sites per year to only three per year of the estimated 150-plus sites.[11]

Nuclear materials remain vulnerable to theft in a number of other countries as well. Although in the past five years some highly enriched uranium has been removed from seven countries (Serbia, Romania, Bulgaria, Libya, Czech Republic, Uzbekistan, and Latvia), there are still over one hundred nuclear research reactors or associated facilities in dozens of countries around the world with enough nuclear materials to make a bomb. In some cases, there is little more protecting the weapons-quality material than a padlock and an unarmed guard.

Even nuclear programs ostensibly under state control can pose a threat. Pakistan's A. Q. Khan is an excellent case study in how nukes (or nuclear material and technical knowledge) could make their way into al Qaeda's hands. As inspectors have been unraveling and retracing A.Q. Khan's global black market network, we now know that Libya was not his only customer. Clearly he traded nuclear secrets and technologies to the North Koreans for their assistance with Pakistani missile programs, and inspectors are still searching for the results of his dozen trips to Iran in the 1990s.

The clincher in the Bush administration's case for war against Iraq turned on the possibility that Saddam Hussein might attack Americans with weapons of mass destruction, particularly nuclear weapons, or transfer them to terrorists like al Qaeda. Yet of the three countries he identified as constituting an "axis of evil," Bush wound up attacking the least nuclear. He rushed to war against a country that—as the CIA had stated clearly—had no nuclear weapons, no collaborative relationship with al Qaeda, and no history of transferring weapons to terrorists. President Bush argued that "if the Iraqi regime is able to produce, buy, or steal an amount of uranium a little bigger than a softball, it could have a nuclear weapon in less than a year." What the president failed to mention is that with the same quantity of highly enriched uranium, terrorist groups like al Qaeda, Hezbollah, or Hamas could do the same thing.

What has happened while the administration's attention has been diverted to the Iraq War? In the past two years, Iran has rushed to complete its factories for producing highly enriched uranium and plutonium. Once Tehran achieves this goal, we face the nightmarish prospect that it might transfer nuclear weapons to its terrorist client and collaborator, Hezbollah, a group that has already killed 260 Americans in attacks in Lebanon and at Khobar Towers in Saudi Arabia.

Certifiably the world's most promiscuous proliferator, North Korea might provide nuclear weapons to terrorists out of economic desperation or spite. Pyongyang has demonstrated that it will sell missiles to whoever will pay, including state sponsors of terrorism, specifically Iran and Libya. It has threatened to sell weapons to others including terrorists.[12] Yet in the months after January 2003, as North Korea withdrew from the nonproliferation treaty, kicked out the International Atomic Energy Agency inspectors, turned off the video cameras that monitored the 8,000 fuel rods that contained enough plutonium for six additional nuclear weapons, trucked the fuel rods to reprocessing plants, claimed to have manufactured nuclear weapons with the material, and restarted its reactor to make more plutonium,[13] the United States simply stood by. President Bush's first-term policy was to threaten North Korea, then ignore it. As a result of this neglect, North Korea may already have eight nuclear weapons and is currently operating its Yongbyon reactor, producing additional bombs' worth of plutonium every year. Al Qaeda, meanwhile, is shopping the black market for a nuclear bomb, and North Korea may soon have bombs to sell. Those who imagine that Kim Jong-Il would stop short of selling nuclear-weapon materials should reflect on a *New York Times* report that Pyongyang may have supplied Libya with enough uranium hexafluoride to make a bomb.

If North Korea demonstrates that it is, in fact, a nuclear weapons state, South Korea and Japan will almost certainly go nuclear in the decade thereafter, fueling an arms race that would be very destabilizing for the Northeast Asia region. As the U.N. High-Level Panel on Threats, Challenges, and Change warns, "We are approaching a point at which the erosion of the nonproliferation regime could become *irreversible* and result in a *cascade of proliferation*." (Emphasis added.) In that future, the prospects for preventing nuclear terrorism would plummet.

Thus, despite progress made on some fronts in the battle against nuclear terrorism, developments in Iraq, Iran, and North Korea leave Americans more vulnerable to a nuclear 9/11 today than we were four years ago.

And despite the president and vice president's clarity in identifying this threat, the gap between the administration's words and deeds remains wide.

The gravity of the potential consequences requires that the president give absolute priority to this challenge. A nuclear terrorist attack on an American city would be a world-altering event. The categorical imperative, therefore, is to do everything technically feasible on the fastest possible time line to prevent it.

PREVENTING NUCLEAR TERRORISM

What is to be done? A comprehensive strategy for reducing the risk of nuclear terrorism would follow the logic of 3 No's: No Loose Nukes, No New Nascent Nukes, and No New Nuclear Weapons States.

No Loose Nukes first requires securing all nuclear weapons and weapons-usable material, on the fastest possible timetable, to make them as secure as the gold in Fort Knox. The United States and Russia should jointly develop such a nuclear safety "gold standard" and then act at once to secure their own nuclear materials. Russian President Vladimir Putin must be made to feel this in his gut and to take the lead. He has to visualize the Chechens who killed 172 schoolchildren at Beslan exploding a nuclear bomb in Moscow. President Bush must use his close personal friendship with Putin to talk him into doing what only the Russian president can do: Guarantee that every weapon and potential weapon is locked up with utmost urgency. Moscow must come to see safeguarding those weapons not as a favor to the United States but as an essential protection for its own country and citizens.

Once Putin is on board, the two countries should launch a new global "Alliance Against Nuclear Terrorism." Its mission would be to lock down all weapons and materials everywhere and clean out what cannot be locked down. This would require engaging the leaders of other nuclear states on the basis of a bedrock of vital national interest: preventing a terrorist's nuclear bomb from exploding in my capital. The target date for the global lockdown of nuclear material should be in twelve or eighteen months—not mañana.

No New Nascent Nukes means no new national capabilities to enrich uranium or reprocess plutonium. A loophole in the 1968 Nuclear Nonproliferation Treaty allows states to develop these capacities in civilian programs, then withdraw from the treaty and declare themselves a nuclear state.

NO LOOSE NUKES

Actions Required for A-level Performance:

- Make preventing nuclear terrorism an absolute priority
- U.S. and Russian presidents must engage each other in a joint program to assure no nuclear weapons or materials are stolen
- Appoint individuals of stature reporting directly to U.S. and Russian presidents as commanders in the war on nuclear terrorism
- Develop new "gold standard" for security of world's nuclear weapons and materials
- Secure all nuclear weapons and materials to the gold standard as fast as technically possible on a set timetable
- Lead a joint U.S.-Russian campaign to persuade other nuclear states to join a Global Alliance Against Nuclear Terrorism
- Draw on previous nuclear cooperation with China to enlist Pakistan in the preventing nuclear terrorism club
- Accelerate Global Threat Reduction Initiative to take back HEU from both Soviet- and U.S.-supplied research reactors on fastest technically feasible timetable

---

The proposition of no new nascent nukes acknowledges what the national-security community is now coming to realize: Highly enriched uranium and plutonium are bombs just about to hatch.

The long-term strategy of the United States should be to build a global consensus around the No New Nascent Nukes principle. That could begin with the worldwide five-year moratorium on building new capacity for uranium enrichment and plutonium separation that IAEA Director Mohamed ElBaradei has proposed. This would allow breathing room to negotiate a more lasting solution.

The crucial challenge to this today is Iran. The administration's naming and shaming of Iran as part of the "axis of evil" during President Bush's first term did nothing to stop Tehran's advancement of its nuclear weapons programs. Yet Iran has shown great sensitivity to the views of other governments. In seeking to avoid an IAEA finding that it violated its NPT commitments, Iran has bargained intensely with the EU-3 (Britain, Germany, and France), observed an eight-month moratorium on all nuclear activity that ended in September 2005, and negotiated valuable oil and gas contracts

NO NEW NASCENT NUKES
Actions Required for A-level Performance:

- Close current NPT loophole that permits signatories to develop nuclear fuel production capabilities
- Orchestrate consensus that there will be no new national HEU enrichment or plutonium reprocessing
- Guarantee supply of reactor fuel to non-nuclear weapons states at prices less than half national production costs
- Organize program to securely store spent fuel from civilian reactors
- Persuade all states to adopt the Additional Protocol
- Limit import of equipment for existing civilian programs to states that have signed Additional Protocol
- Provide resources to help states implement UNSCR 1540
- Expand Proliferation Security Initiative
- Make grand bargain with Iran: in exchange for dismantlement of enrichment and reprocessing facilities, offer fuel-cycle agreement, acceptance of Bushehr, relaxation of trade sanctions, and security guarantee
- Pose credible threats to Iran sufficient to persuade it to accept grand bargain
- Accelerate and highlight deep cuts in U.S.-Russian nuclear arms, and minimize role of nuclear weapons as fulfillment of NPT Article IV
- Resume Fissile Material Cutoff Treaty (FMCT) negotiations

with China, India, and others. However, Iranian President Ahmadinejad's leverage of $8 billion in oil deals with Europe and a $22 billion natural gas contract with India did not prevent the IAEA Board of Governors in September 2005 from declaring Iran's actions in noncompliance with IAEA safeguards and worthy of U.N. Security Council attention.[14]

It is unrealistic to hope that the new Iranian government, or any future government, will permanently foreswear its "right" to nuclear technology. The United States should target not aspirations or even this asserted "right," but rather the actions of Tehran. Specifically, the objective should be for Iran to accept a deal to forgo any reprocessing or enrichment.

The EU-3, Russia, and the United States must develop a common strategy on Iran. The group of five should then present Iran with two alternative futures, neither of which includes nuclear weapons. In the first, Iran keeps its civilian nuclear program, minus the ability to enrich uranium or reprocess plutonium, and the EU–3 and the United States deliver an array of carrots. The EU–3 are prepared to offer important economic benefits, including financial support for an oil transit route through Iran and Central Asia, and an extensive EC/Iran Trade and Cooperation Agreement.[15] What Iran wants most from the United States is a credible assurance that the United States will not attack it to change its regime by force. Given the potential consequences of an Iranian nuclear weapon, the United States must be willing to give that security guarantee as long as Iran refrains from enrichment and reprocessing.

Iran will also demand an assured supply of low-enriched (i.e., non-weapons-grade) uranium to power its civilian nuclear reactors. The United States, EU–3, and Russia should sign a binding agreement guaranteeing Iran's purchase of fuel for all new reactors and removal of spent fuel (and notably the plutonium encased therein) at bargain prices. The agreement would include both assurances that Iran's fuel services could not be cut off for any reason other than a violation of NPT or IAEA commitments, and standby arrangements with other nuclear suppliers or the IAEA. The United States has agreed to contribute seventeen tons of low enriched uranium to an "assured fuel supply arrangement" for precisely such a purpose. Purchasing nuclear fuel and services would be far less expensive for Tehran than producing the fuel indigenously.

These guarantees would assure Iran that its civilian program could not be interrupted or subjected to pressure over nonnuclear issues like Israel, human rights, or terrorism.

Successful negotiation with Iran will require close collaboration with Russia, the country that provides the Islamic Republic with its nuclear fuel. Russia is well positioned to be the leading supplier of additional nuclear power reactors to Iran. The current ten-year contract to supply fuel rods for the Bushehr reactor and to retrieve the spent fuel should be the first step in a major new business for Russia—storing spent fuel from the global nuclear power industry. Putin would have the satisfaction of taking a lead in dealing with a major national security challenge.

Carrots alone will not suffice. Crucial to sealing this deal will be a judgment by Iran's leaders that they have no realistic prospect of completing their enrichment and reprocessing facilities at this time. Essential to that judgment is a credible military threat to destroy the facilities before they can produce weapons-grade material. The United States is not the only country that poses such a threat, Israel does as well. The country also has a very direct interest in the issue, in light of President Mahmoud Ahmadinejad's vitriolic statement that Israel must be "wiped off the map," Israel's Chief of General Staff, Lt. Gen. Dan Halutz, has called the combination of an irrational Iranian leadership and nuclear capabilities "Israel's sole existential threat." Acting Prime Minister Ehud Olmert has put an even finer point on it: "Under no circumstances and at no time can Israel allow anyone with malicious designs against us to have control of weapons of destruction that threaten our existence."

What remains for this deal to come together is for the United States to step up as determined dealmaker, assemble the full array of international carrots, and package a deal Iran cannot reasonably refuse.

No New Nuclear-Weapons States draws a line under the current eight nuclear powers and says unambiguously "no more." The immediate test of this principle is North Korea. To prevent Pyongyang from becoming a Nukes "R" Us for terrorists will require both carrots and sticks, including a bilateral nonaggression and normalization promise should Pyongyang concede the nuclear issue, and a credible military threat to the country's nuclear facilities should negotiations fail. The great powers share real national interests here, because each fears nuclear weapons in the hands of terrorists, whether they are al Qaeda or Chinese separatists.

In the case of North Korea, sharp internal divisions paralyzed the first term of the Bush administration. As a result, it followed a policy of insult and neglect, refusing to offer any carrots or threaten any sticks. In Vice President Dick Cheney's words, "We don't negotiate with evil; we defeat it." Despite the tough talk, however, the administration let the problem fester while Pyongyang added to its arsenal.

In its second term, the Bush administration has made a much stronger start on this agenda. The six-party talks of September 2005 resulted in forward movement: North Korea agreed in principle to "abandoning all nuclear weapons and existing nuclear programs and returning, at an early date, to the Treaty on the Nonproliferation of Nuclear Weapons and to IAEA safeguards." The breakthrough was possible only because the second-term team exchanged an unsuccessful ideological approach toward Pyongyang for a new pragmatism.

The six parties must now agree on the sequencing for a North Korean nuclear stand-down. The five (United States, China, Japan, South Korea, and Russia) have an array of carrots that North Korea wants: fuel oil shipments and humanitarian assistance, the normalization of diplomatic relations, removal from the state-sponsors of terror list, a nonaggression pledge, a reduction in America's military posture in South Korea, a peace treaty

NO NEW NUCLEAR STATES
Actions Required for A-level Performance:

- Draw bright line under today's eight nuclear powers and declare: no more
- Subordinate all policy objectives on North Korea (e.g., regime change) to this goal
- Send Secretary of State Rice to Pyongyang for candid private discussions
- Offer carrots in exchange for verifiable dismantlement: bilateral non-aggression pledge, expansion of food aid, resumption of Japan-South Korea fuel shipments
- Describe further phased benefits: financing for natural gas pipeline, construction of two light-water reactors, aid for infrastructure reconstruction, North Korean Nunn-Lugar, eventual normalization of relations
- Pose credible threat to North Korea sufficient to persuade it to choose freeze and start down path to eliminate nuclear weapons
- Ratify Comprehensive Test Ban Treaty (CTBT)

ending the Korean War, financial support for a natural gas pipeline from Russia to South Korea that would cross North Korea, and a light-water nuclear energy reactor. North Korea would earn carrots or slices of carrots, as it moves in a step-by-step, reciprocal process: freezing the production of further plutonium at its 5-megawatt Yongbyon reactor, halting the reprocessing of spent fuel rods, ending the reconstruction of its unfinished 50-megawatt reactor that could make enough plutonium for ten bombs a year, rejoining the NPT and accurately accounting for all previous nuclear activities and nuclear materials, and, eventually, allowing IAEA inspectors to verify the complete dismantlement of North Korea's entire nuclear weapons infrastructure, including all uranium enrichment facilities.

Pyongyang and Washington each believe they were cheated by the other in the 1994 Agreed Framework. Both sides can thus be expected to adopt a negotiating position of "distrust but verify." Third parties will play a crucial role in assuring the full implementation of the September 2005 pledges. IAEA inspectors can verify North Korea's denuclearization pledges and monitor any future light-water reactor to assure it is not used for the production of fissile material. China can use its leverage as North Korea's largest trading partner and treaty-bound ally to enforce Pyongyang's commitments. Beijing will also have to use its position as the emerging diplomatic broker for East Asia to assure that others, including the United States, fulfill their commitments, particularly if Congress or some in the Bush administration are tempted to renege. Whether the pragmatism of President Bush's second-term team will stretch to such broad concessions remains to be seen.

The "No New Nuclear Weapon States" piece of the challenge will be easier in the long run if the United States and other nuclear weapon states devalue nuclear weapons. Article VI of the Treaty on the Nonproliferation of Nuclear Weapons legally requires nuclear-weapon states to make "good faith" efforts toward disarmament. Steps such as reducing the overall number of deployed warheads from their current levels, and forswearing new nukes, including the so-called "bunker busters," would give the United States, Russia, and the other nuclear haves greater credibility in building a global consensus around the Three No's. Other lower-hanging fruit for legislators could include legislation to ban nuclear weapons testing for a ten-year period (if the CTBT proves too much of a stretch), and adopting the necessary laws so that the Additional Protocol to the IAEA safeguards agreement can take effect in the United States. The United States would also have much greater moral authority to deal with Iran if Washington agreed to a Fissile Material Cutoff Treaty—essentially reminding the world that if the United States has no need for new fissile material, then neither does Iran.

Preventing a terrorist nuclear attack on an American city is not an issue for Republicans or Democrats. As the nation has learned from Hurricane Katrina, when disaster strikes, citizens will ask what everyone with authority did—or failed to do. In an age when terrorists target civilians with acts of unprecedented destruction, preventing nuclear terrorism cannot be pushed off into the "too hard" category. All elected leaders must understand the agenda of actions necessary to prevent nuclear terrorism and continually drill down on tasks left unfinished. What is needed to earn an "A" is clear. Politicians from both sides of the aisle must keep up the pressure on the president and his renewed administration to rise to this challenge.

NOTES

1. This chapter was adapted from Allison, Graham, "The Gravest Danger," *The American Prospect*, March 2005, with assistance from Angelina Clarke.

2. Commission on Presidential Debates, "The First Bush-Kerry Presidential Debate," September 30, 2004, www.debates.org/pages/trans2004a.html.

3. For Americans to fully grasp what an act of nuclear terrorism would mean, they should imagine such an event happening in their own neighborhood. To assist in that effort, www.nuclearterror.org allows one to put in his or her own zip code and visualize the consequence of the explosion of a small (10 kiloton) nuclear bomb. From the epicenter of the blast to a distance of approximately one-third of a mile, temperatures reaching 540,000 degrees Fahrenheit would vaporize every structure and individual instantly. A second circle of destruction extending three-quarters of a mile from ground zero would leave buildings looking like the Murrah Federal Building in Oklahoma City. Fires and radiation would scorch the earth up to a mile away.

4. *The 9/11 Commission Report: Final Report of the National Commission On Terrorist Attacks Upon The United States* (New York: W.W. Norton, 2004).

5. Baker, Peter, "Pakistani Scientist Who Met Bin Laden Failed Polygraphs, Renewing Suspicions," *Washington Post*, March 3, 2002.

6. Khan, Kamran; and Molly Moore, "2 Nuclear Experts Briefed Bin Laden, Pakistanis Say," *Washington Post*, December 12, 2001.

7. Secretary Condoleezza Rice, "Remarks on the Second Anniversary of the Proliferation Security Initiative," Washington, D.C., May 31, 2005.

8. U.S. House, Committee on the Judiciary, Hearing on the Department of Justice, 108th Congress, 1st session, Serial 59, June 25, 2003; CBS News, "Bin Laden Expert Steps Forward," 60 Minutes, November 14, 2004; "CIA Official Challenges Agency on Terrorism," *Los Angeles Times*, November 9, 2004.

9. See Norris, Robert S. and Hans M. Kristensen, "NRDC: Nuclear Notebook: Russian Nuclear Forces, 2005" in *Bulletin of the Atomic Scientists* 61, no. 2 (March/April 2005): 70–72, and Albright, David, "Global Stocks of Nuclear Explosive Materials: Summary Tables and Charts," September 7, 2005, available online at www.isis-online .org/global_stocks/end2003/summary_global_stocks.pdf; accessed November 20, 2005.

10. The United States Senate. Nomination of Condoleezza Rice to be Secretary of State. 109th Congress, 17th Session. Washington, January 25, 2005.

11. Finlay, Brian, and Andrew Grotto, *The Race to Secure Russia's Loose Nukes* (Washington, D.C.: The Henry L. Stimson Center/Center for American Progress, 2005), p. 25.

12. Reportedly, a North Korean Foreign Ministry official told Assistant Secretary of State for East Asian and Pacific Affairs James Kelly that Pyongyang will "export nuclear weapons, add to its current arsenal or test a nuclear device." (Bill Gertz, "N. Korea Threatens to Export Nukes," *Washington Times*, May 7, 2003, A1.)

13. Foreign Ministry Statement, carried by the Korean Central News Agency: "We . . . have manufactured nukes for self-defence to cope with the Bush administration's evermore undisguised policy to isolate and stifle the [North]." Quoted in "North Korea: We have nuclear weapons to defend from U.S.," *Guardian*, February 10, 2005.

14. International Atomic Energy Agency. Board of Directors. *Implementation of the NPT Safeguards Agreement in the Islamic Republic of Iran.* Resolution adopted on September 24, 2005. GOV/2005/77.

15. See "EU offering to back Iran as major oil route," Reuters News, August 7, 2005, and International Atomic Energy Agency, "Communication dates August 8, 2005 received from the Resident Representative of France, Germany, and the United Kingdom to the Agency." INFCIRC/651 (August 8, 2005).

7

PAKISTAN'S CHOICE: PARTNER OR PROBLEM?

Stephen J. Solarz

Few countries in the world are more important to the success of America's struggle against jihadist terrorism than Pakistan. Its cooperation in the campaign against the Taliban was the logistical foundation for our successful effort to eliminate the safe haven al Qaeda had established in Afghanistan during the 1990s. And its willingness to cooperate with us in the search for Osama bin Laden and Ayman al-Zawahiri, the al Qaeda leaders who have reputedly fled Afghanistan for Pakistan's Pushtun tribal areas, is essential if we are going to capture or kill them.

But while Pakistan's importance may begin with the hunt for bin Laden, al-Zawahiri, and the remnants of the Taliban who have also fled to the relative safety of the Northwest Frontier Province, it doesn't end there. The United States needs Pakistan to drain the swamps inside its own borders that serve as breeding grounds for jihadi terrorists. We need Pakistani cooperation to prevent the proliferation of nuclear weapons, since the head of Pakistan's own nuclear establishment was the primary supplier to an international nuclear weapons supermarket in the 1990s. We need Pakistan to refrain from providing support to terrorist groups intent on destabilizing its Indian neighbor if the Asian subcontinent is to avoid the frightening prospect of another war between two nuclear powers. And if the United States is to succeed in its overriding foreign policy objective of promoting political freedom in Muslim countries, we need the current government of Pakistan to move much more unequivocally and expeditiously toward the establishment of a genuine democracy.

The Bush administration has chosen to designate Pakistan as a "major non–NATO ally," But it could easily slip into the status of a rogue regime intent on openly and actively assisting the international jihadist movement. With Pakistan already in possession of a growing nuclear weapons arsenal, such a development has to be considered one of America's worst nightmares. The truth is that Pakistan is as much a part of the problem as it is part of the solution. For everything Pakistan has done to help us in our struggle against jihadi extremism, it has either pursued policies that contribute to the terrorist challenges we are trying to overcome or has failed to take the actions that are essential if it is going to become a truly responsible member of the international community.

Yes, Pakistan has ostensibly committed itself to the effort to apprehend the arch al Qaeda terrorists who have presumably taken refuge on its territory. But it has done so in a halfhearted way, leaving the impression that it may not actually want to be seen by its own people as being responsible for the capture or killing of terrorist leaders such as bin Laden and al-Zawahiri, who are far more popular in Pakistan than President George W. Bush, or even Pakistan's president, General Pervez Musharraf. When *Time* magazine asked Musharraf whether he thought bin Laden would ever be captured, he replied, "One would prefer that he's captured outside of Pakistan. By some other people."[1] And Pakistan has done virtually nothing to keep the Taliban from reconstituting itself in the tribal areas where they enjoy the sympathy of their fellow Pushtuns.

Yes, Pakistan has put the notorious A.Q. Khan, the father of its nuclear weapons program, under house arrest following the disclosures about the nuclear weapons bazaar he was running. But it has refused to grant the United States, or even the International Atomic Energy Agency (IAEA), access to Khan so he can be questioned about his efforts to provide North Korea, Libya, Iran, and perhaps other countries and even terrorist organizations, with the technology and designs to make their own nuclear weapons.

Yes, Pakistan did assist us in the overthrow of the Taliban, which it supported in the civil war that erupted after the Soviet Army left Afghanistan in 1989—and which it continued to back until 9/11, when the United States gave it an ultimatum that it was either with us or against us in the war we had declared against jihadi extremism. But while Pakistan has engaged in efforts to hunt down al Qaeda leaders hiding out in the tribal territories, it has acquiesced in the remaining Taliban's use of that rugged terrain as a staging ground for efforts to destabilize the new and democratically elected Karzai government in Kabul. As Taliban incursions have risen, so have U.S. casualties. By late December 2005, the Pentagon reported that 89 Americans were killed "in and around Afghanistan" that year,[2] more than double the number of combat deaths recorded in the year before.

Yes, Pakistan also has pledged to bring the multitude of madrassas, which the Pakistanis themselves acknowledge have been a breeding ground for the recruitment of jihadists, under effective government control. But it has done virtually nothing to prevent the promulgation of the jihadi ideology in those theological institutions which continue to provide recruits for the jihads being waged in Kashmir, Afghanistan, Chechnya, and Iraq. The *Chicago Tribune* provided a glimpse inside these militant theological institutions in November 2004:

> Abdul Basit, 23, who just graduated, says he will go to Afghanistan or Iraq to fight America if ordered by a religious leader. "Every religious man would go to defend our brothers," Basit says. "I would like to go there."
>
> "Why not? I am ready for it," adds Azam Khan Tanoli, 23. "Whenever our leaders say."[3]

Yes, Pakistan recently entered into a dialogue with India presumably designed to resolve the many differences between them, and it has even agreed to a few tangible tension-reducing measures, such as allowing a bus route to operate between the two countries. But its public pledge not to permit jihadists to cross the Line of Control separating the Pakistani and Indian areas of Kashmir has been honored more in the breach than the observance, leaving New Delhi and Islamabad only one more major terrorist attack away from what could well be another full-scale war between them.

Yes, President Musharraf, who came to power in a 1999 military coup, has promised to guide Pakistan toward genuine democracy by the time of the next presidential election in 2007. But he continues to prevent the two main secular political parties from effectively participating in the political process, has arrogated to himself the power to dissolve Parliament whenever he chooses, and has entered into political alliances with Islamist parties that, because of the absence of meaningful secular competition, have come to power at the provincial level in Baluchistan and the Northwest Frontier Province.

Indeed, the man who holds the future of Pakistan in his hands has built a worrisome record of major miscalculations and dissembling. It was

Musharraf, after all, who as chief of staff of the Pakistani Army conceived the plan for the incursion into the Kargil sector of Kashmir in 1999, which brought India and Pakistan to the brink of the fourth war between them in the last half century. That maneuver, intended to establish Pakistani control over a strategically significant part of the Indian State of Jammu and Kashmir, had egregious political consequences. It took place shortly after Musharraf's own government had agreed to negotiate peacefully its outstanding differences with India, and thus squandered a promising opportunity to move the peace process forward.

There is also reason to believe that Musharraf was fully aware of A.Q. Khan's efforts to peddle Pakistan's nuclear weapons technology to other countries during the time he served as chief of staff of the Pakistani Army.[4] That may explain his refusal to permit Khan to be questioned by U.S. or IAEA interrogators. If they were able to establish links between the Pakistani military and Khan's activities, Musharraf himself could be exposed to international condemnation. These concerns might be dismissed as ancient history, if not for the fact that Musharraf continues to talk out of both sides of his mouth on such issues as cracking down on the madrassas, cutting off support for the jihadis operating in Kashmir and Afghanistan, and restoring democracy in Pakistan.[5]

To be sure, the problems we face in Pakistan are not all of Musharraf's making. They are a reflection of deeply rooted historical forces and societal trends that have produced a clerical class deeply hostile to the West, a military establishment whose sense of mission stems from what it perceives to be the enduring hostility of India, and a population increasingly prone to bouts of anti-Americanism.

It is also important to remember that prior to 9/11, Pakistan was a country in serious economic straits: The military's historic domination of politics has created a deeply distorted economy, with huge expenditures on defense in place of spending on health, education, and infrastructure for economic growth. Nor has the often-corrupt civilian political elite governed much better. Since 9/11, aid, debt write-offs, and macroeconomic reforms have produced solid growth, but Pakistan is still desperately poor, with a per capita income of around $600, and an adult literacy rate below 50 percent. Buried within these figures are deep gender inequalities: Female literacy in remote areas like the Northwest Frontier Province or Baluchistan has been measured as low as three percent.[6] The 2005 United Nations Human Development Report, an index of health, education, and income indicators, ranked Pakistan 135th out of 177 countries—a rank that is bound to fall further after last year's devastating earthquake.[7]

Pakistan's weak and military-dominated political institutions help explain its economic troubles. But they also explain much of the current security problem. Radical Islam and the state-sponsored insurgency in Kashmir have been fomented by Pakistani military rulers unable to legitimize their rule by improving living standards. Military leaders have also boosted political Islam by marginalizing the larger moderate parties. And the preference for defense over social spending has opened the door for radical groups—often Saudi-funded—to provide basic social services to the Pakistani people, including the madrassas.

Clearly, Pakistan is an unstable and troubled polity. But short of washing our hands of it entirely—an option we don't have—we have little choice in pursuing our pressing national security goals but to find a way of securing real commitment and cooperation from Musharraf. Absent another military coup, or the emergence of a democratic government when presidential elections are held in 2007, Musharraf will remain the dominant figure in Pakistani politics for some time. Under the circumstances, the key to a fundamental transformation in the views and values of Pakistan lies in a series of policy changes that are much more likely to be initiated from the top down than from the bottom up.

The Bush administration has paid lip service to urgent issues such as Pakistan's support for jihadist terrorism in Kashmir, its dangerous state of tension with India, its cancerous madrassas, and its need for democratic political reform. But the unfortunate truth is that the administration has put the limited cooperation we've received from Pakistan in the hunt for the remnants of al Qaeda ahead of everything else. The White House has been unwilling to jeopardize the assistance we have been receiving, inadequate as it is, by making it clear to Musharraf that our relationship depends on his full cooperation in addressing the totality of our policy agenda. It has shown neither the imagination nor the toughness necessary to secure genuine support for any other priority. To be sure, U.S. policy options are severely limited. Jawboning, which is what the administration has mostly relied on, clearly hasn't worked in the past and is unlikely to work in the future. Sanctions, which failed to prevent Pakistan from developing nuclear weapons in the 1980s and 1990s, are more likely to further inflame Pakistani opinion against us than bring about the changes we seek in the policy of the Pakistani government. And the use of military force, after what we've experienced in Iraq—but in this case against a country with nuclear weapons—is not even worth considering. The time has come for a definitive diplomatic test of the proposition that you can "catch more flies with honey than with vinegar."

If we're going to be successful in enlisting Pakistan's support for our policy objectives, it will probably be necessary to put forth a proposal sufficiently attractive to convince Musharraf that he and his people will be better off by giving us the complete cooperation we seek than the limited support we've received so far.

Such an approach will probably require a much more substantial package of aid and trade concessions than the one Pakistan currently receives. Right now, it is slated to receive $3.5 billion in economic and military assistance over the next few years. While generous, it still leaves Pakistan far short of the resources it needs which, in combination with essential economic and political reforms, would be needed to truly lift living standards for the great majority of the Pakistani people. The current aid package also fails to provide Pakistan with sufficient access to the American market, or sufficient capital investment, which more than anything else could lead to significant and sustained economic progress.

The United States should put together an international consortium of countries to create a robust, $10 billion Fund for the Future of Pakistan, akin to the program we developed for Europe after World War II. We should also offer Pakistan something it urgently desires—a free trade agreement with the United States. Hopefully, such a package would be sufficiently attractive to the Pakistani people to enable Musharraf to overcome the political opposition to the steps he would be obligated to take for Pakistan to qualify for the assistance on offer, and to persuade Musharraf to take the political plunge into the uncharted waters of full cooperation against terrorism and a complete commitment to the democratization of his own country. Under the terms of such a package, Pakistan would be expected to completely cooperate in the search for bin Laden, al-Zawahiri, and their al Qaeda associates hiding out in its tribal areas, while denying the use of these territories to the remnants of the Taliban. It would be expected to establish effective control over the madrassas to make sure they provide legitimate religious as well as secular educational opportunities, and cease their efforts to generate recruits for jihadi campaigns. It would be expected to make A.Q. Khan available for interrogation by American or IAEA investigators, to determine the full scope of his proliferation activities. It would be expected to close down the terrorist training camps on its territory and terminate the material assistance it continues to provide the jihadists operating in

Kashmir and Afghanistan. And it would be expected to hold genuinely free and fair elections by international standards, with full participation by secular political parties that have previously been forced to sit on the sidelines. Without meeting these conditions, which would have to be certified by President Bush and the leaders of the other countries involved in the consortium, none of the trade and aid benefits on offer would be made available.

This would admittedly be a series of tough pills to swallow for Musharraf, whose political legitimacy as president is already questionable. Having been the target of two failed assassination attempts, and as the leader of a country where anti-Americanism is rampant, he has been understandably cautious when it comes to taking bold initiatives that could engender considerable popular opposition. Complying with these conditions would inevitably encounter stiff resistance from several quarters, including Pushtuns in the tribal areas who are sympathetic to al Qaeda and the Taliban; the clerical establishment, which resists any effort to establish government control over the madrassas; military officers, who may have been complicit in A.Q. Khan's efforts to profit from the sale of Pakistan's nuclear technology, and who would be reluctant to once again cede power to an elected civilian leadership; and the leaders of the Islamist parties that have benefited from the marginalization of Benazir Bhutto's Pakistan's Peoples Party and Nawaz Sharif's Muslim League. Yet these reforms and policy changes are necessary if Pakistan is to finally emerge from its status as a crypto failed state. Moreover, it is just possible that Musharraf could sell the Pakistani people on the prospect of a potentially transformative international aid package which, among other things, could be used to create a nationwide system of public education for both boys and girls that would give their parents a secular alternative to the currently dominant madrassas.

But such a "grand bargain" must be accompanied by a reinvigorated U.S. and international effort to resolve the Kashmir problem. After all, the Kashmir dispute has driven Pakistan's support for terrorist movements in the subcontinent, and has led Pakistan to engage in activities that not only continue to threaten war with India but which also have prevented the stabilization of the security situation in Afghanistan. If the Kashmir conflict could be resolved, it would eliminate any justification for Pakistan to continue supporting the jihadists in Kashmir and Afghanistan while also facilitating a return to the barracks by the military who continue to dominate the politics of their country.

But how to resolve the Kashmir conflict? That question continues to haunt those who recognize the debilitating consequences it has had for both Pakistan and India. Left unresolved, it could well lead to another war and even the possibility of a cataclysmic nuclear exchange.

For over fifty years, Kashmir has been a zero-sum game from the perspective of Islamabad and New Delhi. To Pakistan, whose creation was based on the proposition that the aspirations of the Muslim community in South Asia could not be satisfied within the framework of a Hindu-dominated Raj, the existence of an Indian province with a majority-Muslim population geographically contiguous to Pakistan appears to challenge the very premise on which Pakistan was established. To India, which prides itself on being a multiethnic and religious state with the third largest Muslim population in the world (and whose president is a Muslim), the idea of relinquishing control over Kashmir simply because a majority of its population is Muslim would ideologically undermine the foundation of its secular democracy and inevitably generate communal tensions elsewhere in the country.

Pakistan insists that a plebiscite be held, according to the terms of a U.N. resolution adopted in 1949, in which the people of Kashmir on both sides of the Line of Control would be given a choice of acceding to either Pakistan or India. The fact that the plebiscite would not give the Kashmiris a choice of independence, even though a majority might well favor such an outcome, does not seem to have troubled Pakistan. India's position is that all of Kashmir should be part of India. New Delhi invokes the decision by the Maharajah of Kashmir to accede to India, after the invasion of his kingdom by "tribal" elements directed by Pakistan following the partition of the subcontinent by the British in 1947, as the justification for its claim to the Pakistani as well as the Indian parts of the former Princely State.

Given the tangled history of the dispute, there is no reason to believe a plebiscite could succeed in providing a basis for a resolution of the Kashmir dispute. From the perspective of New Delhi, any plebiscite that could lead to a decision on the part of the Kashmiri people to depart from India would run the risk of exacerbating separatist tendencies in other parts of India and could conceivably lead to the disintegration of the Indian Union. It would also generate an anti-Muslim backlash throughout India, triggering communal violence on a scale that could dwarf the scale of the bloodletting that accompanied the disintegration of Yugoslavia. Moreover, any Indian government that agreed to such a proposition would be voted out of office in less time than it took for the ink on the document ratifying such an agreement to dry.

The only realistic way of resolving the conflict between India and Pakistan over the future of the territory is to convert the existing Line of Control into an international border leaving "Azad" Kashmir in Pakistan and "Jammu and Kashmir" in India. A settlement along these lines would necessarily have to include Pakistan's cutting off support for terrorist organizations fighting in Kashmir, followed by a major drawdown of the Indian security forces currently deployed there. It would also require fully implementing existing provisions in the Indian constitution that grant autonomy to the State of Kashmir and the establishment of a "soft" border between India and Pakistan so Kashmiris on both sides of the current Line of Control can visit and do business with their kinsmen on the other side.

There is every reason to believe that most Indians would be willing to accept such a formula. On the Pakistani side, Musharraf himself has all but flatly admitted that a plebiscite may no longer be a realistic way of solving the problem. What the Pakistani government needs is a politically palatable way to sell a territorial solution to the Pakistani people in which it relinquishes its dreams of acquiring all of Kashmir.

One way of providing Pakistan the political cover it needs would be for the United States to take the lead in securing a new Security Council resolution on the issue. Such a resolution would need to repeal the previous U.N. demand for a plebiscite and replace it with a new call for a negotiated settlement between India and Pakistan based on the principles described above. Persuading the Security Council to adopt such a resolution would not be easy. Yet, given the international community's interest in reducing tensions on the subcontinent and preventing another war, it may not be impossible. If the United States were prepared to push such an initiative, there is a reasonable chance of persuading the British, Russians, and French to go along with us. The main problem would be China, which has historically been close to Pakistan, and would be reluctant to alienate Islamabad by supporting such a resolution. Yet if Beijing were reminded that the holding of a plebiscite to determine the future of Kashmir would create a precedent that might come back to haunt it in Taiwan and Tibet—and was also reminded that the prevailing winds in South Asia would carry the radioactive fallout from a nuclear war into China—it's not beyond the realm of possibility that China might be willing to refrain from vetoing such a resolution.

If a resolution calling for a political settlement of the Kashmir conflict by converting the Line of Control into an international border were adopted by the Security Council, thus rendering the call for a plebiscite legally and politically moot, it could potentially provide President Musharraf with the political cover he would need to accept such an arrangement. By making it clear that the international community was not prepared to support Pakistan's efforts to dislodge Jammu and Kashmir from Indian control, it could finally free the people of Pakistan from the grip of the illusion that they might one day succeed in bringing all of Kashmir into their embrace, thus setting the stage for a resolution of their conflict with India and the political and economic rebirth of Pakistan.

There is, of course, no guarantee that such a strategy would work. It might be impossible to convince the Security Council to move in this direction. And even if we succeed in mustering the necessary majority in favor of such an approach, it is possible that either Pakistan or India, or both, would find a reason to balk. Yet leaving the resolution of this conflict to the Indians and Pakistanis themselves is even less likely to produce a satisfactory solution than a strategy designed to create an international context in which compromise becomes not only possible but desirable. Given the consequences of a failure to bring this long-simmering and potentially explosive conflict to an end—not only for the people of South Asia but for the entire international community—it would appear that an American initiative to resolve the conflict through the Security Council would be well worth the effort.

Such an initiative, combined with the offer of a grand bargain designed to induce Pakistan to become a full partner in the struggle against extremist violence and act on its rhetorical commitment to democracy, would be fully compatible with both American interests and ideals. Compared to what we're now spending in Iraq, the amount of money involved would be a pittance, and the results it could produce would make it a bargain worthy of national celebration.

Pakistan today is balanced precariously between two worlds. It's time for more forceful American leadership to tip that balance toward peace, democracy, and a full partnership in the struggle against terrorism.

NOTES

1. "Ten Questions for Pervez Musharraf," *Time*, October 3, 2005.
2. "Operation Enduring Freedom—Military Deaths from October 7, 2001 by Date of Death as of December 10, 2005," U.S. Department of Defense, October 10, 2005, http://web1.whs.osd.mil/mmid/casualty/oef_date_of_death_list.pdf.
3. Ahmed-Ullah, Noreen S., and Kim Barker, "Schooled in Jihad," *Chicago Tribune*,

November 28, 2004, www.chicagotribune.com/news/specials/chi-0411280298nov 28,1,4893220.stor y?page = 2&coll = chi-newsspecials-hed.

4. Ansari, Massoud, "Islamabad Dispatch: Daddy's Girl," *New Republic*, March 29, 2004.

5. For an example of Musharraf's failure to crack down on madrassas, see Massood, Salman, "Pakistanis Back Off Vow to Control Madrasas," *New York Times*, January 2, 2006.

6. Easterly, William, *The Elusive Quest for Growth: Economists' Adventures and Misadventures in the Tropics* (Cambridge: MIT Press, 2001), p. 232.

7. *Human Development Report 2005*, United Nations Development Program (New York: UNDP, 2005), http://hdr.undp.org/reports/global/2005/.

III

TRANSFORMING OUR MILITARY

8

FIGHTING UNCONVENTIONAL
WARS

James R. Blaker and Steven J. Nider

The wars in Iraq and Afghanistan have highlighted the contemporary paradox of American power. On the one hand, the U.S. military is by far the world's best when it comes to fighting conventional wars. On the other hand, our armed forces are not well designed to meet the new array of unconventional threats that have taken center stage in America's post–9/11 foreign policy. The Bush administration's policies have put enormous strains on our military while failing to confront this mismatch between old force structures and doctrines and new security requirements. Progressives should fill this vacuum of leadership by offering plans for fundamentally revamping and adapting America's armed forces to the new demands of national defense.

The new security challenges we face include transnational terrorism, a threat not subject to traditional methods of deterrence; rogue states determined to acquire nuclear and other weapons of mass destruction; failed and failing states that engender chaos and mass violence, or become havens for terrorists; and China's rapid rise to power, which will require vigilance to maintain the balance of power in East Asia. Tackling these realities will require profound changes in the way the military organizes, equips, and operates its forces.

The United States still needs a military that can win conventional wars decisively. That need could arise, for example, on the Korean peninsula or in the Taiwan Strait. But our country's new foreign policy goals require an enlarged and reshaped force that is also capable of more effective counterterrorism, counterinsurgency, counterproliferation, and postconflict stabilitization and rebuilding. These missions require a more agile, more situationally aware, more strategically mobile and tactically effective force. They also demand more emphasis on language skills and region-specific knowledge, greater facility in operating with other U.S. government agencies at home and abroad, and better collaboration with the militaries of other nations. The Pentagon must make bigger investments in new technologies, such as improved drone aircraft, computer network defenses, and measures for countering biological or chemical attacks. Finally, America's post–9/11 force needs strengthened capacities for homeland defense and disaster relief.

Defense Secretary Donald Rumsfeld has long spoken of the need to transform America's cold war military into a lighter, nimbler force capable of using stealth, skill and technology to fight terrorism and low-intensity conflicts. Many military experts had hoped the 2006 Quadrennial Defense Review (QDR)—and the accompanying FY 2007 defense budget—would lay out a detailed roadmap to achieve this transformation and fundamentally change the Bush administration's previous spending priorities. They were sorely disappointed. While the review does a good job of diagnosing the challenges facing the United States and the U.S. military—placing greater emphasis on irregular warfare while still dissuading major power competitors—it leaves intact legacy weapon systems that continue to gobble up the lion's share of the Pentagon's procurement budget. And while its call for more Special Operations Forces is welcome, the QDR does not come to grips with the reality that we can no longer afford to substitute technology for manpower. Stretched to the limits in Iraq and Afghanistan, the U.S. military is simply too small to take on all the missions that the QDR envisions. The plan fails to emphasize America's urgent interest in enlisting traditional and new allies in today's global counterterrorism efforts and other mutual security tasks. And it fails to devote sufficient resources in the form of doctrine, training, and equipment for the new challenges of nation-building and fighting counterinsurgencies.

Rumsfeld's technocentric interpretation of transformation at first seemed to be vindicated in Afghanistan, where a small, fast-moving U.S. force was able to empower indigenous militias and rout the Taliban. But in Iraq, it has been exposed as an incomplete vision. After its initial decisive victory over Saddam Hussein's conventional forces turned into a grinding counterinsurgency mission, the U.S. military has shown that despite its impressive capabilities, dedication, and élan, it remains ill-equipped, ill-trained, and ill-suited to meet the demands of postcombat stabilization, reconstruction, and nation-building. The Congressional Budget Office estimates that the bill for worn-out equipment is climbing at a rate of $8 billion per year.[1] Major shortages have cropped up in Iraq, such as batteries, tires, vehicle track shoes, body armor, meals ready to eat (MREs), Humvees with extra armor, and add-on armor kits for Humvees.[2] Meanwhile, the National Guard is short on the resources it needs to respond to domestic emergencies like Hurricane Katrina.

A MILITARY UNDER STRESS

Nowhere is the war's stress more evident than in the Army. In December 2004, the head of the Army Reserve, Lt. General James R. "Ron" Helmly, sent a sharply worded memo to other military leaders expressing "deepening concern" about the continued readiness of his troops and warning that his branch of 200,000 soldiers "is rapidly degenerating into a 'broken' force."[3] The Army is keeping most of its soldiers from retiring or leaving for civilian jobs, but has had to increase its bonuses to retain some highly skilled soldiers. For example, the war has made special operations troops so attractive to private contractors that the Pentagon is offering unprecedented reenlistment bonuses of up to $150,000.[4]

Army units are failing to meet Pentagon guidelines that recommend two years at home for every year overseas. Recruiting is at a crisis level. The active-duty Army and the part-time Army National Guard and Army Reserve all missed their 2005 recruiting goals by 8–20 percent; they fell short by a combined 24,000 enlistees. The Army met its recruiting goals in October, the first month of the 2006 fiscal year, but at the expense of lower quality: A disappointing 12 percent of its recruits scored in the lowest category on military entrance tests on science, math, and language skills. The Pentagon is hoping that new recruiting incentives, including bonuses of $20,000, and enlistments as short as fifteen months will turn things around in 2006.[5]

The legacy of the Bush-Rumsfeld approach to national defense is an unfulfilled vision of transformation, a stubborn insurgency in Iraq, a volunteer force under severe stress, and a serious deficit in civil reconstruction capabilities. Progressives can do better.

Specifically, we propose three key steps for a true transformation of America's armed forces that will better align them with the new demands of U.S. foreign policy:

First, we must enlarge the active U.S. military force by at least 40,000 members. Our current force structure is simply too small to tackle both the new security challenges and the enduring requirements of conventional warfare.

Second, we must reorganize our armed forces around the key defense imperatives of the United States in the post–9/11 era, especially: preventing conflicts, intimidation, or humanitarian disasters; defeating foes where prevention fails; and rebuilding civil order and basic infrastructure in failed or failing states, or at home after natural disasters or terrorist attacks.

Third, we must improve our military's ability to work with NATO and other close allies on counterterrorism, counterproliferation, nation-building, or whatever our mutual security interests demand.

Enlarge and Better Equip U.S. Forces

Active duty forces are currently being worn down by constant rotations through Afghanistan and Iraq, and the National Guard and Reserves are feeling the strain as well. Since September 11, 2001, well over a million U.S. troops have fought in Afghanistan and Iraq, approximately one-third the number of troops ever stationed in or around Vietnam during fifteen years of that conflict.[6] And of the troops who have served in Iraq or Afghanistan, one-third have been on more than one tour, according to the Pentagon.[7] In the regular Army, for example, 63 percent of the soldiers have been to war at least one time, and almost 40 percent of those soldiers have gone back.[8]

Not since World War II have so many Guard units been pressed into service abroad. Guard and Reserve troops represent nearly 30 percent of U.S. military men and women in Iraq. The huge deployment is redefining the nature of Guard service, transforming weekend warriors into something closer to full-time soldiers who regularly leave behind their jobs, businesses, and families for extended periods of time.

President Bush and Secretary Rumsfeld have resisted any permanent personnel increase because they insist that the spike in overseas deployments is only temporary, even though the war is in its fourth year and the QDR now talks of "the long war." Rumsfeld is instead reassigning soldiers from artillery and air defense billets to military police, intelligence, and civil affairs, while reluctantly increasing the Army's size by 30,000 on a temporary basis, and moving civilians into jobs now performed by uniformed personnel. In this way, the Army looks to increase the number of active-duty combat brigades from 33 to 42 by the end of fiscal 2007.[9]

These moves are half measures that will not solve the problems of a military that is maintaining a punishing tempo of operations. The United States should increase the size of the military by 40,000 service members— making permanent the 30,000 that Rumsfeld intended to be temporary reinforcements, and then adding an additional 10,000. This will not be cheap. Adding 40,000 people to the regular military—three quarters of whom should go to the Army, and a quarter of whom should go to the Marine Corps—will cost $4.5 billion to $5 billion a year in added pay,[10] plus $2 billion to $3 billion more in benefits needed to attract and keep recruits. Overall, this represents about two percent of the roughly $2.3 trillion the nation will spend on its military forces over the next five years. Some of the cost can be offset by cutting back on the size of procurements of big-ticket items, such as the F/A-22 fighter, the Virginia-class submarine, DD(X) destroyers, the Trident submarine, and the Trident II nuclear missile.[11] But even with some cutbacks, the military budget—which currently consumes a much smaller percentage of U.S. GDP than it did during the cold war, on average—will probably need to grow in the short term.

U.S. forces must have the best equipment available, which too many U.S. units, especially those from the National Guard and Reserves, did not have at the outset of operations in Iraq. Many suffered unnecessary casualties because they lacked "uparmored" Humvees and trucks and bulletproof vests. The military also needs to extend its broadband information network down to the soldiers on the ground. Doing so, among other things, makes small-unit collaboration and synchronization much faster and better, allows much more efficient real-time linkages with airborne surveillance (manned and unmanned), and helps immensely in coordinating the kind of operations that dominate the problems of counterinsurgency and stabilization. Getting the best communications and information technology in the hands of the troops on the ground saves American lives, reduces collateral damage (particularly important in counterinsurgency operations), and gives our troops immense tactical advantages.

Prevent, Defeat, and Rebuild

Real transformation requires a more fundamental revamping of our military than the Bush administration seems to have contemplated. Progressives should call for reorganizing the Pentagon around three key imperatives: preventing threats from materializing; sustaining effective, high-intensity combat when prevention fails; and assisting the transition from armed conflict to stability abroad as well as disaster response at home. The U.S. military today has many of these capacities, but the balance among them is skewed. It still favors high-intensity conflict at the expense of preventing threats or stabilizing postcombat or postdisaster situations.

To correct the balance, the Department of Defense should build its preventive and stabilization capabilities faster than its sustained combat capacities. It should move toward a new kind of triad—an integrated, threefold joint military force structure composed of "prevent," "defeat," and "rebuild" components (see figure 8.1). This would involve more than an adjustment of the defense budget or a realignment of manpower and units. It calls for considerable organizational, structural, and operational transformation. While all three components would have different mixes of active and reserve forces drawn from all four military services, each would have different characteristics and missions.

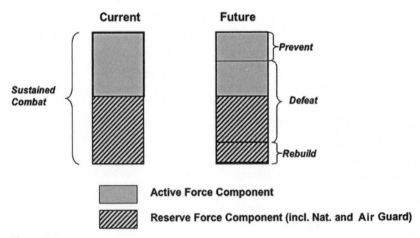

Figure 8.1.

The Prevent Component

Perhaps the most strategically significant characteristic of the new security threats America faces in the twenty-first century—particularly the threat of terrorist attacks by nonstate actors—is that they cannot be deterred by traditional means. Transnational terrorists usually leave no return address, and suicide killers by definition cannot be dissuaded by the threat of retaliation. Therefore, the United States needs to develop a more robust capacity to strike at hostile actors before they can strike at us. While properly skeptical of the Bush administration's attempts to make military preemption a new defense doctrine, progressives should view it as a tool to be used prudently but resolutely to protect Americans from imminent attacks. There are a number of plausible scenarios that illustrate when preemptive action might be needed: striking terrorist cells or training camps in places where local authorities either can't or won't shut them down; destroying weapons of mass destruction and perhaps the means to produce them in rogue states with hostile intent; and preempting aggression against an ally or an area of great economic importance to the United States.

To undertake these missions, our military needs forces dedicated to rapid strikes against distance targets. The prevent component outlined here would include about 20 percent of the active duty manpower strength and a small portion (less than 5 percent) of reserve manpower, and it would perform two functions. One would be to prevent by preemption—to remove or disrupt an opponent's capacity to attack or otherwise harm the United States before he attempts to do so. The forces that would be most effective in these operations would be those with the best expeditionary capabilities, accompanied by cutting-edge joint command, control, communications, computers, intelligence, surveillance, and reconnaissance, along with precision weaponry, high mobility, and personnel trained in their use. As such, large portions of the nation's special operations forces (Army Special Forces, Navy SEALs, Air Force Special Operations) would be rotated through the prevent component for two-year stints. Having a prevent component capable of effective preemptive action does not mean you have to use it. But it can be the big stick that backs up coercive diplomacy and offers new ways of deterring new threats.

The prevent component's second function would be to act as the military's vanguard to transformation. It would have units from all the military services, and it would be largely sea-based and air-deployable from strategic distances. Units would be assigned to the prevent component for roughly two years, during which they would train and operate together, and prior to leaving the component, experiment together to better meld new technology with more effective organization, structure, and operational concepts.

The Defeat Component

The defeat component would be the component most similar to what we have today: the central repository of the U.S. military capability to defeat conventional military opponents in major armed combat. As such, it would remain the core of our ability to deter the aggressive use of military forces by other nations. As with today's force, the defeat component would include the majority—roughly three quarters—of active and reserve forces, including National Guard and Air Guard units, which would be equipped, trained, and organized similarly to the active units they would reinforce when mobilized. It would be able to conduct a wide spectrum of military missions, but it would be best prepared for sustained combat against regular military opponents. It would remain the largest of the three components for probably a decade or more for two reasons. First, it would grow from today's force. The defeat component's modernization and rate of change would probably be faster because its personnel would be rotating through the prevent component and returning with advanced training and experience in joint operations. But the United States would almost certainly want its traditional military services to maintain the esprit de corps and service traditions that currently define them and that make today's force so effective in traditional warfare. Second, it would serve as a hedge against the kind of conflagration today's force is oriented toward. The possibility of armed conflict on the epic scales of the wars of the last century seems remote, but cannot be entirely dismissed. Iran could threaten Persian Gulf shipping or threaten Israel with the nuclear arsenal it seems bent on developing. A U.S.-China conflict over Taiwan is hardly far-fetched, nor can we ignore the possibility of massive fighting on the Korean peninsula.

The Rebuild Component

The rebuild component would be the primary agent through which the U.S. military would aid in post-major combat transitions from war to peace, and for restoring infrastructure and institutions in the event of highly destructive domestic terrorist attacks or natural disasters. Its primary function would be to assist in policing, restoring infrastructure, and providing medical services and other civil administrative activities. Personnel assigned to it would have military training and would be armed and operate as military units, but it would differ from the other two components. While it could provide traditional combat service support, its training, equipment, and focus would be on stabilization, restoration, and reestablishment of civil authority. Manpower for the stabilization component would come mostly from the National and Air Guard units not assigned to the defeat component; roughly a quarter of National Guard (approximately 70,000 personnel) would eventually move under this umbrella.

Relying heavily on National and Air Guard personnel for responses to domestic crises is consistent with the traditional role of the Guard. Both are naturally disposed to work with the civil structures primarily responsible for stabilization, restoration, and support of civil authority in response to domestic disasters. For the same reason, it makes sense to use Guard units in the new "rebuild" component to carry out stabilization missions abroad. Their mission should no longer emphasize being able to take the place of active forces in full-scale combat. They should adjust their training, equipment, and organization to increase their effectiveness in postcombat stabilization or in response to domestic crises. In practical terms, they should trade in their tanks for ambulances and bulldozers.

New Command Structures

Moving toward this "prevent," "defeat," and "rebuild" force-design triad would involve adjustments to the chains of command the U.S. military has in place today.

The Strategic and Special Operations Commands (STRATCOM and SOCOM) are best suited to the task of directing the new "prevent" component's operations. Since the cold war ended, STRATCOM has assumed a growing role in planning long-range, conventional military strikes. SOCOM, meanwhile, already exercises direct command in operations associated with the war on terrorism. Joint Forces Command, now responsible for allocating troops and equipment to the regional commands for joint experimentation in the field, would be the natural candidate for overseeing the last phase of duty in the "prevent" component, which focuses on experimenting with new joint operational concepts and new equipment.

For the "defeat" component, the transformation plan outlined here would not represent a dramatic departure from today's chain of command for the major U.S. regional combatant commands (such as the European, Pacific, and Southwest Asia commands) and the major functional combatant commands (those that have responsibilities that are not necessarily restricted to a specific geographical region, such as the Transportation Command).

Northern Command would play a more active command-and-control role over forces in the "rebuild" component when they respond to domestic crises, such as natural disasters or terrorist attacks. But the "rebuild" component would also carry out stabilization and reconstruction missions overseas. In those missions, they would continue to operate under the authority of regional commands.

IMPROVE ALLIES' CAPABILITIES

No matter how much bigger and better our armed forces are than others, we cannot fight terrorism or stop the proliferation of weapons of mass destruction or even protect our homeland alone. Building our allies' capacity to operate with U.S. forces is in our interests. That includes both traditional allies, such as western European countries that may join us in large-scale combat or stabilization operations, and nontraditional allies, such as tribal forces that may be capable of winning regional conflicts with specialized U.S. assistance. Afghanistan, the Balkans, and the 2005 tsunami relief efforts are examples of where collaboration has worked well.

But to make it work better everywhere means extending military-to-military interactions and giving our allies greater access to U.S. intelligence, surveillance, and reconnaissance capabilities, and to U.S. expeditionary logistics, operational planning, and communications support. A positive step in that direction is the work of Allied Command Transformation (ACT), headquartered in Norfolk, Virginia, which oversees the transformation of NATO's military capabilities. It looks to enhance training, develop new doctrines and operational concepts, and promote interoperability throughout NATO.

Today, there is an increasing disparity between our ability to pass information to and among U.S. military forces and our ability to do so with allied forces. This is in part a product of our proprietary hardware, particularly the U.S. military's space-based communications satellites. It also reflects a conscious decision to exclude access to U.S. capabilities, in part for traditional concern about hiding sources and methods, and in part to guard against intrusions to the information systems our forces depend on. But both the U.S. military and the rest of the world are moving toward greater use of Internet protocols to facilitate the flow of information across different hardware systems. In short, the technical reasons for the communications disparities between the United States and its allies are diminishing, and it is now time to revisit the reasons for excluding wider access to the information assets of the U.S. military.

Accelerate Force Transformation

Finally, we need to develop clear measures to assess how fast transformation is occurring, and apply them as part of the Pentagon's planning processes. There is broad agreement that military transformation involves more than new technology—it also includes adjustments in military organization, structure, and operational concepts. We should facilitate these adjustments by expanding joint experimentation and using the "prevent" component to facilitate integration of new technology with new organizations, structures, and cultures.

Figure 8.2 illustrates how to do this. Units assigned from the sustained combat force component should go through four phases when assigned to the "prevent" force component. The first two phases would focus on training for operations and conducting them, particularly expeditionary operations (when they must bring everything they need with them) or preemptive operations (when they are focused on precise goals that can be carried out quickly). They would train and work closely with each other, using the best, most advanced equipment available. Following a recovery period, the units would enter a final, joint experimental phase. Here, the focus would be on discovering new ways of using the equipment and new ways of organizing. Successful experiments would be used to make appropriate modifications to the bulk of the military. After this final phase of their assignment to the "prevent" component, units would return to the sustained force component. But they would return as change agents, familiar with highly integrated joint operations and acquainted with new organizational structures and equipment.

CONCLUSION

Many of our proposed improvements apply as much to large conflicts as they do to small ones. But the primary impetus for change is the need to

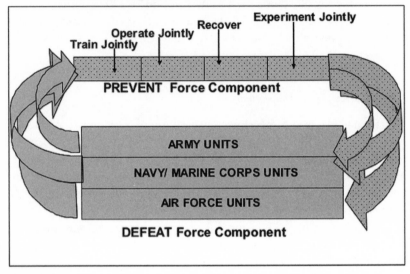

Two-Year Rotational Pattern
Units Assigned to Prevent Component

Figure 8.2.

prevail over today's global jihadist insurgency, and to forestall the possibility that weapons of mass destruction might fall into terrorists' hands. Rather than repeating the mistakes of the past, the Pentagon now has the opportunity to put to rest the ghosts of Vietnam—not only by achieving a successful outcome in Iraq, but by overcoming its longstanding reluctance to reorient itself toward the unconventional operations that are likely to define much of its future mission, and by pushing the reorientation into different military organizations, structures, operational concepts, and cultures.

In 1947, to meet the challenge of Soviet communism, a Democratic administration—President Harry Truman's—presided over the most sweeping redesign of U.S. military and national security capabilities in American history, unifying the armed services under a single Department of Defense, setting up a new National Security Council, and formally authorizing the Central Intelligence Agency. Today's progressives should follow Truman's example and be the authors of a comprehensive military transformation strategy to confront the new, unconventional threats of the twenty-first century.

NOTES

1. U.S. House Committee on Armed Services, Subcommittee on Readiness, testimony by Douglas Holtz-Eakin, "The Potential Costs Resulting from Increased Usage of Military Equipment in Ongoing Operations," April 6, 2005, www.house.gov/hasc/schedules/Holtz-Eakin-04-06-05.pdf.

2. "Actions Needed to Improve Availability of Critical Items during Current and Future Operations," Government Accountability Office, April 2005, www.gao.gov/new.items/d05275.pdf.

3. Graham, Bradley, "General Says Army Reserve Is Becoming a 'Broken' Force," *Washington Post*, January 6, 2005.

4. Moniz, Dave, Matt Kelley, and Steven Komarow, "War's Strain Wearing on Army Troops, Tools," *USA Today*, November 27, 2005, www.usatoday.com/news/world/iraq/2005-11-24-war-strain_x.htm.

5. Moniz et al., "War's Strain."

6. Benjamin, Mark, "How Many Have Gone to War?" Salon.com, April 12, 2005, www.salon.com/news/feature/2005/04/12/troops_numbers/index_np.html?x.

7. Benjamin, "How Many Have Gone to War."

8. Benjamin, "How Many Have Gone to War."

9. Tyson, Ann Scott, "Army to Slow Growth and Cut Six National Guard Combat Brigades," *Washington Post*, January 19, 2006.

10. Bruner, Edward F., "Military Forces: What Is the Appropriate Size for the United States?" Congressional Research Service, February 10, 2005, www.fas.org/sgp/crs/natsec/RS21754.pdf.

11. For additional information on possible cuts, see O'Hanlon, Michael, "More Bang for the Buck," *Foreign Policy*, February 2005.

9

RECONCILING DEMOCRATS AND THE MILITARY

Melissa Tryon[1]

I was no one's idea of prime military material: a violinist inclined to neighborhood tutoring and humanitarian studies, someone who had never touched a rifle or imagined killing anything bigger than household pests. But the humanitarian crises of the early 1990s seemed to prove that suffering could not be alleviated without recourse to a strong and just military, so I started officer training at West Point, mentally prepared for some culture shock.

In addition to standard Army troop leadership, I spent several months with Navy officers and midshipmen, and also some limited time with Marine and Air Force personnel while deployed. I've grown to value the practical wisdom, understated resolve, and offbeat humor of military life. The quality and goodwill of many of even the youngest troops amazes me, and several more traditionally minded colleagues have become lifelong friends. However, the cultural chasm between my progressive ideals and new military surroundings turned out to be much deeper than I expected.

Instead of stereotypical "steely eyed soldiers," I found mainly thoughtful individuals who reminded me of civilian friends. But I also discovered that a set of deeply ingrained assumptions about "liberals" that began in the Vietnam era has calcified into military folklore and been passed on from one generation to the next, with all the nuance expected of "war stories":

- Liberals make America weak and impose dangerous ideas about limited war. Remember how President John F. Kennedy set the military up to fail in Vietnam by not letting us go in and kick butt?
- Liberals in the 1960s either shirked responsibility by running to Canada, or stayed and spat on veterans when they returned home scarred. Then President Jimmy Carter had the balls to pardon the shammers while veterans dealt with their nightmares.
- President Ronald Reagan showed the communists who was boss, rebuilt the military, and restored American pride.
- At least President George H. W. Bush knew how to fight, win, and go home.
- President Bill Clinton was a draft dodger who slashed the military, compromised mission effectiveness by focusing on peacekeeping operations instead of the true "war" mission, and flouted moral precepts by conducting liberal social experiments.
- Iraq may or may not be going well, but there's no excuse in voting for a presidential candidate who betrayed his own brothers-in-arms by coming home from Vietnam and telling lies about them.

The fact that I heard the "Vietnam betrayal" comment most recently from a 20-something Navy officer highlights the power of these assumptions. Factually, of course, much of this collective memory is misinformed: Plenty of Republicans opposed the Vietnam war, and plenty of Democrats supported it; President Kennedy developed U.S. Special Operations Forces; President Carter began the military build-up that President Reagan continued; and President Clinton bequeathed President George W. Bush the high-tech, post-cold war force that fought so brilliantly in Afghanistan and Iraq.

But the facts don't always matter when soldiers banter while loading equipment or waiting for trucks to show up. The enormous demands on a service member's time don't allow for much outside contact and external information beyond one's own unit or military town. And it doesn't help that military televisions seem to be tuned exclusively to Fox News, while competitors like CNN (a.k.a., the "Clinton News Network") are shunned.

To counter such deeply ingrained stereotypes, Democrats cannot simply trot out some retired generals at election time. In order to heal the dangerous divide between progressives and the military[2]—a divide that weakens our country and our democracy, not just one political party—progressives must undertake a broader, deeper embrace of the military community. Progressives must learn to understand military culture, and forge the relationships that will allow shared beliefs and values to overcome these caricatures. Many of the reasons for estrangement between Democrats and the military have been examined elsewhere.[3] What follows is a brief overview of the divide from a military insider's perspective, a primer on military values and culture, and recommendations for how to restore progressives' credibility with the armed forces.

THE PROGRESSIVE-MILITARY GAP

The disconnect between the military and progressives has two components: a demographic divide and a cultural schism. Demographically, few serving officers have friends and relatives who are Democrats. While enlistees are less likely to be Republicans than officers, the increasing trend of recruiting from the rural South and Midwest is intensifying the military's conservative tilt. The growing social distance between progressives and the military—at both mass and elite levels—leads to misconceptions that could be changed simply with greater dialogue and interaction.[4]

Culturally, the Democrat-military gap is an exaggerated version of the widely acknowledged civil-military gap. For many in uniform, the values of a hedonist, acquisitive, and rights-centered society are in tension with a mission-driven military that gives priority to concepts of duty, discipline, solidarity, and results.[5] Liberals are seen as extreme individualists who do not like constraints, do not bend to duty, do not acknowledge the seriousness of the threats we face—and no longer join the forces that guard the freedoms they treasure.[6] Liberal slogans such as "books not bombs" are seen by the military as facile, devaluing of military service, and frighteningly irresponsible when troops are exposed daily to real threats. For their part, liberals often view the military through the narrow prism of the culture wars, including issues such as gays in the military, and see the military as a bastion of social reaction. Since military elites lean heavily Republican while civilian elites lean Democratic, the cultural schism further feeds the demographic divide.[7]

These two trends have turned an institution that is supposed to be politically neutral into a strongly conservative force. In the Vietnam era, the military was culturally conservative, but politically neutral. Now, the military's leadership is strongly partisan, and Republican. The Triangle Institute for Security Studies (TISS) Project on the Civil-Military Gap confirms the growth after Vietnam of Republicans among serving officers (see figures 9.1 and 9.2).[8]

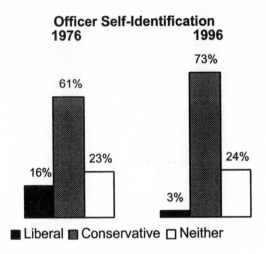

Figure 9.1.

Over the last three decades, Republican parents have been more likely than Democrats to encourage their children toward military service.[9] ROTC programs were driven off Ivy League campuses during Vietnam and are now disproportionately located in the South, which is heavily Republican. Officers in particular come from politically conservative families, and high school seniors seeking officer training (future military elites) have been 5–15 percent more likely to self-identify Republican than those intending to enlist.[10]

The mass military (new recruits and junior enlisted), however, enters the service generally reflecting the demographics of working-class America. Their politics are moderate and their party affiliations are evenly divided.[11] Recruits (by definition, enlisted ranks) are disproportionately from counties with median incomes that are low by either national or state comparison; and disproportionately from the South and Midwest, where it is the motivated youth who often join the military, seeking an alternative to poverty and factory life.[12] (While the military is more attractive to disadvantaged households, it is important to note that service members do not enlist simply for financial or social gain. The poor who enlist believe wholeheartedly that the country's well-being is dependent on its fighting force, and make the choice to join out of the same pride that motivates officers and well-off recruits.) These recruits tend to be religious and culturally conservative, but are relatively apolitical and nonpartisan.

Yet military socialization pushes enlistees toward more conservative

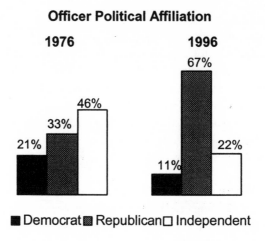

Officer Political Affiliation

1976   **1996**

■ Democrat■ Republican□ Independent

Figure 9.2.

views. The pervasive conservatism of military leaders (both officer and enlisted) creates a conformist climate that leads junior enlisted troops to become increasingly conservative and partisan with time in the military.
Isolation from the moderating influences of the larger society reinforces this
dynamic. Most enlisted families spend the vast majority of their service time
on military bases and/or in strongly military communities. The result is an
increasingly polarized and politicized military. In the 2004 election, for example, service members preferred President Bush to Senator Kerry by
72–17 percent, according to a *Military Times* poll.[13] Enlisted troops, most
from relatively apolitical backgrounds, leaned Republican 49–16 percent,
while officers reported themselves 66 percent Republican and 13 percent
Democrat.[14]

Progressive views enjoy more private support within the mass military
than one might think, however. Because those views are sometimes derided
by supervisors, many service members keep their opinions to themselves.
But even among libertarian-leaning officers, there is disillusionment with
the Republican Party over issues like the ballooning national debt and politicians' preoccupation with social policy. More significantly, Iraq is slowly
replacing Vietnam as the centerpiece of collective memory. Service members are prepared for sacrifice, but the protracted and unclear nature of Iraq
deployments—and discrepancies between official, optimistic reports and
their own experiences—are causing some to question the folklore that says
conservatives are the strongest leaders.

But progressive critiques have not yet solidified in the military, since disillusioned veterans lack ideological support systems, and even constructive criticism is often mistaken for disloyalty or cowardice.[15] The Uniform Code of Military Justice's prohibition of contempt toward the civilian chain of command is often interpreted as a categorical prohibition against public dissent at all.[16] The Army Officer's Guide explicitly warns against any political involvement—which is also interpreted as an injunction against criticizing a sitting administration.[17]

The ugly realities of war, critical shortages of equipment, and the contentious political debate over Iraq nonetheless are stirring latent unrest within the military. Such tensions could snowball into an internal challenge to the military's prevailing conservative orthodoxy—but only if progressives can find leaders with the credentials and self-confidence to address the military's all-too-real dilemmas.

MILITARY CULTURE

Understanding military culture is the first essential step for progressive leaders who wish to earn the respect of the armed services. The military has a uniquely encompassing organizational culture. Extended workdays, month-long training exercises, and multi-year deployments require that most of a service member's social and family life revolve around the military. The values and norms of military life reflect the imperatives of building a fighting force that can fulfill its duties with maximum efficacy. To bridge this cultural divide, progressives must learn to appreciate, not denigrate, the warrior ethos.

The "Warrior Ethos"

Each service has a version of what the Army calls the Warrior Ethos: acceptance of personal risk and discipline in order to survive and prevail in combat. Recognizing that "the more you sweat in peace, the less you bleed in war,"[18] military leaders strive to develop behaviors and values that will prepare their troops to perform under stressful wartime conditions. Officially stated values change often,[19] but the following fundamental cultural motifs are held across services:

Decisiveness. Since military actions require innumerable split-second decisions under stressful conditions, waiting to act until one has all the facts, or until conditions are "optimal," can cost lives. The military therefore values decisiveness—even when a slower decision might occasionally result in a better outcome. Junior officers and enlisteds constantly hear the phrase "Make it happen!" and common bumper stickers in military towns read "Lead, follow, or get out of the way." Military people lack patience with perceived stalling and excuses—they want decisions, and they want action, not explanation. Nuanced analysis seems a luxury to forces that need to know when to start shooting at dangerous enemies—and when to stop.

Pride and honor. Service members see the defense of our country as a calling, and as one of the greatest forms of service. Pride and honor are further cultivated by the military to keep service members focused on completing their missions despite personal losses and combat stress—so even service members who might have been drawn to the military for the college education are filled with a sense of deeper purpose, often religious as well as civic. Perceived slights—including the sense that they are being pitied, are "victims" of an administration or policy, or are serving out of a lack of better options—are tremendously resented by the military. This pride, when over-cultivated, leads some in the military to see their society as better than "soft" civilian society, and contributes to the civil-military divide.

Moral certainty. War is a bad place for self-doubt. Service members learn to accept absolutes—one of the only ways of being comfortable with the possibility of taking or losing life for any cause. This moral certainty provides inner strength and pushes service members to value "the harder right over the easier wrong." It also means that the military wants reassurance that its missions are morally justified. Soldiers tend to be open about religion, and are very comfortable expressing right and wrong in absolute terms—as well as suspicious of civilians who seem unclear or uncomfortable with these concepts. Since they assume that the use of force can sometimes be morally justified—and morally preferable—this certainty can also lead to disdain for liberal ambivalence about the use of force at all.

Community. Combat and military training are stressful and require time away from family and local communities. Service members learn to rely on each other—even if they have never met before—and their families go out of their way to help out on short notice, expecting nothing in return. The unparalleled sense of "family" within the serving community means that service members are more comfortable with other service members—even when out of uniform. Conversely, the sense of community is born from a strong "us" and "them" paradigm, which can cause distrust for anyone who has not served in the military. The lack of serving Democrats as Hill staffers, political consultants, and other political jobs creates a barrier to easy conversation, even when the topic is not defense-related. Moreover, service members are apt to be fiercely protective of others in the military community, championing leaders seen as supporting the military and quick to turn against anyone perceived as denigrating the military—including former service members.

Commitment to winning. In combat, there is no "can't"—every mission given must be accomplished. The can-do attitude fostered includes a commitment to getting a job completed no matter what. It leads to anger at what is widely seen as "defeatism" among those who declare that the Iraq war is "unwinnable." It also explains why "Bring Troops Home Now" slogans fail to resonate with service members, even when they'd personally like nothing better than to return home. No one in the military wants another Vietnam or Somalia—which are seared in collective memory as humiliating retreats without victory. That's why most reject the idea of withdrawing from Iraq according to a politically determined timetable. What service members want most is to see America succeed in Iraq.

Traditionalism. Fundamental principles of war have not changed from times of Sun-Tzu or Clausewitz; so learning from Napoleon Bonaparte's operational genius, Robert E. Lee's battlefield command, or Hal Moore's improvisational tactics at Ia Drang increases preparedness for future conflicts. The experience of combat is sufficiently unique that service members feel a kinship with those who have gone before, those who will come after, and the timelessness of rituals they share. This traditionalism also has a dark side in resistance to even positive change, and an unwillingness to try ideas that come from the "outside." Experimentation, after all, may have lethal consequences for military personnel. The progressive impulse to test new ways to solve problems may appear to undermine time-honored routines that have worked. This value makes the military naturally conservative, and can be seen in an anti-intellectual light.

The salience of these values in military life explains why Republican rhetoric resonates strongly with soldiers. Republicans, for example, rarely use the language of victimization to describe service members, because they understand that such characterizations offend soldiers' pride. Meanwhile, Republicans justify use-of-force decisions by reference to military-friendly values such as duty, toughness, boldness, and decisiveness. Moreover, the Republican openness to religion resonates with a generally religious and increasingly evangelical military. For progressives, this could be cause for alarm. However, it is better seen as encouragement to be clear about the moral foundations of their own beliefs.

Common Ground, High Ground

In fact, progressives and members of the armed forces share many core values. Though they may not agree on narrow issues like gun control, they share a commitment to individual liberty, equal opportunity for anyone willing to work hard, advancement based on merit rather than advantages of birth, and the equal right of all Americans to live with dignity. Both the military and progressives champion defense of the defenseless. Most progressives value West Point's iconic "Duty, Honor, Country" even if they do not publicly highlight those terms as often. With rare and regrettable exceptions, the average service member takes no pleasure in any human bloodshed. Like progressives, though, he or she believes that some causes are worth fighting for. Progressives therefore, can begin to reconnect with the military through the articulation of some common values:

Service. It was a great Democratic war hero who first implored Americans to "Ask not what your country can do for you; ask what you can do for your country." Democrats and the military agree that all Americans have a duty to make this country a better place. The military is more than a paycheck; most join to be part of something larger than themselves. Yet Republicans after 9/11 have not called for a renewed national commitment to service, despite foreign and domestic catastrophes. This fact has not been lost on service members, who increasingly feel that the whole burden of the administration's "war on terror" has been placed on their shoulders. They've carried that burden valiantly, despite strained resources and decreasing active moral support from the rest of America.

This service ideal is a strong potential link between Democrats and the military, which after all is comprised of volunteers. But we don't see many progressives in uniform, and military members generally aren't exposed to organizations like AmeriCorps and Peace Corps, which have tended to attract young progressives. The military generally only sees humanitarian workers under hostile circumstances, when the military perceives itself as "bailing them out," rather than as equals in service. Thus, the military failure to appreciate progressives' commitment to public service is more a problem of institutional interaction than ideology, making it an excellent starting point for expressions of common ground.

Morality. Clearly, progressives believe strongly in morality and justice.

"Right" is central to many liberal views. Again, lack of exposure to progressives—and civilians in general—makes it difficult for the military to perceive progressives' commitment to moral issues. However, this is another potential bridge, if progressive politicians and policy makers can begin to phrase their arguments boldly in the terminology of right and wrong, rather than simply facts or pragmatic interests. Even though the areas of "right" and "wrong" may at times clash, the military will appreciate firm moral commitments more than moral equivocation.

Community. Military leaders of all ranks emphasize the importance of taking care of each other, especially the lowest ranking. The idea of mutual dependence and responsibility is a core element of progressive philosophy, which stresses that we are not born as atomized individuals, but have obligations to each other and our society. This idea, however, needs to be couched in terms of duty, brotherhood, and our shared community as Americans, rather than the patronizing language of victimization.

Freedom and American values. The military prides itself on its duty to "fight for freedom." Though the language of human rights has become a stumbling block because of perceived insults against the U.S. military by Amnesty International and similar groups, service members fundamentally believe in the civil rights and freedoms that America is founded upon.[20] Progressives would find resonance with the military in the idea that America needs to maintain physical security, but stands for more than that—we stand for ideals that must be defended at home and advanced abroad.[21] Framing human rights as integral to individual liberty and democracy will help military people to see that they, and progressives, are fighting for common cause. Progressives, for example, should continue to insist on humane treatment of captives and a ban on torture. Like them, most members of the military believe that a superpower possessing the most powerful military in history must hold itself to the highest standards of conduct in order to be deserving of that power.

These shared values suggest some practical steps that progressives can take to close the cultural chasm between them and the U.S. military.

ACTION PLAN FOR CLOSING THE DIVIDE

Because many Democrats do not regularly interact with individual service members, previous and recent well-meaning Democratic attempts to reach out to the military on policy issues have been poorly received by those in uniform. For instance, when Democrats tried to fight for proper military equipment, pay, or benefits, the phrasing and the Fox News spin led many politically neutral service members to resent the perceived implication of themselves as victims—despite their real desire for better equipment and the benefits they deserve.

Service members do not want "fair weather friends" who pander to them for political advantage—or to be used as tools by either party. Progressives must show sustained interest to create a foundation of trust that will help the military move toward its own ideal of a truly nonpartisan force. Solutions to the overall problem eventually require military-savvy policies—but first the cultural barriers must be addressed. Reconnecting with the military will require long-term strategy, patience, and determination. It will not be achieved in an election cycle—but it must be started now. Here's how:

Forge Strategic Relationships with Credible Messengers

A long-term solution requires sustained contact between Democrats and the military community in order to discover common ground and get past negative spin. For example, Democrats should cultivate strong relationships with veterans' groups and with organizations that can legitimately speak for current service members, groups that can frame progressive arguments in military ideology—providing Democrats with the military-credible social network of those who have "walked the walk."

- Groups such as Operation Truth, Veterans for Common Sense, VETPAC, Vietnam Veterans of America, Veterans and Military Families for Progress, and the Gulf War Resources Council are moderate-progressive groups committed to advocacy for veterans of all generations who would be immediately open to dialogue. These groups have excellent access to recent service members' insights and frustration with current policies and shortfalls.
- More historically conservative groups such as Veterans of Foreign Wars, the American Legion, and Disabled American Veterans (DAV) are increasingly frustrated with the lack of funding for veterans' immediate health needs. DAV has bluntly criticized the current administration's handling of veterans' health. If approached with sensitivity, abstract ideological differences with veterans' organizations take a backseat to their mission: helping veterans.

- Progressive but nonpacifistic religious leaders should build bridges to the U.S. military, to challenge conservative evangelicals' monopoly on religious morality. God must be decoupled from the Republican Party for soldiers who dislike Republican policies but see no other voting options as moral Christians. The spiritual foundations of military service—as personal motivation and moral compass—are simply too important to disregard.[22]

Finally, there is absolutely no substitute for actual military service.[23] Many in uniform are reluctant to take seriously defense-related ideas from "experts" who lack military experience, reasoning that the stresses of military action cannot be understood without a walk in those boots. Especially during wartime, military service must be a serious option for all citizens, regardless of politics or social status.

Liberals' and elites' disinclination to military service is often interpreted as indifference toward national security—and troops themselves. Kathy Roth-Douquet notes that less than one percent of today's Princeton and Harvard graduates have military experience—from a high of 50 percent in 1950.[24] This imbalance in representation weakens our defense systems as well as our national community. For long-term, strategic reconnection with the military, Democrats must:

- Encourage a generation of idealistic Democratic youth to join ROTC programs, attend service academies, or enlist.
- Encourage smart young Democrats to seek defense-related internship programs and entry-level jobs, especially those with regular interaction with enlisted ranks.
- Recruit recent veterans for positions of leadership and staff.
- In the absence of military experience, every Democratic leader needs at least one staff member who has spent enough time in the military community to "speak military." An informal veteran/military advisory panel might be a solution when such staff is impractical. Members of Congress should strive to take advantage of the Military Fellow program for increased dialogue.
- Recruit more military veterans to run for public office.

Focus on Policies That Matter to Soldiers

Much Beltway "military" debate is rightly focused on grand strategy and the use of force. But most service members are too far removed from strategic decisions to actively follow such issues. At the most abstract level, service members want to know that the armed forces will be sent to serve whenever needed, for a good mission, and never misused. However, the military majority is far too busy with daily tasks to pay attention to foreign policy debates that go deeper than assessing confidence in the judgment and basic principles of their commander in chief. Arguments about whether the United States should have invaded Iraq—or who is to blame for miscalculations—are mostly useless to service members. They must focus each day on surviving present realities and finding resolutions to existing problems.

The military community cares intensely about day-to-day challenges and shortfalls. Practical military issues concern lower ranks and injured veterans intensely, since they directly affect health and family well-being—and others in the community care about these serving members. Issues of immediate concern are not new weapons systems or even grand strategy, but:

- Severely overstretched forces resulting in unit exhaustion, deteriorating mental health, stop-loss, and ultimately more personnel shortfalls;[25]
- Poor quality of life for families, substandard housing especially for lower enlisted Marines and Army, family strain from repeat deployments, doubling and tripling divorce rates among different subgroups from 2001 to 2004;[26]
- Poor resources, inadequate training time, rushed preparation, and old, failing equipment;
- Poor medical care from a severely overtaxed Veterans' Administration, shortfalls in VA funding resulting in catastrophic cuts in caring for legitimate, military-related physical and mental problems;[27] and
- Unclear Rules of Engagement, with no consistent guidance on treatment of local populations and detainees.

Such frustrations open a window of opportunity for Democrats to reach out to the military community and show genuine empathy toward its concerns. A young Navy reservist may be too proud to complain about "Stop-Loss," but wants leaders who understand that indefinitely prolonging his service may mean losing his small business back home. "High optempo" means missed anniversaries, increased mental strain from returning to combat without dealing with emotional wounds from the last deployment, insufficient equipment maintenance, and rushed training.

Most importantly, progressives need to understand how personally the military community takes public support, because of the emotional, sometimes overwhelmingly uncertain nature of military deployments. The deployed airman who disagreed with the Iraq invasion in the first place still does not want to abandon the mission and come home, because of the devastating consequences of another military defeat. To his wife, a lifelong Democrat who thinks of him constantly with intense pride and worry, antiwar protests can be difficult to perceive as anything other than a lack of respect for their sacrifice.[28]

Remember That Actions Speak Louder Than Words

Both the military and public are often reminded in sound bites that "We are a nation at war." But service members never see sacrifices other than their own. Many grow disappointed or frustrated at the notion that the military alone bears the costs of the war on terror, while nobody in power cares about the military's strain, insufficient equipment, and shrinking benefits. The military feels increasingly neglected by both political parties and grows increasingly skeptical of words and promises.

Democratic leaders and progressive groups must make the effort to "show up" to support military ribbon-cuttings, hospitalized seamen, and airmen stranded in institutional cafeterias on holidays.[29] Yellow ribbons or quick "fly-by" congressional visits, though noted, are no longer enough. Local Democratic chapters must interact with the flesh-and-blood military and listen to complaints and opinions—especially among enlisted troops and without fanfare, monitoring, or editing by military supervisors. Such outreach can run from volunteering in military hospitals, to progressive churches following evangelicals' example of adopting deployed units or individuals, sending written and home-baked encouragement.

Eventually, Democratic leaders must be comfortable enough to be able to introduce thoughtful military initiatives: a modified national service program to distribute sacrifice and take long-term domestic burdens off the military; informed opinions of military restructuring for twenty-first-century demands, for instance development of a quick-strike force, constabulary force, and humanitarian and nation-building forces; or an overhaul of military medicine and VA care to provide future veterans with the support they deserve. But any great, high-level idea must start with increased visibility and tangible support.

Democrats Must Present a Coherent Vision for National Security Based on Common Beliefs

Many individual Democratic comments and initiatives on defense have been excellent. Unfortunately, they are not yet consistent enough to overcome the louder, consistent yet clearly imprudent demands of the extreme left. Democratic leaders must find a way to coordinate messages on defense and speak with one voice, or else their thoughtful positions simply will not be heard. Aside from obvious political benefits of a unified message, Democrats must remember that service members look at all candidates as those who may someday decide their fate; voting any Democrat into office will be much more attractive if security-oriented voters know what underlying beliefs, priorities, and actions they can expect from today's Democrats.

CONCLUSION

The estrangement between the military and progressives has deep roots and will require significant, focused effort to overcome. But the situation is hopeful. Much of the divide is based on misperceptions and lack of interaction, and can be overcome. Moreover, the current military is in transition and turmoil, and is desperately seeking strong, responsible leadership.

Reestablishing a solid Democratic-military relationship will require focused effort to reconnect culturally, listen to military opinions of all ranks, forge institutional ties with like-minded organizations within the military community, and eventually present a consistent Democratic vision for a strong, sustainable, morally grounded defense policy. Despite increasing cynicism, military personnel are diverse, thoughtful, and pragmatic enough to respond to Democratic defense initiatives if grounded in common ideals and phrased to avoid sore points.

A nation at war, facing huge challenges and potential threats, deserves a healthy and vigorous debate on security issues—between both parties. Understanding the military and tapping into progressive military thought will strengthen Democrats' ability to publicly address national security challenges and stake their own ground in defense issues. Democrats do not need to give up their own values to reforge their relationship with the military. They must remember that America's ability to support democratic ideals in the world—as well as at home—is intrinsically intertwined with the strength and health of America's fighting forces.

NOTES

1. Opinions expressed are the author's own, and do not represent the official view of the U.S. military. The author is registered Independent and does not officially endorse either political party. The author would like to thank Ross Chanin, a Truman Associate, for his assistance with research for this article. The author also greatly appreciates the assistance of Kathy Roth-Douquet, Phillip Carter, and Dick Klass in reading and offering their advice on earlier drafts. Any mistakes that may appear in this essay, however, are the author's alone.

2. The term "military" here addresses Air Force, Army, Marine, and Navy personnel serving in an active duty capacity (including activated Reserves and National Guard). "Military community" also includes veterans and retirees, who have been socialized into many of the same norms, usually identify with current troops, and are often active in military towns—and the spouses who share many decisions and sacrifices.

3. See, for example: Hurlburt, Heather, "War Torn," *Washington Monthly*, November 2002, www.washingtonmonthly.com/features/2001/0211.hurlburt.html.

4. Sappenfield, Mark, "Where Recruiting Runs Strongest," *Christian Science Monitor*, July 19, 2005, www.csmonitor.com/2005/0719/p01s03-usmi.html.

5. Feaver, Peter D., Richard H. Kohn, and Lindsay P. Cohn, eds., *Soldiers and Civilians: The Civil-Military Gap and American Security* (Cambridge: MIT Press, 2001).

6. Military leadership does understand that these tensions undermine the respect necessary between a republic and its all-volunteer military; professionalism, political neutrality, and submission to civil authority are explicitly emphasized during officer training. Sadly, the view "on the ground" is sometimes different.

7. General David Petraeus, quoted in Desch, Michael C., "Explaining the Gap: Vietnam, the Republicanization of the South, and the End of the Mass Army," in Feaver et al., *Soldiers and Civilians*.

8. Holsti, Ole R., "Of Chasms and Convergences: Attitudes and Beliefs of Civilians and Military Elites at the Start of a New Millennium," in Feaver et al., *Soldiers and Civilians*, p. 28.

9. Holsti, Ole R., "A Widening Gap Between the U.S. Military and Civilian Society? Some Evidence, 1976–1996," *International Security* 23 (1999): 5–42.

10. Segal, David R., et al., "Attitudes of Entry-level Enlisted Personnel," in Feaver et al., *Soldiers and Civilians*, p. 177.

11. Segal et al.

12. Brunswick, Mark, "In the Ranks of Recruits, Who Bears the Load?" *The Star Tribune*, November 3, 2005.

13. Feaver, Peter D., "Whose Military Vote?" *The Washington Post*, October 24, 2004, www.washingtonpost.com/wp-dyn/articles/A25656-2004Oct11.html.

14. "Annual Year-end Polls and Special Surveys," *Military Times* Poll, 2005, www.militarycity.com/polls. However, this data is skewed by the nature of *Military Times'* readership: career officers and enlisteds who lean farther right than junior officers and enlisteds.

15. Contrasted with robust right-leaning organizations such as Officers' Christian Fellowship (OCF), an evangelical outreach group available to American officers worldwide. I have had wonderful experiences with OCF officers, but the publicized zeal of the Air Force Academy chapter highlights the concern regarding a strong social group, on a relatively isolated military base, with no progressive counterpoint.

16. Sensitivity to this regulation is clearly uneven: Criticism of President George W. Bush has been unwelcome amidst post–9/11 patriotism, while several military state-

ments about President Bill Clinton bordered on contempt. Despite a strong professional ethos, officers are human. President Clinton's perceived willingness to send American troops to war, when he had avoided service, seriously weakened legitimacy as commander-in-chief in military eyes.

17. Bonn, Ltc. Keith E. *Army Officer's Guide*, 48th Edition (Mechanicsburg, PA: Stackpole Books, 1999), p. 105.

18. Proverb often quoted in the military; attributable to many.

19. The Army's most current official values are Loyalty, Duty, Respect, Selfless service, Honor, Integrity, and Personal courage, spelling L[ea]D[e]RSHIP.

20. The military is still uncomfortable with extended military actions for ideological purposes without a direct benefit for America, because of lack of resources. They fear that a liberal, crusading ethos will use them in ways that fail to achieve missions and weaken the military in the pursuit of fruitless goals. In standing for freedom, Democrats must also stress achievability. Carter, Phillip, and Paul Glastris, "The Case for the Draft," *Washington Monthly*, March 2005, www.washingtonmonthly.com/features/2005/0503 .carter.html.

21. Again, the military will be more accepting of "fostering ideals" if clearly noted that such missions will not be primarily a military burden. This is best illustrated by General Colin Powell's resistance to Madeleine Albright's notion of using the military for nonmilitary action, paraphrasing, "because we can." Powell, Colin, "Why Generals Get Nervous," *New York Times*, October 8, 1992.

22. For more on spiritual aspects of service, see Toner, James H., *True Faith and Allegiance: The Burden of Military Ethics* (Lexington: University Press of Kentucky, 1995).

23. See: Roth-Douquet, Kathy, and Frank Schaeffer, *AWOL: The Unexcused Absence of America's Upper Classes from Military Service—and How It Hurts Our Country* (New York: HarperCollins, forthcoming 2006).

24. Roth-Douguet and Schaffer, *AWOL*.

25. McNaugher, Thomas L., "Chapter 8, The Army and Operations Other Than War: Expanding Professional Juristiction," in Snider, Don M., and Gayle L. Watkins, eds., *The Future of the Army Profession*. Project Directors: Don M. Snider and Gayle L. Watkins (Boston: McGraw-Hill, 2002).

26. Crary, David, "Iraq War Takes Toll on Army Marriages," Associated Press, June 29, 2005.

27. Wilson, Arthur H., "VA Health Care Budget Crisis," *DAV Magazine*, September/October 2005, 3.

28. I must stress that antiwar attitudes are not inherently resented; many individual service members could see Cindy Sheehan in their own mothers. But massive demonstrations on the Washington Mall were eerily reminiscent of the Vietnam era, and are clearly confusing to the military's perceptions of the Democrat mainstream.

29. Avoid VIP visits that are "announced" or in combat zones; they breed resentment because of the time spent cleaning and preparing for the visit, or because of the resources consumed providing security.

IV

STRENGTHENING COLLECTIVE SECURITY

10

WHY AMERICA NEEDS
A STRONG EUROPE

Ronald D. Asmus

As Democrats work to reshape America's post–9/11 foreign policy, they should look to their own past and the reasons why past Democratic leaders were successful and effective national security leaders. During and after World War II, visionary leaders like Franklin Roosevelt, Harry Truman, George Marshall, and Dean Acheson laid the foundations for a unified West and created an American-led liberal world order through institutions such as NATO Alliance, the World Bank, the International Monetary Fund, the General Agreement on Tariffs and Trade (GATT), and the United Nations. These tough-minded Democratic leaders were neither embarrassed by nor afraid of power. They knew how to use America's unique combination of strengths to attract allies. They understood that U.S. global leadership would be welcomed if it was not just devoted to pursuing narrow national interests but broader and shared objectives.

The most important legacy of these Democratic statesmen was the transatlantic alliance between the democracies of North America and Europe. In the aftermath of September 11, the United States was once again presented with an opportunity to reshape that alliance as part of a broader effort to confront the war on terrorism. But the Bush administration chose a very different path than the architects of the postwar system, disdaining allies and institutions, and putting its faith instead in America's ability to go it alone and rely on its preponderant military power. The U.S. today is paying a heavy price for the fracturing of the Western alliance and the squandering of this historic opportunity.

An alternative Democratic vision should recognize that we again face a "Trumanesque" moment, when America has the opportunity to use its vast margin of power to reshape and update our alliance with Europe to confront new threats and create a more cooperative and secure world order. America's future freedom, prosperity, and security are still linked to that of the old continent in fundamental ways. Our new strategic imperatives, in fact, should lead the United States to seek even closer transatlantic cooperation than in the past, albeit in different fields than during the cold war.

Instead of dismissing "Old Europe" as irrelevant, as Defense Secretary Donald Rumsfeld famously did during the run-up to the Iraq war, Democrats must put a revitalized transatlantic alliance at the center of U.S. foreign policy. The United States will never be able to effectively defend our homeland against new terrorist threats, support democratic transformation in the Greater Middle East, or manage the rise of China and work toward regional security in Asia without a unified West. There will never be a well-functioning international system without a strong alliance as its backbone and absent close cooperation between the world's leading democracies in North America and Europe. If the United States does not want to be a unilateralist power, it needs a strong and self-confident Europe as a partner. Renewed cooperation between the United States and Europe is crucial not for reasons of shared history or lingering cultural attachment, but because it is once again a basic American interest—perhaps more so than ever before.

The point of departure for a new Democratic approach to Europe should be the following question: What kind of Europe does America want and need as a strategic partner in the twenty-first century? And what kind of new partnership should Democratic leaders be committed to supporting and helping to create across the Atlantic? The answer to this question should be self-evident. The United States today needs a strong, confident Europe capable of keeping and expanding peace and freedom on its own continent yet also outward looking, open to close cooperation with Washington, and capable of coherent action against a new set of security challenges that are global in scope.

Whereas transatlantic cooperation in the past was focused on military security and cooperation in Europe, today it needs to be expanded to a much broader set of issues around the world. Fortunately, on the major issues facing U.S. foreign policy—from defeating Islamist extremism to managing the rise of China, to fighting nuclear proliferation, to dealing with an increasingly authoritarian Russia, to fighting world poverty and pandemic disease—American and European interests are still fundamentally aligned.

Conservative unilateralists claim that Europe is neither interested in nor capable of stepping up to this kind of partnership. To be sure, Europe's ability to become a stronger partner today is in doubt. The continent is absorbed with its own problems: last year's rejection by French and Dutch voters of the European constitution, which has stymied progress toward political integration; relatively slow economic growth and chronic high unemployment on the continent; the failure to assimilate Muslim immigrants economically or culturally; and the reluctance of European governments, facing aging populations and soaring welfare costs, to invest more in modernizing their armed forces.

But the United States cannot afford to stand aloof and wait for Europe to resolve its dilemmas. On the contrary, progressives should make clear our determination to see Europe succeed as a political and economic community as well as a U.S. security partner. As a party, we need to return to the mixture of idealism and principle that led presidents from Harry Truman to John Kennedy to support a united and strong Europe in alliance with the United States.

THE NEW AGENDA

There are four critical areas that should be at the center of a new and revitalized alliance: homeland defense, Middle East reform, the extension of democracy to Eurasia, and China's emergence as a global power.

Homeland Defense

The glue that held us together during the cold war was the threat to our homelands. Today these homelands are threatened again, albeit in a very different fashion. A series of vivid images over the past two years—the 3/11 Madrid bombings, the July 2005 bus and subway bombings in London, the murder of Dutch filmmaker Theo van Gogh—demonstrate that while the United States is the main enemy, Europe is also a major target of jihadist rage. It is only too likely that America, Europe, or both will suffer a catastrophic terrorist attack in the years ahead. We already know from simulations conducted on a possible nuclear, chemical, or biological attack that the consequences of such an attack on either side of the Atlantic would be horrific and rapidly overwhelm national capabilities. The ensuing political and economic consequences could destabilize the economies and polities of the West more generally.

The terrorist threat we face is transnational and so must be our response. Homeland security is the modern-day equivalent of NATO's Article 5 (which guarantees that members will come to each other's defense) and it should receive that kind of priority. As opposed to areas where we are searching for a common view, this is an area where strategic convergence across the Atlantic often exists. Both sides of the Atlantic have, however, been slow in capitalizing on this and still view homeland security in national terms. There is ample room for expanded cooperation—starting with closer intelligence and law enforcement cooperation, extending to the setting of common norms for protecting our vulnerable infrastructure and industry on both sides of the Atlantic; coordinated responses to catastrophic terrorist attacks that will almost certainly overwhelm national capabilities; or joint research and development of the kinds of vaccines and antidotes we will need against chemical or biological attacks in the future.

But we also need to think about homeland security in broader terms. Americans and Europeans are discovering their dependency upon the policies of the other side of the Atlantic in new ways. Europeans often complain that Washington pursues policies in the Middle East that have a direct impact in Europe and with Muslim immigrant communities. Today many European countries are bracing for a feared round of blowback from the war in Iraq, as a new generation of European-born Muslims are either radicalized or, worse, return to Europe after having cut their teeth in an anti-American insurgency. Americans, in turn, are waking up to the risk of Islamic radicalism in Europe. Key 9/11 terrorists like Mohammed Atta were radicalized in Europe, and the London bombers also called attention to homegrown European terrorism. There is mounting evidence that this is or could become a broader pattern. According to Marc Sageman's study of 400 al Qaeda members, over 70 percent were radicalized while living abroad, many in Western Europe.[1] Jihadists from Western Europe can gain access to EU passports and at times visa-free entry into the United States. American terrorist experts have already started sounding the alarm bells regarding the terrorist threat emanating from Europe.

Americans are also discovering their interest in Europe's ability to successfully integrate its own disaffected Muslim populations and limit the risk that young native-born European Muslims turn to terrorism directed against the United States. Radical Islam's appeal in Western Europe stems in part from the fact that it offers a feeling of identity to alienated Muslim youth detached from the cultures of their parents yet unwilling or unable to assimilate into modern European society. An intense public debate has emerged across the continent, spurred by the realization that neither the "multicultural" model as practiced in Britain and the Netherlands, nor the French version of race-blind citizenship and strictly enforced *laicité*, have thus far succeeded in giving the children of postwar Muslim immigrants a place in modern European society. The outcome of that debate will potentially affect American security in a critical way and is a reminder of how our destinies across the Atlantic remain intertwined in the twenty-first century. And here we have much to offer our European friends. While there are many lessons, good and bad, to be drawn from America's experience in assimilating large waves of immigrants from all parts of the world, our success in economic integration and religious pluralism are particularly relevant to the challenge facing Europe.[2]

Reform in the Middle East

The most profound foreign policy and national security policy challenge facing the United States and Europe for the foreseeable future is the broader Middle East. The paradox here is the potential convergence of interests across the Atlantic on precisely the topic that has strained the alliance the most in recent years. The future relationship between the West and the Islamic Middle East is one of the central strategic issues of our time. It is only logical that a renewed transatlantic alliance should be centered on—but not limited to—the fight against Islamic extremism in the region, because it poses the greatest threat to our respective societies today.

Achieving America's key foreign policy goals in the broader Middle East—keeping Iran from making nuclear weapons, stabilizing Afghanistan, spurring political and economic reform, and dealing with a Hamas-dominated government in Palestine—will be close to impossible in isolation and without strong contributions from Europe. The political transformation of the Middle East is an enormous task on a par with Europe's post-war reconstruction. It will be far easier if Europe's political, economic, and military weight, its long cultural and historical ties, and its trading relationships, are harnessed to support common goals. In fact, Europe's success in spurring change among post-Soviet bloc states may furnish a promising model. By holding out the prospect of membership in the European Union, it has enticed a broad range of neighboring countries, as differing as Poland and

Turkey, to undertake political and economic liberalization. Obviously EU membership isn't in the offing for Middle Eastern states, but the United States and Europe could create the prospect of a privileged partnership—with open market access, reduced farm subsides, immigration privileges, aid, debt relief, and investment—which would be available only to countries that make demonstrable progress toward reform.

Democrats must realize that the main problem with the Bush administration's approach in the Middle East is not its diagnosis of the problem but how it has gone about the solution. Europeans, too, increasingly recognize that the status quo in the region is rotten and must change. As long as the Middle East is mired in a crisis of failed governance and economic stagnation, it will continue to export both emigrants and toxic anti-Western ideology to Europe. Demographic projections show that the problem is only going to get worse: As historian Timothy Garton Ash notes, the population of the Arab world is slated to rise from 280 million to as many as 460 million by 2020.[3] Meanwhile, the National Intelligence Council predicts that Europe's Muslim population will double by 2025.[4] But before Europeans join the United States in a common reform project, they need to be convinced that our policies are likely to decrease and not increase instability and the risks to their own countries. This is yet another reason why Democrats must not only criticize the failings of the Bush administration's policies in the region, but develop their own clear and more competent alternatives for reaching many of the same goals.

Democracy in Eurasia

While working to confront jihadist terrorism and other new challenges, the United States and Europe also need to cooperate closely in consolidating peace on the continent and the extension of democracy and prosperity deeper into both Eurasia and the wider Black Sea region. Today it is often taken for granted that Europe has ceased to be a theater of geopolitical conflict and competition. In reality this is an extraordinary accomplishment. Just imagine what the world would be like if today Washington—in addition to the problems of the broader Middle East and Asia—were also confronted with strategic turmoil on the continent. Locking that stability in and extending it beyond Europe's current borders is a profound American interest and must be a pillar of future U.S.-European cooperation.

The Rose and Orange Revolutions in Tbilisi and Kiev have opened the vista of a third wave of democratization extending deeper into Eurasia and the Black Sea region, and potentially redrawing our mental map of Europe and the West. Succeeding in the Balkans, integrating Turkey, and anchoring these other critical countries on Europe's periphery are keys to influencing and perhaps halting the slide toward authoritarianism in Russia. America's political and strategic role in assisting democratic breakthroughs in these countries has been critical, but ultimately it is Europe and the European Union with its more comprehensive integrationist policies that does most of the heavy lifting to help lock in enduring change in these countries. We want and need the EU to be a magnet radiating influence beyond its borders and helping to anchor young and still fragile democracies to the West.

China

Beyond the challenges of a wider Europe and the wider Middle East lies the challenge of the rise of China and future security in Asia. Acting together, America and Europe still have a window of opportunity to help shape and build a new world order that is largely based on the universalist values we share. Pooling our many resources, including political and moral legitimacy, will give us the best chance to help build peace and stability in the broader Middle East and influence the historical trajectory of countries like Russia, India, or China. But that window will close in the decades ahead as our overall influence in the world diminishes relative to that of rising non–Western powers like China, India, and Brazil.

EMBRACING THE EU AND
REORIENTING NATO

The core of a new Democratic approach toward Europe must be the recognition that the transformation of the U.S.-European partnership is the logical and natural extension of the original vision that led American and European leaders to come together after World War II to create NATO and launch the European project. Today the United States needs a new policy toward the European Union and reform of NATO based on the new threats we face in common, an enlarged Europe's new economic and demographic challenges, and the complementarity of European and American strengths.

It is time to rethink American policy toward the European Union. America's national interest lies in seeing the emergence of a strong, politically cohesive, outward looking, and Atlanticist EU capable of becoming a global partner in confronting the common challenges we face around the world. Democrats need to pursue policies that encourage and support such a historical trajectory for the EU, and support those forces in Europe that are working to achieve this vision. Philosophically, the United States needs to return to the spirit that guided U.S. policy in the 1960s under President John Kennedy, when Washington was unabashedly in favor of European integration because U.S. leaders believed the process could produce a unified and Atlanticist Europe. As opposed to being hostile or agnostic about the EU as so many conservatives are, let alone opting for a policy of trying to keep it down, Washington should be seeking to help build it up while encouraging it to be as outward looking and Atlanticist as possible.

This is an issue where Democrats will have to lead. Many Republicans have been walking away from America's historical commitment to working with Europe. Some commentators on the right have asserted that U.S.-European strategic cooperation has become passé. Cooperation during the cold war, they argue, was driven by a specific strategic need in a unique historical context. It is an illusion, they claim, to think that we can extend the same kind of cooperation to other issues and areas, since our threat perceptions, interests, and strategic cultures are inevitably diverging. The United States therefore should not look to Europe as a close strategic partner in the future but recognize it has no choice but to go it alone. Some have even argued the United States should even seek to prevent the emergence of a strong and unified Europe lest it become a competitor.

The political consequences of this argument have been hugely destructive, feeding the worst crisis in U.S.-European relations in decades. This logic contributed to the Bush administration's early unilateralism and its decision to squander NATO's initial Article 5 offer of assistance in the wake of September 11. It is the rationale that legitimated Secretary of Defense Donald Rumsfeld's vision of "coalitions of the willing" replacing NATO; and which led to loose talk of opposing European integration and a policy of so-called "disaggregation" vis-à-vis the European Union. While the Bush administration in its second term has moved to repair transatlantic ties, such policies have, along with war in Iraq, contributed to the current wave of public estrangement vis-à-vis the United States in Europe. These voices and views remain a potent force in American conservative circles. Paradoxically, they find their counterparts in an unholy alliance with Europe's own unilateralists—more often found on the left on the continent—who argue that Europe must emancipate itself from American influence and go its own way.

Democrats must reject the new Euroskepticism of the American right and the anti-Americanism of the European left and reestablish themselves as the party of internationalism and alliances. For the United States, seeking a stronger Europe means greater willingness to work through the EU as well as NATO. This will require a change of attitudes: While American support was vital to the birth of the European project, Washington later became worried that the EU would either undercut NATO's key defense role or could become a vehicle for Gaullist plans to counter American influence. But those fears have proven largely unfounded, as EU expansion has diluted Gaullist dreams, and worries about European defense forces replacing NATO have faded.

The reality is that the European Union as it exists today is not yet oriented to play a major world role. It is slowly struggling toward mechanisms for collective foreign policy action. But this process is essential: It must emerge as a coherent and outward-looking actor willing and able to project influence beyond its borders. The foreign policy reforms contained in the constitution—an EU foreign minister, a diplomatic service—would have helped. These can probably be implemented despite the constitution's defeat, and they should be.

NATO is the cornerstone of the transatlantic alliance, and it must be at the center of any U.S.-European effort to fight terrorism, especially in the Middle East. Here, too, NATO can play a stabilizing role, for example, by increasing cooperation with Israel—and eventually even admitting it as a NATO member.[5] A useful precedent is the Partnership for Peace, which helped forge cooperation on security matters between NATO and Central and Eastern Europe after the breakup of the Soviet Union. Iraq has shown the limits of the Bush/Rumsfeld paradigm of unilateral, high-tech war with few troops and little postconflict reconstruction. The United States has been harshly reminded of the limits to its military power. But NATO's future importance is not based on the limits to American power, but on the fact that American and European military strengths can complement one another. America defense spending dwarfs European budgets, of course, and American capabilities are far greater, especially in high-tech weaponry and long-distance power projection. This capabilities gap has unbalanced the alliance politically, leading American military leaders to prefer unilateral action, and frustrating European leaders as they realize that their strategic weight is a fraction of their economic and political influence. So any major reform of NATO should include increased European military spending, as well as a shift toward expeditionary capabilities. In a world where virtually all threats come from outside the continent, European forces need to be deployable to and sustainable in those regions where they are most needed.

Yet there is no need for Europe to match America's military power at a time when Washington is spending more on defense than the rest of the world combined. European military power, experience, and capabilities are all still important to the United States. The Iraq war has demonstrated vividly that the American military is not well suited to the tasks of policing and stabilizing postconflict situations and rebuilding state institutions. But European nations, with different strategic doctrines, defense budgets, and military technology, already provide ten times as many peacekeepers as the United States does.[6] NATO's ability to fulfill this type of mission is currently being tested by its assumption of control of the International Security Assistance Force (ISAF) in Afghanistan. To ensure its relevance as a military alliance, NATO must be re-oriented around this transatlantic complementarity of warfighting and postconflict capabilities, with an expanded rapid reaction force, a robust stabilization and reconstruction component, and possibly a new Special Operations force.

CONCLUSION

For much of the twentieth century Europe was among the most unstable and violent continents of the world, spawning two world wars and the cold war. It was the national security problem par excellence that generations of Western statesmen and diplomats wrestled with. Today and thanks to the success of institutions like NATO and the European Union, Europe is more peaceful, democratic, and secure than at any time in recent memory. For the first time in nearly a century an American president goes to work without having to worry about war taking place on the continent.

But the debate over Europe's place in American foreign policy is as controversial as ever. There can be little doubt on which side of this debate the Democratic Party should stand and why. Democrats should support the creation of a strong, unified Europe that can become our global partner in managing the problems of the twenty-first century. The idea that the democracies of North America and Europe form a natural coalition to confront threats to our common values and interests lies at the core of what this party has stood and worked for during the last half century. When President Bill Clinton in the 1990s went to war in the Balkans and decided to expand NATO into Central and Eastern Europe, he did so not only to help lock in a new post-cold war peaceful order in Europe. He also believed that a peaceful and more unified and confident Europe could eventually step up to global responsibility as a partner with the United States.

It is time for the Democratic Party to put forth a vision and strategy for a new U.S.-European strategic alliance for the twenty-first century. We need to be as big and bold today in remaking this relationship as Democratic leaders were in creating it half a century ago.

NOTES

1. Sageman, Marc, *Understanding Terror Networks* (Philadelphia: University of Pennsylvania Press, 2004), p. 135.

2. Ackerman, Spencer, "Why American Muslims Haven't Turned to Terrorism," *New Republic*, December 12, 2005.

3. Ash, Timothy Garton, *Free World: America, Europe, and the Surprising Future of the West* (New York: Random House, 2004), p. 139. Garton Ash quotes these figures from the 2002 Arab Human Development Report (New York: UNDP, 2002), pp. 37–38.

4. Quoted in Savage, Timothy, "Europe and Islam: Crescent Waxing, Cultures Clashing," *Washington Quarterly* (Summer 2004): 33.

5. See: Asmus, Ronald D., "Contain Iran: Admit Israel to NATO," *Washington Post*, February 21, 2006.

6. Moravcsik, Andrew, "Striking a New Transatlantic Bargain," *Foreign Affairs* (July/August 2003): 87.

11

REINVENTING THE
UNITED NATIONS

Anne-Marie Slaughter

The United Nations is at a low ebb in world affairs. Notwithstanding the efforts of one of the most charismatic secretary generals in decades, the organization is mired in scandal, seemingly intractable political divisions between the permanent members of the Security Council over major global crises such as Iraq and Darfur, widespread global perceptions of either its illegitimacy or its ineffectiveness, and fierce resistance to major reform. Even its building is crumbling.

At the same time, however, the U.N. is the only truly global organization—191 members—committed by treaty to establishing and maintaining global peace and security, international human rights, democratic government, and social progress and global prosperity. Over its history, the U.N., for all its failings, has done a great deal to translate these paper promises into practice. Just as Democratic visionaries were able to forge a bipartisan coalition in 1945 to make the U.N. Charter a reality, so today must progressives re-envision what the U.N. could and must become as a global collective security organization for the twenty-first century.

This new vision should go substantially beyond the bundle of reforms developed over the past two years in a process launched by Secretary General Kofi Annan in September 2003. These include recommitting the U.N. to achieving the Millennium Development Goals; expanding the Security Council; defining terrorism and condemning it unequivocally; preventing repressive regimes from leading bodies like the Human Rights Commission; recognizing the responsibility of all governments to protect their citizens from the most serious human rights abuses and authorizing the international community to intervene when governments fail this responsibility; and streamlining the U.N.'s ponderous bureaucracy. The United States has made serious mistakes in handling even these commonsense reforms, missing opportunities to lead the organization to a new level of both representativeness and effectiveness. This is hardly surprising, given that many members of the Bush administration have been openly hostile to the United Nations. As a case in point, consider these musings by our *Ambassador* to the U.N., John Bolton: "There is no such thing as the UN. There is an international community that can be led by the only real power left in the world, and that is the United States, when it suits our interests and when we can get others to go along."[1]

To be sure, the U.N. is not an end in itself; indeed multilateralism is not an end in itself. Ever since President Woodrow Wilson, however, it has been an American article of faith, pioneered by Democratic presidents but also affirmed and advanced by many Republican administrations, that America could best advance its interests in the world by working through international rules and institutions, by committing ourselves to working with others to advance common goals and aspirations. This faith was grounded not in airy beliefs in global harmony, but rather in hardheaded calculations about how best to reassure our allies and deter our enemies.[2]

Today, it is vitally necessary to restore the damage done to U.S. interests—and to existing international institutions themselves—by the absence of U.S. leadership and even engagement. But it is not enough simply to restore the status quo ante George W. Bush. It is time to rethink and reestablish the basis for U.S. commitment to multilateral institutions based on clearly identified U.S. policy goals and clearly specified ways that international institutions can help us achieve them. On the U.N. itself, we must look beyond the current reform agenda and start afresh with a set of big ideas about the principal requirements of an effective global collective security system for the twenty-first century.

The vision set forth below emphasizes economic and social development achieved through a balance of trade and social security within nations, affirmative responsibility for stopping violence and individual accountability for starting it, and an overriding emphasis on preventing conflict before it starts. Achieving this vision would require a radically reformed United Nations with a clear mandate to stabilize and strengthen weak and failing states, and with a caucus of democracies pushing for further reform, including expansion of the Security Council. At the same time, NATO members should agree to expand NATO into a global collective security alliance. That would serve as a catalyst for U.N. reform, and provide a security alternative should reform fail, or should stalemate ever develop, even in a reformed U.N. Members of the new NATO would have to be stable liberal democracies. They would be committed to defending one another; to fighting terrorism; to nonproliferation of nuclear, chemical, and biological weapons; and to holding themselves and other nations responsible for protecting entire populations from massacre and mass atrocities.

REDEFINING COLLECTIVE SECURITY

In September 2003, five months after the United States and Britain invaded Iraq without specific authorization from the Security Council, Kofi Annan addressed the General Assembly and announced that the 191 members of the U.N. had "come to a fork in the road."[3] He harked back to "a group of far-sighted leaders, led and inspired by President Franklin D. Roosevelt, [who] were determined to make the second half of the twentieth century different from the first half."[4] They created a whole new set of international rules and institutions—the U.N., the World Bank, the International Monetary Fund (IMF), NATO, and the Organization for Economic Cooperation and Development (OECD)—to serve this purpose. But at the dawn of a new millennium, Annan argued, the nations of the world must "decide whether it is possible to continue on the basis agreed [in 1945], or whether radical changes are needed."[5]

Kofi Annan himself sought sweeping reform. Shortly after the 2003 General Assembly he appointed a sixteen-member "High-level Panel on Threats, Challenges, and Change." The panel, according to one of its members, former Australian foreign minister Gareth Evans, was informed by the view that:

> what you have among the permanent members at the moment are two nineteenth-century powers, Britain and France, two twentieth-century powers, the US and Russia, and only one twenty-first-century power, China. That might be putting it a little bit harshly, but clearly not to have an India, a Brazil, any African country, a Japan, is to have a Security Council that is not remotely representative of the balances of credible power, authority, and contribution, in the world as it is today.[6]

Yet in September 2005, when the heads of state from 191 countries gathered at a "world summit" to launch the 60th annual meeting of the General Assembly and to decide on a comprehensive reform package resulting from two years of work by the high-level panel, the secretary general himself, and various state delegations committed to reform, they produced a mouse. There was no action on a definition of terrorism, although Annan had proposed one; no action on abolishing the Human Rights Commission and replacing it with a far more legitimate body; and no action on Security Council reform.

The member states did agree to create a new Peacebuilding Commission and to recognize a responsibility on the part of all U.N. members to protect their own peoples from genocide, crimes against humanity, and serious war crimes, although without conferring this responsibility on the international community should a member state fail in its obligation. More important, from the point of view of the majority of U.N. members that are developing countries, the summit achieved a significant victory by outlining a set of development commitments and promises, thereby underlining the importance of development to international peace and security.

Overall, however, the summit fell far short of expectations, and even further short of the potential opportunities. The United States was far more committed to blocking proposals advanced by other states (such as a commitment by advanced countries to devote 0.07 percent of GDP to foreign aid) than to advancing positive reforms. The four states that sought permanent membership on the Security Council—Germany, Japan, Brazil, and India—were unable to regroup after their efforts were defeated. And at the last minute, familiar spoilers such as Cuba and Libya worked behind the scenes to block any serious reform of rules that allow dictators to head the Human Rights Commission. In short, the collective assembly lacked the will, the leadership, or the vision to rise above politics as usual.

Above all, what was missing—or at least what participants in the summit were unable to articulate—was a few big ideas to drive the scores of smaller recommendations. There was no common understanding expressed about the nature of security itself, both for humans and for states. The three ideas presented below could serve that purpose. They are distilled from the thousands of pages of paper generated by official and expert commentary on U.N. reform. Taken together, they could just propel the world toward an expanded and effective collective security system for the twenty-first century.

Global Security Requires Trade Balanced with Social Security

In 1945, following two horrific wars triggered by one state invading another, collective security meant state security—the protection of nation states from violations of their territorial integrity and political independence. The chief instrument of such protection was the pledge contained in article 2(4) of the U.N. Charter, committing all U.N. members to "refrain from the use of force against the territorial integrity or political independence of any state," except in self-defense, and the provisions in Chapter VII of the Charter giving the Security Council authority to act collectively, including the use of force, in response to "any threat to the peace, breach of the peace, or act of aggression."[7]

In 2005, after a decade witness to millions of deaths worldwide from genocide, ethnic conflict, civil war, state failure, the AIDS pandemic, and famine, in addition to thousands of deaths resulting from individual acts of terrorism, collective security means the security not only of states but also of the individuals who live within them. An organization dedicated to the creation and preservation of international peace and security must be able to recognize and stop the violence occurring within state borders as well as across them. Further, it must be able to recognize and stop preventable deaths that result not from violence but from disease and hunger on a massive scale. For human beings dying by the millions in their youth, midlife, and even childhood, the mode of death matters less than the fact of it.

In January 1941, as Europe and Asia were engulfed in war, President Franklin Roosevelt described the conflict in his State of the Union address as pitting freedom against despotism. He spoke first of "the foundations of a healthy and strong democracy."[8]

The basic things expected by our people of their political and economic systems are simple. They are:

Equality of opportunity for youth and for others.
Jobs for those who can work.
Security for those who need it.
The ending of special privilege for the few.
The preservation of civil liberties for all.
The enjoyment of the fruits of scientific progress in a wider
and constantly rising standard of living.

For a nation emerging from the Great Depression, the foundations of national security included a healthy measure of social security. So too for the world. Roosevelt next spoke of "the future days which we seek to make secure," in which "we look forward to a world founded upon four essential human freedoms." He spoke of freedom of speech and expression and freedom of worship, but also freedom from fear and freedom from want. Freedom from want, he said, "translated into world terms, means economic understandings which will secure to every nation a healthy peacetime life for its inhabitants—everywhere in the world."

In 2005, Kofi Annan self-consciously drew on President Roosevelt's text in titling the report containing his proposals for U.N. reform *In Larger Freedom*. He focused specifically on freedom from want, freedom from fear, and freedom to live in dignity. As noted above, his central point was to equate security as much with development within states as with the avoidance of violence between them. But Roosevelt had something more in mind. After the economic devastation wreaked by the Smoot-Hawley tariff in the United States and the corresponding wave of protectionism worldwide, Roosevelt sought a global system of "economic understandings" that would secure the benefits of trade to people all over the world, while at the same time allowing national governments to provide a safety net to their citizens.

In 1949, developed countries began a series of trade negotiation rounds to reduce tariffs with one another, but always with a set of waivers and escape clauses that allowed them to safeguard measures and policies they had adopted to protect their citizens at the domestic level. This is what scholar and later U.N. Under-Secretary General John Ruggie called "embedded liberalism."[9] What is most important in today's context was the basic assumption that trade would advance prosperity far more than aid; that the route to economic prosperity was empowering individual citizens to support themselves through imports and exports.

Following that formula for developing nations today would mean a different agenda for both the General Agreement on Tariffs and Trade (GATT)—which is now the World Trade Organization (WTO)—and the IMF. It would mean a far more concerted and aggressive approach to dismantling tariffs and subsidies in developed countries that block imports from poor country farmers and manufacturers. At the same time, however, it would require the IMF to take a far more nuanced approach to its demands that developing countries end subsidies that provide a social safety net for their citizens.

To generate political support for these measures in developed countries requires a deft hand as well, with a mix of gradual transitions, retraining, and aid for citizens of the countries most affected by these adjustments. Some protective measures could thus be adopted by developed country governments to cushion their citizens disproportionately bearing the brunt of this round of trade liberalization, but only based on a demonstration of real need. Small farmers would get help and retraining. Agribusiness would not.

In both cases—developing and developed countries—aid must be largely focused on enabling trade. Aid—whether foreign or domestic—must be spent on building the physical and intellectual infrastructure that will support economic activity. Governments cannot do this alone, however. As the success of micro-finance has proved, private sector actors, from banks to corporations, have an important role to play in partnership with governments and international organizations.

So where does the U.N. come in? One very important role is articulating collective aspirations and providing a framework for achieving them, as the U.N. has done with the Millennium Development Goals. A second role is to provide a forum in which developing countries can participate in shaping the global security agenda, as they in fact have done with the emphasis on human security as part of state security in the U.N. reform process. But a third, critical role concerns the particular plight of very weak and failing states—states that essentially require global rescue to prevent them from sliding into chaos, civil conflict, or simply islands of urban control in an unpoliced country. Here the U.N. is very well placed to coordinate the different kinds of political, economic, and social assistance—working together with the World Bank, the IMF, and the many specialized U.N. agencies, as well as with nongovernmental organizations and the private sector—to craft and implement both short- and long-term strategies for the provision of the most basic levels of physical and social security.

Collective Security Requires Affirmative Responsibility and Individual Accountability

In 1945, collective security meant protecting one state from another; in 2005 it often means, in practice, trying to protect groups of citizens from their own state. But within the international legal framework developed in 1945 and succeeding decades, it is not actually permissible for the U.N. to authorize the rescue of a people from genocide perpetrated by their own government unless a credible case can be made that the genocide qualifies as a breach of or threat to international peace and security. This has left the

U.N. tragically toothless in the face of massacres and systematic atrocities in places like Bosnia, Rwanda, East Timor, and Darfur.

Collective security today can no longer mean just a negative pledge to refrain from attacking other nations. It must also include an affirmative responsibility on the part of all governments toward their own citizens. Moreover, since this age of terrorism is too frequently marked by incidents of individuals from one country launching attacks against citizens of other countries, a government's affirmative responsibility should extend to protecting the citizens of other nations from attacks originating on its soil.

The mechanisms for fulfilling these twin responsibilities are very different. A government pledging to protect its own citizens must restrain its own behavior. A government pledging to protect the citizens of other nations from attacks originating on its soil must work very closely with intelligence and law enforcement officials from many different nations to fight global terrorist and organized crime networks.

In both cases, however, carrying out these responsibilities means developing effective domestic and international systems for holding individuals—both tyrants and terrorists—to account. A key example is the International Criminal Court. By accepting its jurisdiction, nations obligate themselves to prosecute any government official who is responsible for grave human rights abuses, or else face international prosecution. No longer would ethnic cleansing or other atrocities be the responsibility of the faceless "state." They would instead be attributable to individual criminals seeking to hide their actions behind the veil of sovereign authority.

Individual accountability for crimes once attributed to states is a principle that extends naturally to a government's responsibility to protect the citizens of other nations from attacks organized on its own soil. Once again, these attacks, such as those carried out on September 11, 2001, can inflict a level of damage on another state once limited to interstate or civil war. Collective security in this regard consists in cooperating and strengthening the capacities of developing nations' judicial and law enforcement systems to be able to bring to justice individual perpetrators of terrorism—Osama bin Laden, Abu Musab al-Zarqawi, or the Bali, Madrid, or Red Sea bombers.

Put Conflict Prevention First

A leitmotif of the high-level panel report and of the secretary general's report on U.N. reform was the overriding importance of focusing resources on conflict prevention. The U.N. has had a relatively good track record in this regard, although its successes often go unnoticed.[10] The old saw about "an ounce of prevention being worth a pound of cure" has been demonstrated time and again when the world's nations gather to act, or refuse to act, in the face of escalating conflict that is both expensive and difficult to quell.

Prevention isn't just a matter of law enforcement. It also requires long-term social and economic development. Citizens need to be able to imagine better lives for themselves and their children if they are to have a stake in quelling violence in their societies. Economic growth, educational opportunity, and political participation are all tools for creating a class of stakeholders in the success of the state.

At the same time, the international community needs better ways to target individuals who trigger conflict directly: by seizing power illegally and jailing political opposition, by spreading ethnic hatred and lighting the match of violence, or, in the worst cases, by organizing massacres. Here prevention requires a range of mechanisms ranging from effective international courts to rapid deployment forces. Serious efforts to provide genuine collective security must meet the challenge of prevention on both fronts.

GETTING THERE FROM HERE: REAL REFORM AND REALISTIC ALTERNATIVES

The U.N. cannot be significantly reformed without major changes to the membership of the Security Council to reflect the configuration of global power in the twenty-first century, rather than the nineteenth and twentieth centuries. A modern Security Council would include one or more seats for the United States, the EU, Russia, China, India, Japan, Brazil, South Africa, and a host of additional countries on at least a rotating basis. For states to have a real stake in U.N. rules and procedures, they must have a stake in the U.N. itself. This fact is widely recognized in the abstract; U.N. members have been talking about and halfheartedly negotiating Security Council reform for decades, including an intensive effort by Germany, Japan, Brazil, and India in the summer of 2005. Yet nothing ever happens. Existing permanent members see no reason to rock the boat and possibly risk their privileges. And each aspiring member triggers as much opposition as support, both from one or more permanent members and from other General Assembly members.

It is time to break the mold. Real reform of the U.N. will not happen without a major shift in the incentives of current U.N. members to make it happen. The best way to achieve that shift is to begin developing realistic alternatives to the current system for accomplishing the goals most critical to international peace and security. The development of these alternatives will raise the stakes of successful U.N. reform immediately. They will either create the pressure necessary for such reform, permitting the continuation of the U.N. as the preeminent international peace and security organization of the twenty-first century, or they will form the basis of a new international security architecture if the U.N. proves incapable of adapting itself to twenty-first-century challenges.

The first step is to focus the U.N. much more on the nonmilitary side of security; on the provision of economic, social and political assistance to prevent conflicts from breaking out, and to stabilize and strengthen fragile social and political institutions. The U.N. specialized agencies and units— from refugees to disaster relief to elections—have developed substantial expertise from experience in virtually every region of the world. The proposed new Peacebuilding Commission is a very promising beginning. A second step is to establish a caucus of democracies within the U.N. that would push hard for Security Council reform along the lines of "Plan B" proposed by the high-level panel—an arrangement that would ensure that the major powers from every region would be continually represented.

But the third and crucial step is to reinvent NATO as the core of a global collective security organization of free nations. Japan, Australia, New Zealand, South Africa, and India could all join NATO. Indeed, several prominent former government officials in Britain, Germany, and the United States have already proposed that Israel join NATO. Just as the OECD transcended its European origins, so could the North Atlantic Treaty Organization become the New Atlantic Treaty Organization, with a group of Atlantic countries at its core, but extending far beyond. Ideally, the new NATO would function as a genuine security arm of a genuinely reformed United Nations. But if that proved impossible to achieve, then it would become an alternative to the U.N. for situations requiring the collective use of force, while the U.N. and the Bretton Woods organizations addressed nonmilitary security.

New Mandate for the United Nations

In September 2005, Senator Joseph Biden (D-DE) argued that the U.N. "is not capable of ending wars in our times, intervening in ways to prevent war most times." Instead, he proposed reorienting "Bretton Woods and the U.N. to the purpose of stabilizing weak states."[11] This makes sense: Weak or failing states are unable to perform basic functions of providing security from violence for their citizens, policing their borders, and enforcing their laws. The result is the creation of havens not only for terrorists but for criminal operations of every sort, the frequent displacement of large populations as anarchy looms, the destruction of the environment, the spread of disease, and frequently the creeping destabilization of neighboring states.

But what would "stabilizing weak states" mean in practice? Five things:

First, a far greater focus on conflict prevention than intervention. That could in turn mean redefining "threats to international security" worthy of Security Council notice to include a set of indicators of government disintegration.

Second, the development of peacekeeping forces trained not to police a ceasefire between armies, but to stop random violence from rebels, criminals, and gangs—enough to give governments and civilians a chance to regain and strengthen civic order.

Third, greater autonomy and resources for U.N. entities such as the High Commissioner for Refugees, the U.N. Development Program, the U.N. Environmental Program, and the U.N. Elections Office to coordinate strategies to sustain and strengthen weak political and economic institutions in failing states.

Fourth, reform of the Economic and Social Council and a mandate for the Council to take charge of efforts to achieve the Millennium Development Goals, working with governments, corporations, and nongovernmental organizations. AIDS, illiteracy, environmental degradation, random violence, organized crime—all the threats to human security listed in the summit declaration—would form a new security agenda to be implemented through trade, finance, and aid.[12]

Fifth, a requirement that membership on the Economic and Social Council be based on a demonstrated commitment to development goals and a concrete pledge of resources (this pledge would be greater for fully industrialized countries than for newly developed or developing countries). Such pledges would require a completely overhauled audit system for U.N. expenditures, of the kind proposed by the U.S.–U.N. Task Force funded by Congress and convened by the U.S. Institute of Peace in the spring of 2005.

DEMOCRACY AND SECURITY

Even if the U.N. were to focus on stabilizing and strengthening weak and failing states, the world would still need an organization dedicated to preventing, containing, and stopping mass violence, whether within or between states. The question is whether the U.N. can actually meet that challenge in the twenty-first century. To find out, we need a two-pronged strategy. The first step is to create a caucus of democratic nations within the U.N. that could press for reform, and provide, in cases of Security Council dysfunction, an alternative forum for legitimating collective action. The second is to create a fallback alternative through expanding NATO as a global collective security alliance.[13] Both options, within and outside the U.N., will help to create the pressure and political will necessary for substantial and sweeping U.N. reform. And if they fail, the democratic nations of the world will still have a collective security institution that works.

The United States, the EU, Japan, South Africa, India, South Korea, Australia, New Zealand, and Canada should join with other like-minded states to create a caucus of liberal democratic states within the General Assembly. The point of the caucus would be to cross-cut the power of the regional groupings and to create a strong constituency for reform and continued oversight of U.N. management practices. This group would also have a strong stake in bolstering the U.N.'s mandate to strengthen weak and failing states.

The key question is which countries get to join the democracy caucus. At a conference in Warsaw in 1999, the Clinton administration strongly encouraged the formation of the Community of Democracies, whose "convening group" included South Korea, India, the United States, Mexico, Chile, Poland, the Czech Republic, Portugal, Mali, and South Africa.

Since then, the Community of Democracies has rapidly expanded to include over one hundred countries, many of which would not strike casual observers as worthy of the term. Ivo Daalder and James Lindsay have suggested using Freedom House's definition of a mature democracy (a country where a return to autocracy is "unthinkable") in their proposal for an independent Alliance of Democracies;[14] alternatively, the caucus could adopt the definition of a liberal democracy currently used by the EU in admitting new members.[15]

At the same time, NATO forms an existing core of what could become a global alliance of democratic nations pledged to protect one another's security. NATO already commits its members to a pledge of genuine collective security and requires its members to be free nations. Members of a new expanded NATO would have to meet these criteria and would commit to the following principles:

- not to use force against one another and to come to one another's aid if attacked
- to agree on a common definition of terrorism and to commit to fighting it through every available means, including acceptance of responsibility for apprehending terrorists operating on national territory
- to forswear chemical and biological weapons and to prevent the spread of nuclear weapons. Members of the Union possessing nuclear weapons would commit to no first use, thereby making clear that their purpose is only as a deterrent.
- to create a standing force comprised of designated national units ready to intervene to stop mass violence at the request of a majority of the members of regional organizations such as the African Union.
- to support regional and international tribunals to bring to justice perpetrators of genocide, crimes against humanity, and serious and sustained war crimes.
- to guarantee civil and political rights for all their citizens and to accept oversight of compliance with these obligations by the Union

To expand NATO along these lines would obviously require changes in the North Atlantic Treaty itself. A more globally inclusive NATO would have a powerful inductive effect, akin to that of NATO and the EU today. Smaller nations would have every incentive to meet the criteria for membership in order to benefit from the collective security provisions. Over time, larger nations would have similar incentives to be able to play a role in taking responsibility for global security.

This is a far-reaching proposal. But should Canada, the EU, and the United States so decide, a new and more effective collective security organization could quickly be born. Equally important, even starting to plan along these lines would create an enormous catalyst for equally far-reaching U.N. reform.

CONCLUSION

The United Nations was born out of the ashes of the worst war the world has ever seen. It was a vision of a new world, in which nations would rule out the use of force in their international relations and in which all the nations of the world would come together in an effort to solve common problems. The U.N. has fallen far short of its founders' hopes, but not of their realistic expectations: the Security Council was composed in part of five permanent members wielding vetoes precisely because the framers of the U.N. Charter understood that a global security institution that ignored the will of great powers was doomed to failure. Often those great powers have indeed stalemated the institution. Yet at many other junctures the U.N. has provided an indispensable forum, great expertise, and global legitimacy for collective efforts to tackle security crises.

The inevitability that any vision of a better world will always be imperfectly realized, often radically so, must not stifle our imagination and our will to tackle current problems. The security of the nations of the world is more collective than ever, as a simple corollary of our extraordinary interdependence. Our hope of future progress depends on transforming the empirical fact of collective security into collective institutions designed to counter common threats and the collective will to make them work.

NOTES

1. Kettle, Martin, "Blair May Be First Buddy, But It's Time He Faced the Facts," *Guardian*, September 12, 2002.

2. Ikenberry, John, *After Victory: Institutions, Strategic Restraint, and the Rebuilding of Order after Major Wars* (Princeton, N.J.: Princeton University Press, 2001).

3. Speech by Secretary General Kofi Annan to the U.N. General Assembly, September 23, 2003, New York. Available at www.un.org/webcast/ga/58/statements/sg2eng030923.

4. Annan, speech.

5. Annan, speech.

6. Speech by Gareth Evans to the Institute of Peace and Conflict Studies, December 15, 2004, New Delhi. Available at www.crisisgroup.org/home/index.cfm?id=3205&l=1.

7. United Nations Charter, Chapter VII, Article 39. Available at www.un.org/aboutun/charter/chapter7.htm.

8. Roosevelt, Franklin Delano, State of the Union Address, January 6, 1941, Washington, D.C. Available at www.libertynet.org/~edcivic/fdr.html.

9. Ruggie, John Gerard, "International Regimes, Transactions and Change: Embedded Liberalism in the Postwar Economic Order," *International Organization* 36, no. 2 (Spring 1982).

10. See, for example, "The Human Security Report 2005," Human Security Centre, University of British Columbia (New York: Oxford University Press, 2005); Dobbins, James, *The UN's Role in Nation-Building: From the Congo to Iraq* (Santa Monica: RAND Corporation, 2005).

11. Speech by Senator Joseph Biden to New American Foundation conference, September 6, 2005, Washington, D.C. Available at http://biden.senate.gov/newsroom/details.cfm?id=245275&&.

12. Former President Bill Clinton's Global Initiative is dedicated to similar aims, working primarily with corporations and nongovernmental organizations. www.clintonglobalinitiative.org/.

13. The weekend before the September 2005 U.N. General Assembly meeting, *New York Times* reporter James Traub published an article proposing a new Peace and Security Union. ("The Un-UN," *New York Times Magazine*, September 11, 2005.) In his proposal, membership in the PSU would be limited to states who could commit to the following three principles: 1) Terrorism must be unambiguously defined and confronted both through police and, where necessary, military means; 2) states have a responsibility to protect their own citizens, which in turn confers an obligation on the membership to intervene, at times through armed force, in the case of atrocities; 3) extreme poverty and disease, which threaten the integrity of states, require a collective response. I have adapted and built on this idea.

14. Daalder, Ivo H., and James M. Lindsay, "An Alliance of Democracies," *Washington Post*, May 23, 2004.

15. In June 1993, the Copenhagen European Council set forth the following conditions for the accession of countries into the EU: "Membership requires that the candidate country has achieved stability of institutions guaranteeing democracy, the rule of law, human rights and respect for and protection of minorities, the existence of a functioning market economy as well as the capacity to cope with competitive pressure and market forces within the Union. Membership presupposes the candidate's ability to take on the obligations of membership including adherence to the aims of political, economic and monetary union." European Council in Copenhagen—Conclusions of the Presidency, June 21-22, 1993), p. 14, available at http://ue.eu.int/ueDocs/cms_Data/docs/pressData/en/ec/72921.pdf.

V

BUILDING OUR
ECONOMIC STRENGTH

12

THE ECONOMIC FOUNDATION OF NATIONAL SECURITY

David J. Rothkopf

The bedrock upon which U.S. national security is built is the strength of the U.S. economy and the vitality of our society. Maintaining them is the key to both ensuring the future of our way of life and to defeating our enemies.

This belief has roots that stretch back throughout the first century and a half of U.S. existence, when economic concerns were seen by U.S. leaders to be the primary driver behind international policies. More recently, it manifested itself during the formative years of U.S. cold war policy. In his historic 1946 "Long Telegram" from Moscow, George F. Kennan helped lay the groundwork for America's grand strategy for containing Soviet expansion. Although he wrote during a far different era, his insights continue to resonate as we debate how to respond to the new threat of global terror.

In assessing the danger that communism posed to the United States, Kennan concluded that "much depends on health and vigor of our own society."

"World communism is like [a] malignant parasite which feeds only on diseased tissue," he wrote. "This is [the] point at which domestic and foreign policies meet. Every courageous and incisive measure to solve internal problems of our own society, to improve self-confidence, discipline, morale, and community spirit of our own people, is a diplomatic victory over Moscow worth a thousand diplomatic notes and joint communiqués."

Elsewhere in his memorandum, Kennan underscored the importance of offering other nations "a much more positive and constructive picture of the sort of world we would like to see than we have put forward in past."

"We must have courage and self-confidence to cling to our own methods and conceptions of human society," Kennan continued. "After all, the greatest danger that can befall us in coping with this problem . . . is that we shall allow ourselves to become like those with whom we are coping."[1]

The analogies between our postwar communist enemies and those who now want to supplant our global influence with their own are clear. Certainly, the threat posed by terrorists worldwide is hardly that posed by an archrival nuclear superpower. Yet Kennan's fundamental points are still valid. Indeed, his recognition that our society's health and vigor were vital to overcoming the most grievous threat our nation ever faced underscores how critical they remain in our current situation.

Kennan, as venerable a policymaker as any we have had in the past century, realized that national security policy must begin by cultivating the economic and social wellsprings of our strength. If we fail to do so, he warned, we risk becoming the authors of our own undoing.

It is not an exaggeration to state that this is precisely the mistake the Bush administration has made in its response to the horrific attacks on September 11, 2001. Rather than shoring up the foundations of our economic and social strength, the administration's policy choices are instead undermining them. Most glaringly, the unprecedented combination of large tax cuts in the face of heavy wartime expenditures has led to skyrocketing deficits, over-reliance on foreign creditors, an exploding trade gap, and untold social opportunity costs.

THE ECONOMIC COSTS OF TERRORISM

The 9/11 attacks were costly on many levels. The human losses were staggering, their impact on our society incalculable in mere numbers. Economically, the New York City Partnership assessment of the losses, cited by the Government Accountability Office (GAO) as the most comprehensive analysis, put the total direct and indirect costs of the attacks at $83 billion. It estimated that $67 billion was covered by insurance, federal payments, or increased economic activity, suggesting the economic net damage to the city and others affected by the attacks was $16 billion.[2]

But the stark reality is that the Bush administration's economic choices following the attacks have been vastly more damaging than anything Osama bin Laden could ever have dreamed of—and this even though bin Laden himself asserted that he sought to sap America's strength by bleeding its economic resources.

Were bin Laden to make the case that he is the author of the greatest damage to the U.S. economy, in addition to the $83 billion cited above, he might claim responsibility for federal spending on the war on terror. He could certainly claim credit for the $73 billion that the Congressional Research Service (CRS) reports was spent through the end of fiscal 2005 on the war in Afghanistan. He might even claim credit for the $214 billion that CRS estimates has been spent in Iraq. He might even take full credit for the total $357 billion that the CRS estimates was spent through fiscal 2005 on the "War on Terror," including the war in Iraq.[3] Of course, he would be disappointed were he to try to claim responsibility for spending on the Department of Homeland Security. Its total costs are actually equal to or less than its component parts when they were housed in other agencies. Still, $83 billion for one attack plus $357 billion (so far) for the war it triggered is a fairly substantial economic toll: $440 billion, an astounding return on an operation that by some estimates cost less than a half million dollars.

Such spending has negative effects beyond the simple allocation of dollars. Because we are running a deficit and have to borrow the money, there is the cost of debt service. The war is likely to go on for some time, producing an additional cost already estimated to be at least $500 billion (a number that is certain to go up). And then there is the opportunity cost of not spending the money in other ways that might have brought us better economic, strategic, or social returns.

To be fair, a Democratic or different Republican administration certainly would have gone after bin Laden in Afghanistan and probably would have conducted a similar war there. The decision to undertake a "war of choice" in Iraq, however, and to spend what may well amount to $400 to $500 billion over time[4] (by comparison, in inflation-adjusted terms World War I cost $200 billion) was mainly a matter of the Bush administration's discretion.

Clearly, Americans will spend whatever it takes to defend our nation and prevail against global terror. But we must acknowledge that the post–9/11 shift from domestic to security-related priorities imposes severe opportunity costs. From 2001 to 2004, for example, overall discretionary spending within the budget shifted from 50 percent defense and international and 50 percent domestic, to 55 percent defense and international and 45 percent domestic—amounting to a difference of nearly $50 billion. Over the same period, spending on major defense capital and infrastructure increased by 34 percent, while non-defense public physical capital investments grew at half that rate.[5] Our economic growth and ability to compete globally depends heavily on such domestic capital expenditures. One of our long-range economic goals, therefore, must be to redress today's imbalance between security spending and investment in future growth.

SELF-INFLICTED ECONOMIC DAMAGE

The administration's relentless and indefensible commitment to tax cuts during a time of fiscal contraction and burgeoning deficits delivered an even worse body blow to our economy and, consequently, to our strength and security.

Ill-considered by any responsible fiscal standard, these cuts had grievous consequences. They limited spending crucial to our competitiveness and strength, dramatically increased our dependence on foreign capital (most of which comes from a handful of Asian nations), and worsened inequity within the United States, producing precisely the kind of social strains against which Kennan warned.

President George W. Bush inherited a balanced federal budget when he took office in 2001. Indeed, in 1999 the federal government had a total surplus of $125.5 billion and an on-budget surplus of $1.9 billion. By 2004, it had a total deficit of $412.1 billion and an on-budget deficit of $567.4 billion.

The Bush tax cuts' costs are far more damaging in the long run than even those dramatic numbers suggest. In April 2004, the well-respected Center on Budget and Policy Priorities (CBPP) wrote, "In the absence of the tax cuts, the deficit picture during the coming decade would look very different. Without the tax cuts, the deficit would be under $100 billion in most years. With the tax cuts, the deficit is projected to grow to more than $675 billion by the end of the decade."[6]

That additional red ink will force programs to be cut or scaled back, damage our competitive edge, and compromise our national security. For example, the money lost to tax cuts would have paid for 59 percent of the cost of all federal legislation passed since 2001, and twice the combined cost of defense, homeland security, and international spending increases.

The real pain of the tax cuts is yet to come. The CBPP estimates that the total costs of the cuts and the interest we'll pay on the money we borrow to make up for them will approach $5 trillion for the period between the first cuts in 2001 and 2014. By that final year, the interest on borrowing to cover the cuts alone is estimated to be $218 billion a year—the average annual cost of the first three years of the war in Iraq. In other words, 1.2 percent of the nation's entire 2014 gross domestic product (GDP) will be devoted to paying for this extraordinary act of ill-considered national self-indulgence.[7] To put that figure into starker perspective, we dedicate roughly 3.3 percent of our GDP to paying for our defense budgets. When you consider that Japan only spends one percent of its annual budget on defense, Germany 1.5 percent, and the U.K. only 2.4 percent, it is even clearer how significant this decision is, given the resources typically available to even rich governments around the world.

The picture becomes even more disturbing when you assess the impact of all the tax cuts implemented and currently suggested by the administration. According to a paper by Friedman, Carlitz, and Kamen published in early 2005,[8] over the next seventy-five years these existing and proposed cuts would produce revenue losses three to six times the size of the projected long-term shortfall in U.S. Social Security resources—one of those numbers that politicians from both parties run from as soon as it surfaces in conversation. (The president's ill-fated proposal to "deal with" the Social Security problem was estimated to produce almost $4.5 trillion of additional borrowing during its first twenty years of operation.)

In 2005 the Congressional Budget Office (CBO) suggested that during the next ten years the administration's tax policies would push total deficits $1.6 trillion higher than the budget office's baseline projections.[9] That's five times the cost of the war on terror to date. If the Iraq war ends up costing between $400 billion and $500 billion, as it very well might, that means the tax choices made by this administration could amount to $2 trillion dollars of deficit spending over the next decade.

Some reputable economists argue that the U.S. fiscal deficit as a percentage of GDP is manageable in historical terms. But during the Bush years, the fiscal deficit has not been the only thing that has burgeoned. We have also seen a breathtaking increase in the "other" deficit, the trade gap. Already $378 billion annually when Bush took office, it is on pace to pass $700 billion when the final numbers for fiscal 2005 come in.[10] At the same time, our current account deficit has grown to almost six percent of our GDP (although analysts differ about the degree to which the fiscal deficit and other factors play in this growth). In turn, this unprecedented current account deficit has raised our net indebtedness to foreign investors to unheard-of levels. As Federal Reserve Vice Chairman Roger Ferguson noted in a recent speech, "in 1985 our foreign assets were about equal to our foreign liabilities, so that our net international investment position was roughly zero. By 1995, our investment position had deteriorated to negative 4 percent of GDP, and by 2004, we estimate this negative position to have reached about one-fourth of GDP. If current account deficits continue to boost the negative international investment position, eventually the cost of servicing that position, which so far has been quite modest, would rise to an unsustainable level."[11]

So, who is paying for all of these deficits? Clearly, given the above statistics and our nonexistent national savings rate (remarkable and disturbing given the structural deficits associated with our aging population), it is not U.S. taxpayers. To whom must we turn when we seek money to recover from natural disasters, for wars, schools, or our seniors' health care and retirement benefits? As it turns out, our deficits, our self-indulgent choices, our payoffs to the rich for their financial support for Republican politicians, are being paid for primarily by foreign economic competitors.

According to the CBO, "almost all official purchases of U.S. assets were made by a handful of Asian governments"—notably Japan and China (including Hong Kong) as well as South Korea and Taiwan.[12] As of October 2005, according to the Treasury Department, Japan held $681 billion in U.S. securities, with China (including Hong Kong) holding almost $300 billion, Taiwan $71.5 billion, and South Korea $63.8 billion.[13] China's holdings of long-term securities have increased 252 percent since 2000, Japan's by 157 percent, South Korea's by 113 percent, and Taiwan's by 151 percent, whereas other formerly important players' holdings such as the U.K.'s and Germany's have remained fairly stable.[14]

GETTING RID OF BLANCHE DUBOIS ECONOMICS

This growing dependence on economic competitors (and in the case of the China, a potentially important geopolitical rival) is an obvious national security concern. How long will they continue to finance our overspending? What would happen if they curtailed such support?

All of these nations sell us goods and services and thus finance our debt out of self-interest. Still, our increasing requirement that they "approve" our policy decisions by continuing to write us big checks is a shift of historic proportions in America's relative strength in the world. (Remember, it was only twenty years ago that we were not a net borrower.) This Blanche Dubois international economic policy, in which we stake our future on the "kindness of strangers," is profoundly reckless.

The shadow that current policies cast over our national future grows darker still when we consider that America faces new competitive threats from around the world—often from the same countries upon whom we are financially dependent. More than a billion workers will enter the global labor force during the next decade, virtually all from the developing world. China has become the economic engine of Asia and soon will become the world's fourth largest economy. Opportunistic (mostly Democratic) politicians have vastly overplayed the outsourcing of U.S. jobs to Asian countries. Still, one cannot ignore their ability to train vast numbers of scientists and engineers and offer their services at a low cost. Nor can one ignore international corporations' and natural-resource providers' increasing dependence on these rapidly growing countries for sales and profits. All of this suggests we should ramp up spending on our own training programs, the expansion and modernization of our own infrastructure, the enhancement of our own research and development capacity, and an improved education system that keeps our kids in school year round and prepares them to compete internationally.

But, of course, we can't do those things, cut taxes, and spend ever-increasing amounts fighting wars of choice in distant locations. Our next president will have to make hard choices to overcome the dreadful record of the Bush administration, which has done more than any recent presidency to undermine the economic and social foundations of our national security.

The American people are uncomfortable with such hard choices. We have been blessed during our lifetimes with sufficient growth and other advantages that have enabled us to always rise to the challenges we have faced. Even today, our stability, innovation, great international brands, quality workforce, and history of economic dynamism have produced enough faith among global investors that we can continue to borrow, thus numbing the pain that would otherwise be caused by our deteriorated financial position.

Rapid economic growth would do the same. But such growth requires foresight: an acknowledgment that our dependence on foreign lenders, our unsustainable spending levels, our spending choices that degrade our competitiveness, our lack of savings, and our unwillingness to grapple with structural deficits are all threats greater than anything al Qaeda could muster. They impair our ability to lead, to create jobs for our children, to preserve our social fabric, and even to protect ourselves.

In fact, they are threats to what Kennan called "the health and vigor of our own society." If we do not address them now, if we continue to mainline the drug of borrowing to provide for the feel-good politics of today, we expose our society to dangers that far outstrip anything a terrorist could imagine.

As former Treasury Secretary Robert Rubin observed in a 2005 speech before the Institute for International Economics:

> Entitlement programs, defense spending, and interest on the federal debt constitute roughly 80 percent of the federal budget. Beyond these functions, the American people want and need government to maintain many activities, such as law enforcement, education, basic research, infrastructure, and many other programs. Meanwhile, tax revenues are roughly 16 percent of GDP, the lowest ratio since roughly the 1960s. Given these realities, reestablishing sound fiscal conditions will be exceedingly difficult both substantively and politically and will require major change, not adjustments at the margin or the time-honored resort of both political parties to unrealistic budgeting projections.[15]

As Rubin so accurately suggests, America's economic security depends on the same crucial element as its national security: courage. Halfway measures, timidity, pandering, and dishonesty are fatal flaws in waging war, whether on terror or any other enemy. So too will they invite defeat economically.

The next president and Congress will face critical choices that far transcend those that arose in the wake of 9/11. They must provide the American people with the kind of leadership we need today and that we owe to our children. They must move beyond incrementalist policies, cease catering to special interests, and embrace bold ideas to enhance our national economic security. These include:

Restore Fiscal Sanity

Budget deficits limit our choices and make us ever more dependent on the foreign lenders underwriting our national spending spree. The Bush tax cuts must be rolled back and the bipartisan consensus that underpinned the fiscal discipline of the 1990s must be restored. We must return to efforts to contain the size of government. A remarkable 377,000 federal jobs were eliminated during the years 1993–2000, a trend reversed by the Bush administration.[16] We need to cut back corporate welfare and wasteful entitlement programs and invest in education, infrastructure, research and development, and energy independence to keep America strong and competitive. (This doesn't mean being short-sighted. Sometimes major investment, like a massive national program to achieve real energy independence, will produce major savings in the long run. Such an investment could help eliminate the costs associated with maintaining our interests in the Middle East, reduce the cost of energy we purchase, reduce costs associated with environmental degradation, and at the same time create new business growth and jobs that will benefit the economy and build the tax base.)

This will mean striking the right balance on the defense budget. On the one hand, we must invest in the capabilities we will need to meet the challenges of this century. We must expand programs that make us more flexible, able to deploy more troops more rapidly to more places in the world, and ensure our leadership with the war-fighting and peacekeeping technologies of tomorrow. Yet, as we do so, we must also recognize that even if we are at war, wasteful spending must stop. It is a terrible drag on limited resources and thus, in itself, a threat to our security. Politicians must stop reflexively defending local military bases and favored procurement programs that benefit their districts and states. There is nothing patriotic about underwriting programs that siphon money from the places we really need to spend it. Every senior commander in the Pentagon knows there is plenty of waste to be targeted. Spending imprudently is worse than not spending at all.

Embrace Real Tax Reform

It was a big mistake to let one party co-opt the initiative for tax reform. It was a bigger mistake to let irresponsible tax-cutting masquerade as reform. The U.S. tax code is a national embarrassment; it is literally incomprehensible to the average American. It must be simplified to create incentives for savings and investment and to encourage those struggling to make ends meet to keep working toward a better future.

The rebuilt code should reflect three principles: fairness (the rich and powerful who had their taxes custom tailored as neatly as their suits need to begin pulling their weight), fiscal responsibility (we should produce the revenue we need while containing the size of government), and a focus on the future (we should create incentives to enhance our strength in years to come). Our focus since 2001 has been the opposite: irresponsible overspending, tax cuts for those who need them least, and borrowing from our children and our grandchildren to pay for our inability to make hard decisions today.

Create a National Competitiveness Strategy

Our generation is not automatically entitled to the global leadership role that our parents bequeathed to us. We will face new rivals and challenges in the twenty-first century that will test us in many ways. History, luck, and an exclusive reliance on the mysterious forces of the marketplace will not guarantee us success in the decades ahead.

Agrarian America remade itself into the industrial giant of the twentieth century through a powerful, visionary partnership of business leaders, workers, scientists, educators, and policy makers. Now we must create a new partnership to reinvent ourselves yet again into the postindustrial leader of tomorrow. Services already represent 70 percent of our economy, yet we hardly know what this means in terms of where to invest for the future, how to create the good jobs of tomorrow, and how to compete with nations and regions with more workers, bigger potential markets, and new pools of scientific, engineering, and other technical capacity.

We need to reassess our comparative advantages in this changing world. We need to get a firmer grasp of government's role in helping business do what it does best. This will mean more spending, as noted earlier, in education and infrastructure. It will also mean reconsidering the basic paradigms in each of these areas and others. We need to begin seeing education as a lifelong pursuit. We need to put the agrarian schedules of limited school days and entire summers off behind us. We need to train more scientists and students who speak more languages and understand the rest of the world better.

We also need to maintain our technological leadership by welcoming the best and the brightest from around the world to America and enticing them to stay. We need to put broadband infrastructure in place and give every child access to the Internet. We need to end absurd debates about whether we should be teaching science in our science classrooms and recognize that when we pass laws based on the marriage of dubious science and dubious theology on issues such as stem cells, we allow other nations to become the leaders in that field of research.

Renew U.S. Economic Leadership

Over the last six decades, U.S. leaders crafted international agreements and built international institutions that regulated and stabilized the global economy. Today, global progress in trade liberalization has stalled. Despite its relative youth, the World Trade Organization (WTO) is in dire need of reform, as are virtually all the international institutions we created in the wake of World War II. As we finalize the Doha Round of Trade reforms built on major and massive elimination of costly agricultural subsidies worldwide, we should also make creating the next generation of rules governing trade and investment—WTO 2.0—a top agenda item. Efforts to conclude regional trade deals like the Free Trade Area of the Americas also need to be revitalized because of the potential for job creation and regional growth, and thus enhanced stability and security, and reduced tensions on the immigration front.

We must assess the failures and missteps of international financial institutions and reinvent them to address the greatest single threat to world peace in the century ahead: the growing chasm that separates the world's haves and have-nots. Failed and failing states are magnets for terrorists and criminals of every stripe. We need to create stakeholders in globalization and global growth among the next generation, nine out of ten of whom live in the developing world. We need to reconcile the divergent needs of the aging north and the youthful south; to find opportunities for complementarity, rather than new sources of tension.

We can't rise to these responsibilities by denigrating the U.N. and other international institutions, by obeying international laws and systems we have created only when it suits us, and by avoiding investing time and money in reinvigorating these critical systems. We must step up to the great and difficult leadership challenge of shaping an international system. At times this challenge may require us to cede some authority to ensure its functioning, and to work within the community of nations rather than above or apart from it. This is a hard sell on Main Street. But we must recognize that the values that are required are precisely those we apply in our own communities, the places where we live, in which we abhor the dominance of self-interested bullies and seek justice as aggressively as we promote individual freedoms.

We must also recognize that twenty-first-century leadership will make new demands on us. For example, at current rates of growth, China's economy will outgrow ours before midcentury. Our focus must not be on trying to constrain its ascension. Rather it must be on understanding that to lead in the future we will have to do it in concert with a new cadre of great nations. Further, we need to formulate policy doctrines for an era in which the great challenge will be that many of our greatest rivals are countries with which we share a deep interdependence. This is very different from the past, when our competition with the Soviet enemy was essentially a zero-sum game: We gain, they lose. China, for example, is a potential rival but also one of our most essential partners. This will require sophistication, nuance, and open-mindedness on the part of policymakers, and that will run contrary to many of the simplistic and emotional arguments traditionally offered by politicians seeking good applause lines.

Declare Energy Independence

We are trapped in the quagmire of the Middle East because of our dependence on foreign oil. Virtually all projections call for that dependence to grow in the decades ahead. Virtually none call for peace or stability to arrive easily or cheaply or any time soon in the region.

It is time to create a national effort to end our dependency on foreign oil. Simple solutions like enhancing fuel efficiency in vehicles can have massive beneficial consequences. The cultivation of alternative fuels and alternative fuel technologies, incentives for the cheaper production of ever more efficient hybrid vehicles, a real exploration of the potential of hydrogen and other experimental approaches are all needed. The potential returns warrant an immediate long-term investment. Now is the time for a massive national commitment to declare energy independence for our children, a program drawing on our scientific, technological, business, and other national resources to comprehensively enhance conservation, promote new technologies, promote alternative energy resources, reform our energy and power distribution systems, enhance competition, create incentives for innovation, and put into place penalties for waste.

Address the Realities of an Aging Society

We can no longer continue to shrug off the contributors to our structural deficit that politicians of both parties have failed to address. We must fix Social Security and eliminate the threat of its bankruptcy. We must calculate and close the gap between what we have promised to pay in retirement health coverage costs and what the real costs will be. The retirement age must be raised to fit today's life expectancies.

We also need to recognize the potential threat posed by underfunded pension programs and government's inability to meet that challenge. We cannot build a system around the idea that bankruptcy is the solution that wipes the slate clean no matter the human cost, or the belief that there is a permanent call on government capital when corporate managers fail to spend or plan wisely. We can take small steps with big consequences—like prioritizing pension obligations above debt obligations in the bankruptcy payment hierarchy, a change that will force creditors and equity holders alike to take the problem more seriously. We should also make the pension system more transparent. Currently, although the government is on the hook to cover pension shortfalls, taxpayers can't even see what the health of individual corporate pension funds is.

Finally, we need to recognize that our broken health care system is a security risk, and a drag on our economy. The only defense against bioterror is a health care system that protects all Americans. Further, given that health care represents a greater portion of the cost of a car than steel, we must acknowledge that placing the burden of providing national health coverage on companies puts us at a huge competitive disadvantage internationally. We are the only developed country that does not have a form of effective national health coverage and it is hurting us on many levels. Despite missteps in the past, a new program providing health care to all is essential, but so too are efforts to make the system simpler and more efficient.

Since the republic's founding, America's security has been built upon courage in the face of great challenges. We have retreated from that tradition during the past five years. A further retreat would be disastrous. It is time to once again mount an offensive: Define our goals, understand our position, summon the will we require, and move forward. This will require leadership, a commodity in short supply in either political party today. We can only hope that today's leaders will depart from politics as usual and begin feeding the wellsprings of America's strength—which after all is where all national security planning should begin in the first place.

NOTES

1. Kennan, George, *Memoirs*, Vol. 1: 1925–1950, (Boston: Little, Brown, 1967), pp. 547–59.
2. "Working Together to Accelerate New York's Recovery: Economic Impact

Analysis of the September 11th Attack on New York City," New York City Partnership and Chamber of Commerce, November 2001, www.nycp.org/reports/ImpactStudy .pdf.

3. "The Cost of Iraq, Afghanistan, and Increased Base Security Since 9/11," Congressional Research Service, October 7, 2005, www.opencrs.com/rpts/RL33110_2005 1007.pdf.

4. "Estimated Costs of Continuing Operations in Iraq and Other Operations in the Global War on Terrorism," Congressional Budget Office, letter to Senator Kent Conrad, June 25, 2004, www.cbo.gov/showdoc.cfm?index=5587&sequence=0.

5. "The Budget and Economic Outlook: Fiscal Years 2006–2015," Congressional Budget Office, January 25, 2005, Appendix F, Table F-7, www.cbo.gov/showdoc.cfm? index=1821&sequence=0.

6. Shapiro, Isaac, and Joel Friedman, "Tax Returns: A Comprehensive Assessment of the Bush Administration's Record on Cutting Taxes," The Center on Budget and Policy Priorities, April 23, 2004, www.cbpp.org/4-14-04tax-sum.htm.

7. Shapiro and Friedman, "Tax Returns."

8. Friedman, Joel, Ruth Carlitz, and David Kamin, "Extending the Tax Cuts Would Cost $2.1 Trillion Through 2015," Center on Budget and Policy Priorities, February 2, 2005, www.cbpp.org/2-2-05tax.htm.

9. "Preliminary Analysis of the President's Budget Request for 2006," letter to Senator Thad Cochrane, Congressional Budget Office, April 4, 2005, www.cbo.gov/show doc.cfm?index=6137&sequence=0.

10. Andrews, Edmund, "Trade Deficit Hits Record, Threatening U.S. Growth," *New York Times*, December 15, 2005.

11. Ferguson, Roger W., Jr., "U.S. Current Account Deficit: Causes and Consequences, Remarks to the Economics Club of the University of North Carolina," Chapel Hill, April 20, 2005, www.federalreserve.gov/boarddocs/speeches/2005/20050420/de fault.htm.

12. "Recent Shifts in Financing the US Current Account Deficit," Congressional Budget Office, July 12, 2005, www.cbo.gov/ftpdocs/65xx/doc6542/07-12-Current Account.pdf.

13. Department of Treasury, Office of International Affairs, Treasury International Capital System, www.treas.gov/tic/mfh.txt.

14. "Report on Foreign Portfolio Holdings of U.S. Securities as of June 30, 2004," Treasury Department, Federal Reserve Bank of New York, and the Board of Governors of the Federal Reserve System, June 2005, pp. 73–83, www.treas.gov/tic/shl2004r.pdf.

15. Speech to Institute for International Economics, Washington, D.C., February 15, 2005, www.iie.com/publications/papers/paper.cfm?ResearchID=27.

16. "Reinvention Remembered: A Look Back at Seven Years of Reform," www .govexec. January 19, 2001, www.govexec.com/dailyfed/0101/011901p1.htm.

13

TOWARD A POST-OIL ECONOMY

Jan Mazurek

In the summer of 1859, the world's first commercial oil well began pumping in Titusville, Pennsylvania. Over the next century, Americans invented the modern oil economy. We fueled our own industrial revolution and two world wars with a healthy petroleum surplus to export. Along the way, as production spread from Pennsylvania to Texas and the Plains states, and as auto manufacturers sold millions of affordable cars to the masses, our distinctly American way of life took hold. Today, we commute long distances from houses in the suburbs, past strip malls and drive-thru restaurants, to jobs in the world's leading economy. Yet our safety and prosperity now depend increasingly on our willingness to break free of our historic reliance on oil.

America has gone from being the largest oil producer to the largest importer. We consume a quarter of the world's oil, and our once-bountiful domestic reserves have dwindled to just three percent of the world's supply. Looking forward, our dependence on foreign oil is only projected to increase. The U.S. Energy Department predicts that by 2025 we will import between 63 and 72 percent of our oil.[1]

This worsening oil addiction poses a triple threat to America's national security, economy, and environmental health. A fifty-year legacy of petrocentric policy decisions has left us deeply entangled in the politically unstable Middle East—the wellspring of jihadist terrorism—because that is where two-thirds of global reserves are located.[2] Meanwhile, our growing reliance on imports means that Americans are sending more dollars overseas, pushing the U.S. trade deficit to record heights. In 1998, Americans spent $50 billion on oil imports; by 2004 the tab had more than tripled, to $179 billion.[3] Occasional spikes in oil prices have thus far done little lasting harm to our economy, but a major disruption of oil supplies—say, from a terrorist attack in the Persian Gulf—could easily trigger a recession. All of this, and our prodigious oil consumption is spurring global climate change, with all of its insidious side effects—from the receding polar ice caps, to increasingly destructive hurricanes,[4] to the potential spread of exotic diseases such as West Nile Virus and Bird Flu.[5]

The spillover costs of our oil habit are becoming prohibitive. It's time to put American ingenuity to work inventing the world's first post-oil economy.

President George W. Bush belatedly admitted in his sixth State of the Union address that "America is addicted to oil." Despite the president's apparent epiphany, however, he and his Republican allies remain firmly wedded to the status quo. They want to reduce U.S. dependence on foreign oil by opening up Alaska's Arctic National Wildlife Refuge, where reserves are difficult to reach and expensive to extract, and where the yield will likely amount to a tiny fraction of our regular demand. Incredibly, the White House and Congressional Republicans last year showered the oil industry and other fossil fuel producers with more than $11 billion in tax breaks, even though they had been reaping record profits because of soaring oil prices. The much-heralded Energy Policy Act of 2005 did practically nothing to change energy consumption patterns in the transportation sector, which accounts for two-thirds of the nation's oil use and one-third of the greenhouse gas emissions implicated in global warming.[6] In signing the energy bill, President Bush consigned the nation to drift slowly toward a clean energy future when we should be accelerating our progress.

Administration critics, meanwhile, have issued ringing but vague calls for a new "Manhattan Project" or "Apollo moon shot" to help America achieve energy independence. They urge adoption of ambitious national goals, such as creating three million more "new energy" jobs,[7] or cutting oil use in half in twenty years.[8] Conspicuously missing from these well-intentioned schemes, however, is a credible road map for getting from here to there.

And so the United States remains suspended between the past and the future, between oil and clean energy, between the administration's more-of-the-same approach to energy and its critics' over-the-horizon solutions.

It's time for progressives to fill in the blanks in their clean energy blueprints. We need to offer concrete ideas for changing the way Americans consume energy in the here and now, not the distant future. And we must recognize that making oil more expensive to burn is the sine qua non of any credible plan for energy security.

What would such a plan entail? The key is a mandatory national cap on greenhouse gas emissions. This longtime environmental policy goal has now become the first imperative of energy policy as well, for a simple reason: The most common greenhouse gas, carbon dioxide, is produced by burning oil and other fossil fuels. So a cap on greenhouse gases would immediately spur the development of alternative fuels and cleaner technologies. When combined with emissions credits that companies could sell or buy, the resulting "cap-and-trade" system would offer a flexible, decentralized, and market-driven way to lower the nation's output of greenhouse gases.

It would also create the framework for several other major steps that could galvanize progress toward a clean energy future: Replacing the stalled auto fuel economy standards with a new regime of "tailpipe trading" that would operate within the national greenhouse gas emissions trading market. By raising the cost of burning fossil fuels, this system would also spur the commercialization of their most attractive alternatives, especially homegrown biofuels. Finally, capping carbon emissions and creating incentives for innovation would also stimulate U.S. efforts to capture the burgeoning global market in clean energy sources and technologies.

The market potential of clean energy—for the heartland states where crops can be grown to produce biofuels; for Detroit, which will need to produce new generations of cars; and for the U.S. economy as a whole—is enormous. By one estimate, the global race to build clean, energy-friendly technologies is already worth more than $600 billion and growing.[9] In the same way oil made horsepower and whale blubber obsolete, these clean technologies point the way toward a post-oil economy.

THE MOUNTING COSTS
OF OIL DEPENDENCE

Since World War II, the United States has assigned high strategic priority to assuring our access to Middle East oil. That has led us to forge close ties to autocratic, corrupt, and unpopular regimes in the region, from the shah of Iran to the House of Saud. Given our longstanding policy of promoting "stability" rather than liberal values in the region, it's little wonder that

President Bush's calls for Middle East democracy are greeted skeptically there.

The United States and its Western allies have developed an especially unhealthy relationship of codependency with Saudi Arabia. We buy Saudi oil and rely on the Saudis, as the dominant players in OPEC, sitting on 78 percent of the world's spare oil production capacity, to provide steady supplies at reasonable prices.[10] Despite the kingdom's extraordinary influence over the world market, however, it has a poor record of delivering on its end of the bargain. In theory, at least, OPEC adjusts spare oil production capacity to prevent oil prices from rising to recession-inducing levels, or dropping below revenue-maximizing levels for oil producers. But it has on several occasions proven unwilling or unable to avert wild price swings, as in 2000, when it cut production, thereby producing price spikes; and, more recently, in 2003 and 2004, when it refused to adequately increase production to accommodate surging world demand due to China's economic expansion, among other factors.[11] Saudi influence over oil prices is the main reason that the United States traditionally has been reluctant to press hard for political reform there, or look too deeply into the kingdom's funding of groups that promote Wahhab fundamentalism around the world, including "charities" suspected of funneling money to terrorist groups.

Oil is a mutually destructive force in another way, too: Throughout the Middle East, it acts as a "resource curse" that stunts democratization and promotes autocracy, which in turn fuels jihadist rage. Consider how liberal democracy emerged in the West: As monarchical states with centralized power emerged and began to tax their populations, property-owning interests in society demanded greater voice in government in exchange for this taxation. Over time, this interplay led to the formation of parliaments, judiciaries, and other institutions of democracy. Oil-rich countries like Saudi Arabia, by contrast, are "rentier" states: They make enough money from oil that they require little tax revenue from their people, who in turn have little standing to demand more accountability or better political representation. Jihadism—directed at Middle Eastern autocracies, and the Western oil clients that underwrite them—is an outgrowth of that dynamic.

Our military presence in the Middle East further inflames jihadist rage. Resentment over U.S. troops stationed in Saudi Arabia, home of Islam's two holiest places, in large part drove Osama bin Laden to his now-famous fatwa directing his followers to "kill the Americans" and drive them "out of all the lands of Islam."[12] And for too long, our inability to change course has prevented us from challenging the autocratic system of government there that creates a constant supply of disenfranchised people all too willing to kill themselves and innocent victims in a twisted rendering of a faith that simply does not condone such practices.

Protecting oil assets in the Middle East has cost the American taxpayer close to $50 billion per year in defense spending, according to the National Defense Council Foundation, a nonprofit research group.[13] That's the equivalent of adding $1.17 to the price of a gallon of gasoline at the pump—a true hidden cost not reflected in today's already record gasoline prices.

Beyond the Middle East, our dependence on foreign oil sources has other strategic disadvantages. For example, it may put the United States on a collision course with China, which is scouring the world for oil to fuel its explosive economic growth. Like the United States, China initially was able to meet its own oil needs with domestic supplies. No longer: China is now the world's second largest oil importer after the United States, accounting for more than half of the growth in world oil demand in 2002 and 2003.[14] And like us, its dependence on foreign oil is only expected to increase. The International Energy Agency (IEA) expects China to import 82 percent of its oil by 2030.[15]

China clearly has made assuring access to oil a top strategic priority, just as the United States did after World War II. Analysts say China is building a blue-water navy and seeking basing rights in other countries to protect oil supply routes. And Beijing is striking up cordial relationships with a motley array of tyrants and rogue states with which the United States is at odds. In fact, competition between China and the United States for oil and influence in oil-rich countries could become the twenty-first-century equivalent of the arms race between the United States and the Soviet Union in the cold war.

China has, for example, forged close ties in recent years with some of the world's least savory regimes: Iran, Syria, Sudan, and Venezuela. And while China has given rhetorical support to international efforts to induce Iran to abandon its plans to enrich nuclear fuels, it has generally resisted calls to place punitive sanctions on Tehran. And China's growing stake in Sudan likewise complicates international efforts to pressure the Sudanese government to stop the ethnic violence that has claimed more than 200,000 lives in the western province of Darfur.

The economic consequences of our oil addiction are just as alarming as the foreign policy and national security implications. Because it runs through the veins of our economy, when something interrupts the flow of oil, it can cause a shock to the entire system, as last year's hurricanes in the Gulf of Mexico showed. By hitting consumers squarely in the pocketbook, oil price spikes limit the amount of other goods people can buy and lead to job losses in industries heavily dependent on consumers. Spikes also hurt other sectors, such as automobile manufacturers, airlines, and the myriad industries that make oil into things like plastic and fertilizer. To illustrate oil's ability to make us less prosperous, consider that nearly every economic recession since World War II has come on the heels of a global petroleum shortage and ensuing price spike.

The good news is that in time, Yankee ingenuity helps us to adapt to oil price shocks. For instance, when the Arab oil embargo focused our attention on energy in the 1970s, we learned how to produce more goods and services with less power. In fact, today it takes about half as much oil as it did thirty years ago to generate one dollar of gross domestic product—a chief reason why the U.S. economy has proved to be far more resilient to recent oil price increases than during the OPEC oil embargo.[16] Nevertheless, even seemingly small disruptions in daily production have the potential to send oil prices skyward, as a recent simulation run by the National Commission for Energy Policy demonstrated. The hypothetical exercise showed that a four percent global shortfall in daily oil supply results in a 177 percent increase in the price of oil (from $58 to $161 per barrel). So although the United States has learned in the last thirty years how to do more with less oil, it is not prepared for cascading price shocks of that magnitude.[17]

The problem is that once we find ways to make do with less energy, energy prices stabilize, as they did during much of the late 1980s and 1990s. Sticker shock fades and we begin buying gas guzzlers and gorging on electricity again, driving energy demand and prices back up. We pretty much forget about energy policy until the next crisis erupts.

But beyond domestic price shocks, America's oil dependence contributes heavily to global environmental problems. As the world's biggest economy and its most prodigious consumer of fossil fuels, the United States is also the most prolific emitter of man-made greenhouse gases, accounting for close to a quarter of the world's total CO_2. But the second biggest emitter, China, is quickly gaining ground. Because of its thirst for oil, China now produces about 13 percent of the world's total CO_2.[18] By 2024, as its demand for cars and trucks grows, it is expected to account for nearly 18 percent of the world's total.[19] Unfortunately, the United States has no standing in the international community to complain about China or any other country's energy and environmental policies, because the Bush administration refused to either work for improvements in the admittedly flawed Kyoto Protocol on Global Warming, or pursue a credible alternative approach to curtailing U.S. greenhouse gas emissions.

A PROGRESSIVE CLEAN ENERGY STRATEGY

The environmental, energy, and strategic challenges posed to the United States by our lingering dependence on imported oil, coupled with China's growing appetite for it, vividly illustrate why it is high time for the president and Congress to come to terms with the reality of our global energy and environmental interdependence. No country exists in a vacuum. The consumption, output, and environmental refuse of one roaring national economy sends ripple effects throughout the world. We must shape our national policies—and engage with the rest of the world to shape international policies—accordingly.

In addition to reengaging with the international partners we shunned by withdrawing from the Kyoto Protocol, the United States must embark upon a far-reaching, four-part clean energy strategy here at home.

Step 1: Cap Carbon Emissions Now

The surest way to both curtail global warming and spur the transition to a post-oil economy would be to establish a mandatory, market-based "cap-and-trade" system for carbon dioxide and other greenhouse gases. In such a system, the government would set a national limit (or "cap") for allowable greenhouse gas emissions, and companies that produce emissions—such as energy companies—would be given emissions credits that they could trade with other companies. Those that keep their emissions below allowable limits would be able to sell their excess credits, and those that exceed allowable emissions limits would have to either buy extra credits from more energy-efficient companies, or pay fines to the government. The system would thus establish a profit incentive to reduce carbon dioxide emissions by consuming less oil—and that profit incentive would trigger investment in clean technologies and alternative fuels.

As an environmental policy strategy, the cap-and-trade approach has already proven to be wildly successful, most notably in the fight against sulfur dioxide pollutants from power plants that cause acid rain. The key to its success is that the policy focuses only on the intended outcome—total emissions levels—instead of mandating specific technologies or practices industries must use to meet that target. Companies are free to find the most innovative ways possible to meet their obligations.

For the same reasons, a cap-and-trade approach that covers carbon emissions will prove to be an effective energy policy strategy. It can serve as the lever that has thus far been missing to push the economy away from oil consumption and toward more sustainable alternatives.

Among its many other benefits, such a system would also be a boon for farmers. It would create new demand for crops such as soy, peanuts, and switchgrass that can be converted into "biofuels." Farmers and foresters could also profit if they are allowed to sell emissions credits based on the amount of carbon dioxide their crops suck out of the atmosphere. And a national carbon cap will give potential biofuel suppliers, such as filling stations and truck stops, as well as end-users, a more powerful incentive to switch to cleaner fuels that help keep U.S. dollars here at home.

The leading proposal in Congress for a national cap-and-trade system has been introduced by Senators John McCain (R-AZ) and Joseph Lieberman (D-CT). They would establish absolute, economy-wide caps on emissions of all six major greenhouse gases (carbon dioxide, methane, nitrous oxide, hydrofluorocarbons, perfluorocarbons, and sulfur hexafluoride), and require large industrial emitters, electric utilities, and oil producers to return emissions of those gases to 2000 levels by 2010. A more modest proposal by Senators Tom Carper (D-DE) and Lincoln Chafee (R-RI) would start with a cap on carbon dioxide emissions by power plants. That could be a valuable first step toward overcoming entrenched political resistance to economy-wide emissions limits such as those envisioned in the McCain-Lieberman plan.

Step 2: Shift from Fuel Economy Standards to "Tailpipe Trading"

For nearly half a century, transportation has accounted for about a quarter of total U.S. energy use and two-thirds of total oil consumption. Tailpipe exhaust remains a leading source of air pollution and accounts for roughly one-third of the nation's emissions of carbon dioxide. Therefore, a national cap-and-trade system should include limits on tailpipe emissions from cars and trucks.

As in cap-and-trade proposals for energy producers, factories, and other big emitters, a tailpipe trading system would give automakers a profit motive to produce cars and trucks that keep CO_2 emissions below national standards. Companies whose fleets miss the mark would have to buy credits from other companies (any regulated company, not just other automakers), or pay fines to the government.

Because of the profit motive it creates, such a policy is far more likely to reduce oil consumption than the country's stalled system of miles-per-gallon standards. Those standards, known as Corporate Average Fuel Economy (CAFE) standards, are mired in Congressional gridlock and are unlikely to be significantly tightened anytime soon, as the 2005 energy bill deliberations proved. One reason for the gridlock is that automakers complain that fuel economy standards force them to make costly trade-offs in terms of vehicle performance and safety, and build vehicles that consumers do not want.

Meanwhile, they have gamed the system by taking advantage of the lower fuel-efficiency requirements for trucks (20.7 mpg) than for passenger cars (27.5 mpg). Since Congress first created CAFE standards in 1975, the share of new vehicles classified as light trucks (including SUVs, minivans, and pickups) has shot up from 20 percent of sales to more than one-half of the market today. The president's proposal to raise truck standards between 1.5 and 1.8 miles per gallon would do little to improve overall fuel efficiency and may actually encourage automakers to build larger, more inefficient light trucks. Not only does the plan give Detroit the green light to potentially build bigger gas guzzlers, it also fails to tighten fuel economy for passenger cars, which remains at 27.5 miles per gallon. Additionally, the plan fails to close a current loophole that leaves no standards for the biggest behemoths—vehicles with a gross vehicle weight of between 8,500 and 10,000 pounds, including the Hummer H2, Ford Excursion, and Chevy Suburban.

These factors combined make fuel economy standards a far less powerful brake on gasoline consumption than they were in the 1970s.

With the spur of a cap on carbon dioxide and other greenhouse gases, automotive advances already at hand can help us double the efficiency of a barrel of oil by 2020. For example, most diesel engines manufactured since 1992 can already run on biodiesel fuel blends.[20] Another way to cut back dramatically on oil use is to build ultralight vehicles with carbon composites or lightweight steel.

Step 3: Replace Oil with Homegrown "Biofuels"

As their name implies, biofuels are made from crops like soy, corn, and peanuts—even plant waste that would otherwise rot and emit methane, a potent greenhouse gas. Biofuels are infinitely renewable, relatively clean burning, safe to handle, and can be produced in abundance here on American soil.

One of the most promising biofuels is biodiesel. In the United States, most of it now comes from soybeans and recycled cooking fats, but those represent only a fraction of potential sources. Others include canola, corn, cotton, mustard, peanuts, sunflowers, and even lard. Like most other vehicle fuels, biodiesel releases carbon dioxide when it's burned. Those emissions, however, are recycled by the crops grown to make new batches of biodiesel. New crops breathe in or "sequester" carbon dioxide in equal or greater amounts to the CO_2 released by combusting biodiesel to run cars, trucks, and heavy machinery. When the U.S. Department of Energy (DOE) studied that closed carbon loop, it concluded that buses using pure biodiesel emit 78 percent less CO_2 than those using petrodiesel.[21]

In fact, homegrown biodiesel may be able to reduce our dependence on foreign oil more than any other alternative fuel. DOE-sponsored research shows that for every unit of fossil energy expended to make biodiesel, 3.2 units of energy are gained. No other vehicle fuel has as high a positive "energy balance." In contrast, it actually takes 1.2 units of fossil fuel energy to yield one unit of petroleum diesel. Studies also suggest that biodiesel production can be a boon to farmers. The U.S. Department of Agriculture concludes that a one-hundred million gallon a year boost in demand for biodiesel would increase revenue for U.S. soybean farmers by more than $112 million.

Energy legislation enacted in August 2005 established tax credits for fuel distributors who blend biodiesel with petrodiesel, and for fuel stations that have biodiesel pumps available to customers. But a cap on carbon dioxide and other greenhouse gases will further spur the transition to alternative fuels ranging from biodiesel to cellulosic ethanol.

Step 4: Capture the Clean Technology Market

In the same way that the birth of commercial oil production helped usher in a new industrial era, we already have at our disposal new energy-saving technologies that may serve as the cornerstone of the next energy era. And in the same way that the oil crisis of the 1970s spurred us to do more with less oil, advances already at hand can help us dramatically reduce our oil consumption. By one estimate, cars made from advanced carbon composite material or lightweight steel can nearly double the efficiency of today's popular hybrid-electric cars and light trucks while improving safety and performance.[22]

Although the future of alternative energy, energy efficiency, and other green technologies—collectively termed "clean tech"—is still somewhat uncertain, many clean energy industries are growing rapidly. For instance, the global solar power market alone generates more than $7 billion per year and is expanding at an annual rate of more than 30 percent.

President Bush has refused to do anything serious about global warming because he says greenhouse gas regulation would wreak havoc on the U.S. economy. That was his main rationale for pulling America out of the Kyoto Protocol, which took effect in February 2005. But the truth is that the clean technologies that can curb global warming represent a tremendous economic growth opportunity—worth $607 billion in 2005.[23]

Unfortunately, by sitting on the sidelines while the rest of the world acts to stop climate change, the United States is ceding this clean technology market to its competitors. For example, even though California is the birthplace of wind power, the American wind market as a whole is now stuck in slow motion. The U.S. wind power generation capacity of 6,370 megawatts—enough for approximately 6 million homes—is dwarfed by Germany's 14,600 megawatts. Similarly, while America was once the largest manufacturer of solar photovoltaic (PV) cells—surpassing Japan's production capacity by an impressive 60 percent in 1996—Japan now produces more than twice as many solar cells as we do. And in the transportation sector, Japanese automakers Toyota and Honda recently took top honors for making eight of the ten most fuel-efficient cars sold in the United States. Germany's Volkswagen makes the other two.[24] In each case, compliance with the much-maligned Kyoto Protocol helps explain why our major trading partners are racing ahead of us in the quest to gain leadership in the clean energy market.

To be sure, Kyoto was a flawed deal for the United States that needed to be improved. But this is an economic lesson we should have already learned. Consider that shortly after Congress created the nation's clean air and clean water laws in the 1970s, they had created 50,000 jobs in the construction industry and 75,000 jobs in other sectors.[25] The sluggish job growth in the months after the 2005 hurricanes triggered oil price spikes was just another reminder of how vulnerable the U.S. economy is to fuel price shocks in general.[26]

If we want to revitalize U.S. growth in the clean technology sector, we not only will have to take steps to cap CO_2 here at home and reengage with our international partners, but also redouble efforts to provide educational opportunities in the sciences and spur new innovation. To do so, the National Science Foundation (NSF) should establish between five and ten new national centers of clean technology excellence at U.S. universities. Funding should be $5 million per university and build on NSF's existing program in engineering research.[27]

Additionally, the U.S. Department of Energy should set up a division of the Advanced Research Projects Agency (ARPA) that is solely devoted to energy research—modeled after similar research initiatives at the Defense Department. Specifically, the agency should support high-risk ventures that the private sector is unlikely to develop on its own. ARPA's new energy division should receive about $300 million in its first year of operation and that budget should increase to about $1 billion over the next five years[28]—a small investment when compared to the more than $200 billion we send overseas annually to pay for our costly oil addiction.

CONCLUSION

Our national security, economic interests, and environmental health demand that we neither accept today's energy policy stalemate nor passively wait for a distant wholesale shift to a clean energy future. Although we are gradually moving away from a fifty-plus year policy of propping up despotic regimes to protect oil supplies, we have yet to supplant that policy with a viable alternative. Despite his admission that America is addicted to oil, President Bush seems basically content with this state of drift, as evidenced by his enthusiastic embrace of the utterly conventional 2005 energy bill. It therefore falls to progressives to champion a post-oil economic plan that will yield real progress now. They must make the case to the American people that no leader or political party should be considered credible on national security unless it puts bold energy reforms at the center of its agenda.

NOTES

1. "Annual Energy Outlook 2005," Energy Information Administration, U.S. Department of Energy, 2005, p. 101, www.eia.doe.gov/oiaf/archive/aeo05/index.html.

2. "Annual Energy Outlook 2005," p. 74.

3. "Monthly Energy Review," U.S. Department of Energy, Energy Information Administration, February 2005, www.eia.doe.gov/emeu/mer/contents.html, quoted in Clawson, Patrick, and Simon Henderson, "Reducing Vulnerability to Middle East Energy Shocks," Washington Institute for Near East Policy, November 2005.

4. Emanuel, Kerry, "Increasing Destructiveness of Tropical Cyclones over the Past 30 Years," *Nature* 436 (2005): 686–688, www.nature.com/nature/journal/v436/n70 51/abs/nature03906.html; "Financial Risks of Climate Change," Association of British Insurers, June 2005, www.abi.org.uk/Display/Display_Popup/default.asp?Menu_ID = 1090&Menu_All = 1,1088,1090&Child_ID = 552. See also: Knutson, Thomas R., and Robert E. Tuyela, "Impact of CO_2-Induced Warming on Simulated Hurricane Intensity and Precipitation: Sensitivity to the Choice of Climate Model and Collective Parameterization." *Journal of Climate* 17 (2004): 3477–3495, www.gfdl.noaa.gov/reference/bibli ography/2004/tk0401.pdf.

5. Kovats, R.S., et al., "Early Effects of Climate Change: Do They Include Changes in Vector-Borne Disease?" *Philosophical Transactions of the Royal Society: A Mathematical, Physical and Engineering Sciences*, 2001, 1057–1068; Reiter, P., "Climate Change and Mosquito-Borne Disease," *Environmental Health Perspectives* 109 (2001): 141–61.

6. "Annual Energy Outlook 2005," op. cit.

7. "New Energy for America: The Apollo Jobs Report," The Institute for America's Future and the Center on Wisconsin Strategy, January 2004, www.apolloalliance.org/docUploads/ApolloReport%5F022404%5F122748%2Epdf.

8. Lovins, Amory, et al., "Winning the Oil Endgame," Rocky Mountain Institute, 2005, www.oilendgame.com/ReadTheBook.html.

9. Industry Facts, Office of Environmental Technologies Industries, U.S. Department of Commerce, 2004, http://environment.ita.doc.gov.

10. Minsk, Ronald E., "The High Price of Oil Addiction," Progressive Policy Institute, May 2004, www.ppionline.org.

11. Minsk, Ronald E., "High Gas Prices, Blame OPEC Not EPA," Progressive Policy Institute, October 2005, www.ppionline.org.

12. "Fueling Terror," Institute for the Analysis of Global Security (IAGS), 2004, p. 36, www.iags.org/fuelingterror.html.

13. "The Hidden Cost of Imported Oil," National Defense Council Foundation, 2004, www.ndcf.org/.

14. Barta, Patrick, et al., "Asian Rivals Put Pressure on Western Energy Giants," *The Wall Street Journal*, January 5, 2005.

15. Ehara, Norio, "Oil Supply Disruption Management Issues," IEA/ASEAN/ASCOPE Workshop, IEA Collaboration with India and China on Oil Security, International Energy Administration, April 6, 2004, www.iea.org/textbase/work/2004/cam bodia/bj_session3.2-Ehara%20presentation.pdf.

16. "Annual Energy Review 2002," Energy Information Administration, U.S. Department of Energy, 2003, p. xvii, http://tonto.eia.doe.gov/FTPROOT/multifuel/038402.pdf.

17. "Oil Shockwave," National Commission on Energy Policy and Securing America's Future Energy, September 2004.

18. "International Energy Outlook 2004," Energy Information Administration, U.S. Department of Energy, www.eia.doe.gov/oiaf/archive/ieo04/index.html.

19. "China: Environmental Issues," Energy Information Administration, U.S. Department of Energy, July 2003, www.eia.doe.gov/emeu/cabs/chinaenv.html.

20. "Powering Energy Independence on Peanuts," PPI State Environment Exchange E-Newsletter, Progressive Policy Institute, September 9, 2004, www.ppionline.org.

21. "Biodiesel," Fuel Blends, Clean Cities Program, U.S. Department of Energy, 2005, www.eere.energy.gov/cleancities/blends/biodiesel.html.

22. Lovins, et al., op. cit.

23. Industry Facts, op. cit.

24. Mohiuddin, Shamarukh, "How America Lost Its Clean Technology Edge," Progressive Policy Institute, December 2004, www.ppionline.org.

25. "Testimony of Russell E. Train," Congressional Joint Economic Committee, November 22, 1974, www.epa.gov/history/topics/costs/01.htm. Rejeski, David, "How New Environmental Technologies Can Stimulate Economic Growth," Progressive Policy Institute, December 2004, www.ppionline.org.

26. "The Hidden Cost of Imported Oil," op. cit. Leonhardt, David, "High Prices for Energy Hold Down Job Growth," *New York Times*, November 5, 2005, www.nytimes.com/2005/11/05/business/05econ.html.

27. Leonhardt, David, "High Prices for Energy Hold Down Job Growth."

28. Leonhardt, David, "High Prices for Energy Hold Down Job Growth."

VI

RENEWING OUR FIGHTING FAITH

14

THE 9/11 GENERATION

Rachel Kleinfeld and Matthew Spence

In the 2004 election, everyone thought they knew where young people stood.[1] They were filling campus courtyards protesting the war. They were filling the campaign coffers of liberal candidates. And they were filling buses headed for get-out-the-vote drives in swing states. Pundits spoke of the reawakening of political youth, and the force that this "baby boomlet" generation would become in American politics. This confluence of far-left politics and grassroots activism left security-minded Democrats in despair. How could the party take responsible, strong national security positions without losing the next generation of voters and alienating our crucial activist base?

But a funny thing happened when we examined the data on youth attitudes. This conventional wisdom turned out to be dead wrong. The traditional dove-hawk, liberal-conservative dichotomies describe little about today's young. Instead, we found that young voters, ages eighteen to thirty, hold a new political orientation that does not fit into old stereotypes. They are simultaneously human rights crusaders and supporters of a strong military. They are more concerned about both traditional and nontraditional security threats, more comfortable with the use of force, and more in favor of free trade than their elders. Indeed, this generation holds complex and nuanced views which straddle traditional lines of party affiliation, income, class, and ethnicity. They are the September 11 Generation, a generation that is quietly but powerfully helping to reshape our national security debate.

DEBUNKING THE MYTHS

The legend of the liberal young is a familiar story that seemed to fit 2004. The picture of politically powerful youth arrayed against the military, against free trade, and against war appeared frequently in the media. But this was a caricature of a new generation drawn from the outdated iconography of the Vietnam era. Casting youth as 1960s-style liberals not only defies the facts; it defines our generation in terms irrelevant to the ways we define ourselves. But before we can see this generation afresh, we must begin by debunking the myths.

Take, for example, military force. Far from being pacifists, people under age thirty were more *pro*-war, at the outset of the Iraq war, than any other age group in America. Despite the images of youth protesters in the media, young Americans supported military action in Iraq by a three-to-one margin, a wider split than any other age group.[2] And while the young were certainly split along partisan lines (young Republicans were nearly unanimous in their support), over 60 percent of young Democrats also supported the war in 2002. In comparison, only 33 percent of Democrats over age sixty-five supported the war.[3] Youth support dropped, of course, as the war faltered, but even by 2005 when a majority of all Americans (57 percent)—and young voters (55 percent)—felt that the war in Iraq was not worth the cost in lives and dollars,[4] a majority of students (54 percent) still supported the military action to remove Saddam Hussein from power.[5]

Or take the Howard Dean phenomenon. The media, following the story of liberal youth, saw Governor Howard Dean as embodying the protest vote of the young. Although Governor Dean's actual platform was hardly as far to the left as the media made it out to be, he was portrayed as the reincarnation of the 1970s antiwar movement—a man who won the hearts of America's young voters by appearing to pull the Democratic Party back to its traditional, Vietnam-era, liberal roots.

But Dean's voters were not primarily young. While photo ops showed fresh-faced activists at campaign stops, only 18 percent of Dean's activist supporters were under the age of thirty (roughly the same percentage as all Democratic voters under age thirty). In fact, youth were the *smallest* age group supporting Dean, aside from senior citizens.[6] The vast majority of Dean's supporters were the middle aged, well-off, and well-educated baby boomers who have held liberal views since the Vietnam war. These numbers support what a separate Pew survey found about the young in general: Young people in the conventional liberal mode are far *less* politically engaged than their peers who identify as conservatives, centrist Democrats, or any other political category.[7]

Moreover, young "Deaniacs" held far more centrist views than their elders within the Dean camp. Most Dean supporters, according to a post-election Pew survey, held a traditionally liberal set of views: they were more secular than most Democrats, believed that military force is to be used only in extremis and not, even when threatened, preemptively, felt allies should have a significant say in U.S. policy, believed that domestic issues should garner greater attention than foreign policy problems, and felt that the war in Iraq was wrong.[8]

Yet, while two-thirds of middle-aged Dean activists favored pulling troops out of Iraq immediately in mid-2005, regardless of the consequences, 61 percent of young Dean supporters favored *keeping* troops there to stabilize the region. That was an even greater percentage than the general population. And while only 13 percent of Dean supporters over the age of fifty felt that military preemption could ever be justified, more than twice as many young Dean supporters felt that it was sometimes justifiable.[9]

In fact, among the under-thirty electorate as a whole, many of those who opposed the war did so not out of knee-jerk pacifism, but for hard-headed security reasons that were not far removed from the calculations of war supporters. Young opponents of the war worried that Iraq was a distraction from catching terrorists—the real threat America faced. (Half of young Americans worried that the war in Iraq might hurt our prosecution of the war on terror, compared to only one third of Americans over age thirty who opposed the war for that reason.)[10] Young people believed that war with allies was preferable because waging war without allies was likely to be ineffective and make us less secure in the long run.[11] Many appeared to believe, quite reasonably, that the Bush administration had ignored the hard realities of nation-building, would not be greeted with roses and garlands, and would leave American troops mired in Iraq, fighting a stubborn insurgency, and contributing to global instability. These assessments were remarkably prescient. In other words, very few young voters who opposed the war fit the conservative stereotype of being weak on security.

Nor did the young—whether prowar or antiwar, express shame about being American, a sadly common perception associated with the Vietnam generation. Young people are overwhelmingly enthusiastic to identify as patriotic Americans. Over the past five years of polling, 87–92 percent of college students (a group generally more left-wing than the total under-thirty population) have consistently described themselves as patriotic.[12]

Finally, on trade, despite the publicized protests against the World Trade Organization since Seattle 2000, there is little truth to the conventional wisdom that paints youth as antiglobalization. In fact, a solid 68 percent of people under thirty believe that free trade is good for America. That is 20 percent *more* support than any other age group in America. Moreover, half say that free trade has either definitely or probably helped their personal financial situation—indicating a personal stake in free trade that is likely to last.[13]

It may be tempting to dismiss such sentiments as reflections of a naïve optimism that will change when the young face firsthand job loss and competition due to outsourcing. But this strong support is probably better seen as a product of the September 11 Generation's new perspective on work. Unlike past generations, today's youth do not plan to have a job for life, an expectation that fuels fears of job loss and outsourcing. Instead, young people expect a great deal of volatility and change in their jobs—and their careers—both from external shocks and from personal choices. This generation knows it cannot expect job stability—instead, they value options. Expanding trade means more options and lower prices as buyers. And while young people expect their careers to be volatile, they know that they will be steady consumers throughout their lives. Thus, the effects of trade on prices are likely to affect young people more than the effects of outsourcing on any particular job they might hold.

Understanding where young people stand on trade points to a larger need. To grasp how this generation thinks about foreign policy, it is not enough to look at discrete issues cast in the terms of old debates. We must try to tap the experiences and expectations that compose this generation's zeitgeist.

UNDERSTANDING THE FOREIGN POLICY OUTLOOK OF VOTERS UNDER THIRTY

The most important insight about the September 11 Generation is simple: *Americans under thirty hold a set of beliefs that cannot be captured in the simple cold war–era liberal-conservative or hawk-dove dichotomies.*

This should not be surprising: Each generation is defined by its own set of catalyzing events, and by different generational moods and beliefs. The generations before us wrestled with the ideological challenge of Soviet communism, the fear of nuclear weapons, and the divisive debate over the

Vietnam war. These events shaped their general worldview. The cold war outlook translated into a set of foreign policy rules of thumb, which carried over into their beliefs and policies on how to face an age of terror.

Similarly, to understand how Americans under the age of thirty think about foreign policy it is important to understand the general beliefs about the world and cataclysmic events that shape our way of looking at the questions, events, and policy challenges we face.

First, we should underscore that the September 11 Generation is hardly a homogenous group. It instead differs by political orientation, by race and ethnicity, and by an attitudinal split between Gen X (those over-twenty-five, comprising a particularly small generation with an especially strong distrust of government and a yen toward entrepreneurship), and Gen Y (those born after 1980, the children of the Boomers who compose a second large "boomlet," who are particularly community-oriented and trusting of authority).[14]

Overall, voters under age thirty still fit conventional stereotypes by identifying more as Democrats (42 percent) than do most voters (29 percent). And far more young voters identify as liberal (34 percent) than do all voters (19 percent).[15] But these numbers break down starkly by race. Young whites are moving away from the Democratic Party. In 2002, for example, 47 percent of white voters eighteen to twenty-four years old identified as Republican—nearly ten points higher than their parents' generation. Meanwhile, young minorities remain on the left, especially African Americans under age thirty, 86 percent of whom identified as Democrats.[16]

Voters under age thirty—particularly those under twenty-five, a large and growing demographic force—are far more conservative than the Vietnam Generation. Protected by attentive parents, they are close to their families and are the first generation to grow up with more conservative sexual, religious, and social mores than the generation immediately preceding them. Sixty-seven percent of voters ages eighteen to twenty-five feel that religion is important in their family lives, and over half attend church at least once a month.[17] They are also more prone to accept authority and trust the government than voters in their late twenties and early thirties. These beliefs help explain why the young Caucasians of this generation lean more Republican than past generations of young people—a fact the Democratic Party would do well to notice.[18]

In addition to their unabashed patriotism, voters under age thirty have deep respect for the military. The numbers are overwhelming: more than 70 percent of college students (the most liberal contingent of this group) trusted the military to do the right thing all or most of the time when polled in 2001, and in 2005, 65 percent still held that opinion. Among the young, the military is the most respected of the major public institutions.[19]

But the September 11 Generation are not old-fashioned conservatives. They distrust large corporations. They have even less confidence in "spin" from the media and from politicians but they believe that the government can—and should—be an active force solving problems in America. They embrace multiculturalism and a multilateral worldview: after all, they have grown up in a truly pluralistic society where many schools enroll students speaking dozens of languages; where Caucasians are often minorities themselves amid other minorities, and where that reality is not threatening.[20] In national security terms, these beliefs matter. While the rest of the population cast a vote for President George W. Bush in 2004 out of fear for American security, the September 11 Generation saw through this ruse and doubted President Bush's claims that he would protect America better. While President Bush won the popular vote in 2004, young voters picked Senator John F. Kerry instead.

These attitudinal trends are cemented by historical events. For voters under thirty, the main catalyzing foreign policy event of our lives has been the fall of the Twin Towers. Hence, on issues of national security, we are collectively the "September 11 Generation." But the tragedy of September 11 begins with the climax of the story—and it is important to start at the beginning.

The September 11 Generation was raised amid enormous optimism. The cold war was distant: a twenty-one-year old in 2005 was only five when the Soviet Union disintegrated. Our first political memory was the triumph of freedom: the fall of the Berlin Wall and the collapse of Soviet communism. American values were strong and spreading: America turned to NATO not just as a cold war alliance of realpolitik, but increasingly as a vehicle to promote democracy and human rights. In school, we learned that we lived in the "end of history," a time when U.S. values, aided by an enormous economic boom and the promise of globalization, would spread peacefully across an improving world.

American power was real, vast, and a force for good. We never knew the pain of military stalemate and the self-doubt of the Vietnam generation. Instead, we watched our first war on television, culminating in the first Gulf War's stunningly rapid victory. That war showed us both the power of military force, and the broad potential of multilateralism—with NATO, the

United Nations, Arab countries, and even our former Soviet enemy united to defeat aggression against an innocent country.

We also saw that inaction and isolation could betray our ideals. We watched the foot-dragging in Bosnia and our failure to address genocide in Rwanda. Yet we viscerally understood that military solutions were not the only answer. Underneath the "end of history," new problems were boiling that seemed unlike the old ones. We did not face Soviet armies in the center of Europe, but instead the threat of AIDS, ethnic conflict, and Samuel Huntington's famous "clash of civilizations," weak states, environmental destruction, and a myriad of new issues that required new, nonmilitary solutions.

Then, September 11 struck. Suddenly, on the cusp of adulthood, we faced the stark reality of a threat. It was not overseas, abstract, and far away—but concrete, and in our cities. The attitudes and history that had begun shaping this generation crystallized into a new security worldview, one that simply does not fit old categories.

Americans under thirty do not doubt that we face a deadly enemy—the burning towers are etched on our generation's collective conscience, and we are not burdened with the blame-America-first mentality that tars some on the left. Yet we are neither "realist" hawks nor conservatives. We do not believe we need to surrender civil liberties at home to keep America safe.[21] And we believe America should be willing to stand for our ideals in the world, spreading hope and preventing genocide. Crucially, perhaps because of the encompassing multiculturalism of our peer groups, young people firmly believe in a world community, despite otherwise conservative security stances. Thus, we care about the United States being respected by other countries, and think that the United States should lead cooperatively, not unilaterally—because it's right, and because it works. In June 2005, over twice as many voters under thirty chose the statement "America's security depends on building strong ties with other nations" (64 percent) over "Bottom line, America's security depends on its own military strength" (29 percent).[22] That was over twice the margin opting for multilateralism than any other age group, and double the margin of American voters overall (who sided with multilateralism by 53 percent to 38 percent).[23]

Young people do not deny the power of terror and hatred. Neither do they blindly accept the Republican strategy for a unilateral, military-led solution. They are engaged in a more difficult pursuit—trying to determine for themselves how best to meet these threats.

While September 11 provides the starting point for the national security vision of this generation, the long-term foreign policy values and policies of those under thirty are still being formed. We are watching, learning from, and—most importantly—*fighting in* the current war in Iraq. That war will easily have an impact that rivals September 11 itself in terms of shaping this generation's vision of national security.

For example, overwhelming confidence in America's military superiority—and even invincibility—catalyzed much of the September 11 Generation's prowar sentiment. Yet polling shows that the struggles of the war in Iraq are giving young people a more nuanced view of what military force alone can and cannot accomplish. Our troops—most of whom are our peers—were eager to go to war, but have been chastened by the realities of occupation and insurgency. They have learned firsthand, and the rest of us have learned at one remove, the limits of military force.

But we have reached a very different conclusion from the ambiguous and painful relationship the Vietnam generation formed with the military. We care about, support, and trust the military to do good in the world. We are, instead, simply becoming aware of its limits, and learning that the military is not a one-size-fits-all tool. Support for the war has gradually dimmed since 2005, as well as support for the necessity of preventative war.[24] Young people are paying attention to what is happening in the world, and changing their beliefs accordingly. We are not becoming more timid and dovish, but wiser.

IMPLICATIONS FOR THE FUTURE OF THE DEMOCRATIC PARTY: TRUMAN DEMOCRATS

Why do the beliefs of the young matter? Voters under thirty cast nearly 20.1 million votes in 2004. Turnout for this age group was the highest it has ever been since the voting age was lowered to eighteen.[25] And as the baby boomlet gathers force, the attitudes carried by this generation will only grow more important: they are just reaching voting age, and by the next decade will comprise 25 percent of the voting public.[26]

We believe that the views of Americans under thirty are beginning to set into a pattern we have seen before. Their belief system has been aptly compared by generational researchers to that of the "Greatest Generation," who fought in World War II and formed the backbone of America afterward.[27] Their views resemble neither President Bush's cowboy triumphalism, nor the pacifism of the Vietnam era, but instead the muscular, value-driven policies of our Greatest Generation leaders like President Harry Truman.

The natural home for a new generation of young people with a worldview similar to President Truman's should rightfully be in Truman's party. But Democrats have drifted in the post-Vietnam era from their tradition of progressive internationalism. Our party has become estranged from the military, successfully caricatured as opposed to the transformative power of American values, and marginalized in the national security debate.

The September 11 Generation seeks a foreign policy that both keeps our nation safe and embodies our values. We care deeply about helping the poor, supporting human rights at home and abroad, safeguarding the environment, creating a real equal opportunity society, and easing the plight of the disadvantaged. More than half of all college students volunteer directly, many college students prize these activities more than their studies, and 68 percent of college students say that they would consider working for a nonprofit for part of their future employment.[28] We want our government to inspire us, not just to keep us safe.

But in foreign policy Democrats have too often ceded our ideals and values to the Republicans. While conservatives have misappropriated core liberal values such as democracy and freedom, many Democratic security thinkers have embraced a narrow pragmatism. Young people see Democrats speaking of technocratic policies and diplomatic processes, not overarching ideals. By talking about pragmatic methods, but failing to link these with values and vision, they fail to provide a coherent, overarching message that can energize America's youth.

Moreover, realpolitik rings unrealistic to us. When facing an ideological threat, the response can only be found in an opposing and galvanizing idea. Young people agree that America's top priority must be to stop terrorists from killing innocent people. Our party leaders should be able to say this. But we diverge with the current administration's tactics. The fight against terror is not a fight against a finite set of terrorists, but a fight against an idea that can garner new recruits catalyzed by new rounds of humiliation. Only a strategy that conveys hope, as well as strength, will be able to overturn the humiliation that engulfs the world from which radicals recruit. And only a vision that grounds idealism in pragmatic means will appeal to today's youth.

To return our party to its own traditions, a group of young Democrats have joined to form the Truman National Security Project. The organization forms the hub of a movement dedicated to reviving the strong security, strong values tradition of the Democratic Party—for Democrats of all ages. Its goal is to rebuild an authentically progressive national security tradition capable of addressing America's vexing national security challenges. This Truman Democratic tradition is, we believe, the natural home of the September 11 Generation.

Truman Democrats believe that promoting human rights and a strong military are two sides of the same coin—not opposing values. We have seen how a strong military was essential to protecting rights in Bosnia, and how its absence allowed genocide in Rwanda. We know that the lack of military protection prevents development in war-torn countries throughout the world.

Truman Democrats also see the world's strongest army bogged down in the deserts of Iraq, and understand that national security cannot rest on military strength alone. We want to see America using our entire foreign policy tool kit to protect our country from terrorism. We know that our security also requires the multiple pillars of a strong economy, strong morale at home, and strong alliances based on shared threat.

Like President Truman, we think that foreign policy draws no clear lines between security, development, trade, and diplomacy—all are necessary for achieving our goals. We must deliver aid, not just armies—so that terrorist groups are not seen in the Islamic world as the only entities delivering charity to the poor; so that weak states are given the ability to patrol their own borders and enforce the rule of law; and so that young men can work and marry, not spend jobless hours idling amidst radical clerics and seeking self-worth in attention-grabbing destruction. And we must fight not just with weapons, but with words and beliefs.

In concrete terms, this means that we should be matching Saudi fundamentalists dollar for dollar in education spending in the Islamic world. We should not let terrorists tell the world who Americans are; we should be funding programs for young people to get out into the far corners of the earth and represent our country, while learning how best to interact with Muslim and Arab culture. And we should not invade countries without the skills to put them back together again.

Truman Democrats, like our namesake, are not afraid of American leadership. We prefer, however, that America lead by adopting policies that seek to benefit, not simply bully, other nations. Gaining the assistance of other nations lessens our security costs, and enables us to build the worldwide net essential to catching terrorists, stopping weapons proliferation, and catching the many threats that don't respect borders.

These are not "soft" security ideas. They are strong and pragmatic means of keeping us safe.

TOWARD A PROGRESSIVE NATIONAL SECURITY MESSAGE

How can Democrats offer a national security message to inspire and tap into the enormous political power of voters under age thirty? In the 1960s, when liberalism seemed to be the dominant ideology of the future, a group of young dissidents gathered on William F. Buckley's ranch to hammer out a credo of conservatism. They articulated guiding principles—lower taxes, limited government, and strong defense—that sustained the movement for years. We now face this situation's mirror image: and it is time for young progressives in the September 11 Generation to do the same.

What would the September 11 Generation's ideology look like? The polling data about specific issues—from free trade to the military—may paint a discouraging picture of a conservative generation soon to be lost to the Democratic Party. But there is another way to speak to this generation, which offers a far more compelling alternative than the Republican vision of national security. A national security message that is responsive to the values of our generation would be grounded in the following premises:

America is an exceptional country and must lead by example.

We believe America can and should lead as a great and vibrant nation whose values, integrity, opportunity, educational system, fairness, and generosity attract the rest of the world. While the conservative unilateralists in the Bush administration seem to believe American exceptionalism resides in our military dominance and our ability to force our views upon the rest of the world, we believe that America's strength comes from the vitality of our ideas and institutions, not our ability to impose these upon others. We strengthen our exceptionalism by following our values, and weaken it through hypocrisy.

America must have a strong military.

We understand the critical role of military force in foreign policy, and deeply respect the sacrifices of our men and women in uniform. But while

Republicans often rush to embrace military force first, we believe that the military should be used only when other options are unworkable, and for missions they are designed to fight. Then, we believe in fighting to win: using all resources necessary for a quick and decisive victory, rather than penny-pinching and starving our fighting force.

America needs allies.

Unlike conservative unilateralists, we believe terrorism can only be addressed when nations of the world band together. Alone, we cannot protect ourselves from problems that cross borders. And we cannot remain powerful by renouncing treaties and thumbing our nose at the rest of the world. With barely 4 percent of the world's population, the United States must again create great alliances, as we did after World War II, to lead other nations toward a world that is safe, humane, and prosperous.

America must use all our foreign policy tools to remain strong.

We need to protect America from threats and rebuild our strength. That requires eschewing ideological differences over using the military, aid, diplomacy, and other implements of power. We must use every tool we have to stop the growth of new terrorists and master other new threats, while using the military to catch the terrorists already in the trenches.

America's security depends on free enterprise and free trade.

We believe a strong economy is as critical a tool of American power as military might. But while Republican policies use trade policy to promote large corporate monopolies, we believe that too much corporate power can smother the entrepreneurial spirit. We believe that many smaller, independent businesses offer greater opportunities, better jobs, and a more dynamic economy. A free trade system built on small businesses strengthens the American economy, bolstering our security. And when this free trade system is fairly applied, it provides opportunity abroad, reducing the hopelessness that can radicalize aimless young men, and building appreciation for America.

America should promote human rights and freedom.

America is a great country that should live up to its responsibilities to support the weak and the needy. We believe that upholding human rights and preventing genocide is the right thing to do. And we believe free countries are less likely to breed terrorists and other security problems that will threaten us. Force alone cannot create freedom—we believe we need to work with people inside autocratic countries, to help them liberate themselves.

These premises, drawn from the ideology of the September 11 Generation, suggests a set of core foreign policy beliefs that could form the basis for a Democratic national security strategy, and offer a clear alternative to the security views of Republicans.

CONCLUSION

The September 11 Generation is coming to political power. But its political identity is not captured in categories created four decades ago. This generation is looking for inspiration from a vision of American national security that neither political party now espouses. The Truman Democratic movement is creating a new home for this new set of beliefs within the Democratic Party. And they are a movement we hope the party notes. More in tune with the general population than their parents, Truman Democrats are capturing the national security beliefs of a new generation. This September 11 Generation will be taking the reins in politics and policy in coming decades. They are strong, they are principled, and they are redefining the lines of our national security debates.

NOTES

1. Throughout this chapter, we refer to "youth," "the young," and "students." The first categories refer to Americans between the ages of eighteen and thirty. "Students" is used when polls refer specifically to college students, primarily the Harvard Student Poll, which is a biannual poll of college students across all categories of higher educational institutions in the country. The "September 11 Generation" is a broader term coined to refer to the set of beliefs held by the majority of those under thirty, for whom September 11 forms our seminal, coming-of-age political memory, as Vietnam or World War II formed for earlier generations. Except where particularly indicated, we analyzed the views of young people across party lines, not those held solely by self-identified Democrats.

2. "Generations Divide over Military Action in Iraq," The Pew Research Center for the People and the Press, October 17, 2002, http://people-press.org/commentary/display.php3?AnalysisID = 57.

3. Ibid. These findings are also supported by a Harris Interactive survey, which

found that 69 percent of teenagers supported military intervention in response to the terrorist attack, though these numbers dropped if the intervention resulted in casualties to the military or innocent civilians. Harris Interactive Survey, September, 28, 2001, p. 28, www.harrisinteractive.com/news/allnewsbydate.asp?NewsID = 366. Support for the war among the young declined precipitously over time, as it became clear that weapons of mass destruction were not present, and that our military was becoming bogged down. We address this change of heart later.

4. Surveys, Democracy Corps, conducted September 5–7, 2005 and October 19– 23, 2005, www.democracycorps.com/reports/. These two surveys are combined in order to give a more accurate picture of smaller groups of respondents, such as under-thirty voters.

5. "A Survey of American College Students," Leon and Sylvia Panetta Institute for Public Policy, May 2005, www.panettainstitute.org/lib/05/Hart_execsum.pdf. To be sure, polls only represent a snapshot of public opinion at any one time and change with new developments in Iraq and at home. However, the core values behind these sentiments of a belief in American power, a strong military, and engagement abroad have remained remarkably stable over time. Moreover, the sentiments in this polling data had been borne out by anecdotal evidence and informal focus groups conducted by members of the Truman Project across the country. For more on focus-group descriptions of young voters' reactions, see the Harvard Student Polls.

6. "The Dean Activists: Their Profile and Prospects," The Pew Research Center for the People and the Press, April 6, 2005, http://people-press.org/reports/display.php3?ReportID = 240.

7. "Beyond Red vs. Blue: Republicans Divided about Role of Government— Democrats by Social and Personal Values," The 2005 Political Typology, The Pew Research Center for the People and the Press, May 10, 2005, http://people-press.org/reports/display.php3?PageID = 944.

8. "The Dean Activists," op. cit.

9. Ibid.

10. "Generations Divide," op. cit. By August 2005, 55 percent of voters ages eighteen to twenty-five felt that the war in Iraq was not part of the war on terrorism, compared to 45 percent who thought it was. "Youth Monitor Frequency Poll," Greenberg Quinlan Rosner Research, August 10–17, 2005, www.greenbergresearch.com/articles/1010/696_YouthMonitorII-Survey.pdf.

11. When students nationwide were given the choice between "going to war in Iraq if the U.N. is not allowed to conduct effective weapons inspections," and going to war "only with the support from its allies in the United Nations," 51 percent chose the latter, and only 18 percent chose the former, while 28 percent felt that we should simply not engage in military action against Iraq. "Survey of Student Attitudes," Institute of Politics, Harvard University, October 18–27, 2002, www.iop.harvard.edu/pdfs/survey/2002.pdf.

12. See "Coming of Age—The Political Awakening of a Generation," Institute of Politics, Harvard University, October 21, 2004, www.ksg.harvard.edu/iop/pdfs/survey/fall_2004_topline.pdf.

13. "Foreign Policy Attitudes Now Driven by 9/11 and Iraq," The Pew Research Center for the People and the Press, August 18, 2004, http://people-press.org/reports/display.php3?ReportID = 222.

14. We owe this generational research breaking down Gen X and Gen Y, also known as the Millennial Generation, to leading social scientists Neil Howe and William Strauss: Howe, Neil, and William Strauss, *Millennials Rising: The Next Great Generation* (New

York: Vintage, 2000); and to Jane Eisner: Eisner, Jane, *Taking Back the Vote: Getting American Youth Involved in Our Democracy* (New York: Beacon, 2004).

15. Voters under thirty identify slightly more as independents (27 percent) compared to all voters (25 percent), and less as Republicans (31 percent of young voters, compared to 35 percent of all voters). Slightly fewer young voters identify as conservative (34 percent) and moderate (31 percent) than does the general public (39 percent combined). September 2005 and October 2005 Surveys, Strategic Analyses and National Surveys, Democracy Corps, www.democracycorps.com/reports/.

16. 2004 Exit Poll Data, conducted by Edison/Mitofsky Research, *New York Times/National Election Pool*, 2004, www.exit-poll.net/.

17. Greenberg Quinlan Rosner Research, Youth Monitor Frequency Questionnaire, April 21–28, 2005.

18. According to the *New York Times* exit polls from 1972 to 2004, more voters ages eighteen to twenty-nine identified as Republican in 2000 (46 percent) and 2004 (45 percent) than since 1988 (52 percent). The percentage of voters eighteen to twenty-nine identifying as Republican had dropped to 34 percent in both 1992 and 1996. Before 2002, exit polls were conducted by Voter News Service (VNS). In 2004, polls were conducted by Edison/Mitofsky Research, op. cit.

19. "Redefining Political Attitudes and Activism," Institute of Politics, Harvard University, November 16, 2005, www.iop.harvard.edu/pdfs/survey/fall_2005_topline.pdf. See also: Sitaraman, Ganesh, and Previn Warren, *Invisible Citizens, Youth Politics after September 11* (Boston: Institute of Politics, 2003).

20. Howe and Strauss, op. cit. Other institutions included in the poll at varying times were: the president, large corporations, the federal government, the United Nations, the media, the United States Congress, government workers, and your local member of Congress serving in Washington.

21. "Eroding Respect for America Seen as a Major Problem," in "Foreign Policy Attitudes Now Driven by 9/11 and Iraq," op. cit., p. 27.

22. Surveys, Democracy Corps, conducted May 17–23, 2005, and June 20–26, 2005, www.democracycorps.com/reports/.

23. June 2005 Survey, Strategic Analyses and National Surveys, Democracy Corps, 2005, www.democracycorps.com/reports/surveys/Democracy_Corps_June_2005_Survey.pdf.

24. "Survey of Student Attitudes," Institute of Politics, Harvard University, 2002–2005, www.iop.harvard.edu/research_polling.html.

25. Turnout was 47 percent. "U.S. Voter Turnout Up in 2004, Census Bureau Reports," U.S. Census Bureau, May 26, 2005, www.census.gov/Press-Release/www/releases/archives/voting/004986.html.

26. Projection from U.S. Census, 2004, Current Population Survey. Tabulated by Lake Snell Perry and Associates, August 2004.

27. Howe and Strauss, op. cit.

28. "Survey of Student Attitudes," 2002–2005, op. cit. Sitaraman and Warren believe that one reason for young people's alienation from public service stems from politicians' inability to convince young Americans that they are there to be public servants and serve these ideals—rather than to serve themselves.

INDEX

United Nations and, 179–88; unity
important for, 12–13; youth and, 223–
25, 227–35. *See also* homeland security
nongovernmental organizations, 61, 62,
65–66, 67n13
North Atlantic Treaty Organization
(NATO): liberal democracy and,
186–87; national security and, 184;
strategic alliances and, 138, 169–72,
177; United Nations and, 177, 184;
war on terrorism, role in, 8–9
Northern Command, 138
North Korea, 105, 106, 111–13
"The Nuclear Bomb of Jihad and the Way
to Enrich Uranium," 104
Nuclear Nonproliferation Treaty, 107–8,
110, 111, 112, 113
nuclear terrorism: Bush, George W., approach to, 101, 102–7, 111, 113; progressive strategy for, 107–14; threat of,
101–2, 103–7, 115, 116, 118, 120–21,
165–66. *See also* weapons
Nunn-Lugar Cooperative Threat Reduction, 105

Officers' Christian Fellowship (OCF),
158n15
oil: alternatives to, 201, 204, 209, 213–18;
Bush, George W., and, 208, 217, 218;
China and, 45–46, 210, 211, 212–13;
dependence on, 207–13; economy
and, 33, 34, 45–46, 201, 204, 207–9,
211–12, 216–18; environment and,
208, 209, 212–18; fuel economy standards and, 209, 214–16; Middle East
and, 33, 34, 201, 209–11; national security and, 207, 209–11, 218; strategic
alliances and, 209–11; trade and,
207–8; transportation and, 208,
214–16
Organization of Security and Cooperation
in Europe (OSCE), 62–63

Organization of the Petroleum Exporting
Countries (OPEC), 210

pacted transitions, 61
Pakistan: Afghanistan and, 115, 116–17,
120–21; al Qaeda and, 115, 116,
120–21; al-Zawahiri, Ayman, and,
102, 115, 116, 120–21; Bush, George
W., and, 116, 119–20; diplomacy and,
120–24; economy and, 118–19,
120–21; foreign aid for, 120–21; India
and, 117–18, 121–24; jihadist terrorism and, 115–17, 118, 119, 120–21,
124; liberal democracy and, 51, 115–
16, 117, 119, 120–21, 124; madrassas
and, 117, 120–21; military of, 119; nuclear terrorism and, 102, 103; Taliban
and, 115, 116–17, 120–21; trade and,
75, 76–77, 120–21; weapons and, 105,
115, 116, 118, 120–21
Palestinian Authority, 28, 39–41, 51, 93
partisanship, 12–13, 59, 113, 143–48,
151–57
Patriot Act, 12
pension programs, 205
Persian Gulf War, 22, 228–29
population, 72, 168
preemption, doctrine of, 135
prevention, 93–96, 132, 134–38, 182–83,
184–85
pride, 149
progressive internationalism: Democratic
Party and, 231–35; economy, strategy
for, 70–71, 79–82, 198–205; jihadist
terrorism, strategy for ending, 24–31;
liberal democracy, strategy for, 57–66;
military, strategy for, 129–30, 132–40,
152–57; national security and, 5–6,
233–35; nuclear terrorism, strategy for,
102, 107–13; oil, strategy for, 208–9,
213–18; overview of, 4–7; Pakistan,
strategy for, 120–24; strategic alliances,

ABOUT THE EDITOR
AND CONTRIBUTORS

Graham Allison is the founding dean of Harvard University's modern John F. Kennedy School of Government and director of the Belfer Center for Science and International Affairs. He was assistant secretary of defense in the first Clinton administration.

Reza Aslan is a writer, scholar of religions, and regular commentator on the religion and politics of the Middle East. His most recent book is *No God but God: The Origins, Evolution, and Future of Islam.*

Ronald D. Asmus is executive director of the Transatlantic Center of the German Marshall Fund of the United States in Brussels, Belgium. He served as deputy assistant secretary of state for European affairs in the second Clinton administration.

Daniel Benjamin is a senior fellow at the Center for Strategic and International Studies, and coauthor, with Steven Simon, of *The Next Attack: The Failure of the War on Terror and a Strategy for Getting It Right.* From 1994 to 1999, he served on the National Security Council staff.

James R. Blaker is a senior fellow at the Progressive Policy Institute, former advisor to joint chiefs of staff vice chairman William Owens, and vice president of Science Applications International Corporation.

Larry Diamond is a senior fellow at the Hoover Institution, Stanford University, and author of *Squandered Victory: The American Occupation and the Bungled Effort to Bring Democracy to Iraq*. He is also founding coeditor of the *Journal of Democracy*, and codirector of the International Forum for Democratic Studies of the National Endowment for Democracy.

Edward Gresser is director of the Trade and Global Markets Project at the Progressive Policy Institute, and a contributing editor to *Blueprint*. Between 1998 and 2001, he served as policy advisor to the U.S. trade representative.

Rachel Kleinfeld is an executive director of the Truman National Security Project. She consults for private and nonprofit organizations on bioterrorism, homeland security, and building police and legal institutions abroad. She is a Rhodes Scholar and holds an M. Phil. in International Relations from St. Antony's College, Oxford, and a B.A. from Yale University.

Will Marshall is president and a founder of the Progressive Policy Institute. After working on Capitol Hill and in U.S. Senate campaigns, he helped to launch the Democratic Leadership Council, where he served as policy director. He is editor of *Building the Bridge: Ten Big Ideas to Transform America* and coeditor of *Mandate for Change* and *The AmeriCorps Experiment and the Future of National Service*. Formerly a newspaper reporter with the *Richmond Times-Dispatch*, he is a member of the District of Columbia's Public Charter School Board.

Jan Mazurek is director of the Progressive Policy Institute's Energy and Environment Project, and a contributing editor to *Blueprint*.

Michael McFaul is director of the Center on Democracy, Development, and Rule of Law at Stanford University, where he is also the Peter and Helen Bing Senior Fellow at the Hoover Institution and associate professor of political science. He is also a nonresident associate at the Carnegie Endowment for International Peace.

Steven J. Nider is director of foreign and security studies at the Progressive Policy Institute, and a contributing editor to *Blueprint*. He is a fellow of the Truman National Security Project and serves on the advisory board of Securing America's Future Energy.

Kenneth M. Pollack is director of research at the Saban Center for Middle East Policy at the Brookings Institution. He has served as director for Persian Gulf affairs at the National Security Council and as a Persian military analyst at the Central Intelligence Agency. He is the author of *The Persian Puzzle: The Conflict between Iran and America, The Threatening Storm: The Case for Invading Iraq,* and *Arabs at War: Military Effectiveness, 1948–1991.*

Jeremy Rosner is partner and senior vice president at Greenberg Quinlan Rosner, a political polling and strategy firm. From 1993 to 1994, he served as special assistant to President Clinton on the NSC staff, running the NSC's speechwriting and legislative affairs offices; and from 1997 to 1998 served as special adviser to President Clinton and Secretary of State Albright, leading the effort to obtain congressional and public support for the accession of Poland, Hungary, and the Czech Republic to NATO. He is the author of *The New Tug-of-War: Congress, the Executive Branch, and National Security.*

David J. Rothkopf is a visiting scholar at the Carnegie Endowment for International Peace and President and CEO of Garten Rothkopf, LLC. He is author of *Running the World: The Inside Story of the National Security Council and the Architects of American Power,* and served as deputy undersecretary of commerce during the Clinton administration.

Anne-Marie Slaughter is dean of the Woodrow Wilson School of Public and International Affairs at Princeton University, and author of *A New World Order.*

Stephen J. Solarz is president of Solarz Associates and senior counselor at APCO Worldwide. He represented Brooklyn's 13th Congressional District for eighteen years, serving on the U.S. House of Representatives International Affairs Committee, as chairman of the Subcommittee on Asian and Pacific Affairs and the Subcommittee on Africa.

Matthew Spence is an executive director of the Truman National Security Project. He has been a lecturer in International Relations at St. Johns College, Oxford University, and a fellow at the Stanford Center on Democracy, Development, and the Rule of Law. He has a Ph.D. in International Relations from Oxford University, where he was a Marshall Scholar, a B.A. and

M.A. from Stanford University, and is now completing his J.D. at Yale Law School.

Melissa Tryon is a veteran of Operation Iraqi Freedom. She is a Rhodes Scholar, a West Point graduate, and a member of the Truman Security Forum.

THE PROGRESSIVE
POLICY INSTITUTE

One person with a belief is a social power equal to ninety-nine who
have only interests.

John Stuart Mill

The Progressive Policy Institute is a catalyst for political change and reform.
Its mission is to modernize progressive governance for the twenty-first cen-
tury. Rejecting tired dogmas and mindless partisanship, PPI generates
"Third Way" thinking that is renewing progressive politics in the United
States and around the world.

The institute fashions new ways to advance enduring progressive principles:
equal opportunity, mutual responsibility, civic enterprise, public sector reform, national strength, and collective security. Its signature policy innova-
tions include national service; a postwelfare social policy that rewards work;
a new twenty-first-century model for public schools based on choice, accountability, and customization; a networked government that uses information technology to break down bureaucratic barriers; pollution trading
markets and other steps toward a clean energy economy; a citizen-centered
approach to universal health care; political reforms aimed at preventing special interests from hijacking our democracy; and, a progressive internationalism that commits America's strength to the defense of liberal democracy.

PPI brings a spirit of radical pragmatism and reform to the challenge of restoring our collective problem-solving capacities—and thereby reviving
public confidence in what progressive governance can accomplish.

U